'Keep On Running *is one of the be*

Gearselected.com

'Phil Hewitt's well written account of his marathon-running addiction (he's up to 25) takes us from his home town of Chichester to the concrete canyons of New York. ... This is the story of a man in love with his sport. ... For those of us fitting running in between job, family and everything else life has to throw at us, this is definitely a book you will make a connection with'

MEN'S RUNNING

'An extremely engaging read'

SUSSEX LIFE magazine

'A charismatic, charming, funny – and, above all, thoughtful – memoir about running, motivation, ambition. Perfect, not just for those who do run – or intend to run – a marathon, but for the hundreds and thousands of us who venture out from time to time to run just a mile or two... A complete delight.'

Kate Mosse, author and broadcaster

'This is a wonderful and frank view of a first-time-marathoner-turned-running-addict. Phil shares the pitfalls and emotions that running a marathon for the first time evoke and how running can grab you and draw you back for more.'

Liz Yelling, double Olympian and Commonwealth bronze medallist

'The pain, perils and utter pleasure of the formidable 26.2 miles by someone who has gone every step of the way... 25 times. Warning: you will seriously want to run a marathon after reading this.'

Rosie Millard, journalist, author and broadcaster

KEEP ON RUNNING

THE HIGHS & LOWS OF A MARATHON ADDICT

Phil Hewitt

summersdale

KEEP ON RUNNING: THE HIGHS AND LOWS OF A
MARATHON ADDICT

Summersdale Publishers Ltd
46 West Street
Chichester
West Sussex
PO19 1RP
UK

www.summersdale.com

Printed and bound in Great Britain

ISBN: 978-1-84953-236-5

Substantial discounts on bulk quantities of Summersdale
books are available to corporations, professional associations
and other organisations. For details telephone Summersdale
Publishers on (+44-1243-771107), fax (+44-1243-786300) or
email (nicky@summersdale.com).

About the Author

Phil Hewitt was brought up in Gosport, Hampshire, where he attended Bay House School. He later gained a first-class honours degree in modern languages and a doctorate in early twentieth century French theatre from Oxford University. He joined the *Chichester Observer* in 1990 and became the newspaper's arts editor four years later. He is now also arts editor for all the *Observer*'s sister papers across West Sussex, including the *West Sussex Gazette* and the *West Sussex County Times*.

Phil lives in Bishops Waltham, Hampshire, with his wife Fiona and children Adam and Laura. A keen runner, he has completed marathons in London, New York, Paris, Berlin, Dublin, Rome, Mallorca and Amsterdam, among others. Since completing this book, he has added the Brighton Marathon and the Portsmouth Coastline Marathon to his tally. Phil is also the author of *Chichester Then and Now*, *Chichester Remembered* and *Gosport Then and Now*.

Phil writes a blog at www.marathonaddictuk.wordpress.com and you can follow him on Twitter at **@marathon_addict**.

With love and thanks to:
Fiona, Adam and Laura, for putting up with me
Michael, for being a true running mate
Pamela, for getting me started
The Stones and The Beatles, for keeping me going
Peter Lovesey, for suggesting this book in the first place

Contents

Introduction
The Boat and the Boy

The rain was lashing down. The wind was bitingly cold. My head hurt. My eyes stung. I could hardly make out the road ahead. All I could see was my chance of running a good race swirling away from me down the storm-filled gutters. And that's when I saw him. Glancing to my left, just by the 37-km marker, I was suddenly aware of a figure coming up beside me, gliding serenely and hideously mocking me with every step – the man with the boat on his head. Not just any boat, but a model yacht, complete with sails and rigging. Calmly, gracefully, he sailed past me, looking the very picture of control. He didn't look back. He didn't need to. On he raced, oblivious to the fact that he'd crushed me. It was the lowest low point in all my years of marathon running.

I had been convinced that I was going to run into my own record books that day. A PB, that personal best which constitutes the Holy Grail of runners everywhere, seemed within my grasp, and that was my mistake. I'd grown too confident, and so the heavens opened. The energy drained out of me, and then came the final straw: the man with the boat on his head. You might strive for a PB, but any time you think you're bigger than the marathon you're running, the marathon will always have the last laugh.

Perversely, though, in the warm light of the Amsterdam changing room afterwards, I realised that it was for moments like these that I run marathons – a moment so miserable at the time and yet so hilarious in hindsight that it went straight into the annals of my own running folklore. Within an hour, I found myself softening towards the man and his boat.

It was a low point, but looking back now, it was a low point every bit as precious as the high point that had sent me smiling over the finish in the London Marathon the year before. Marathons can crush, but so too can they send your spirits soaring with little moments that will equal anything else that life will ever throw at you.

In London, I had been struggling, desperately needing help. I had turned into Parliament Square with just under a mile to go, but I was in a state of near collapse, succumbing to increasing confusion and feeble-minded despair. All that was keeping me going was thrusting my chest towards randomly selected spectators in the hope that they would read the name on my vest, shout it out and urge me on. The noise was intense, but in that moment all I could hear, loud and clear above the roar of the crowd, was the voice of a little boy standing at the corner. 'Come on, Phil! You can still win this!'

It was a sublime moment, so absurd and so true, so crazy and so perfect. Win it? I was heading for a finish nearly an hour and three-quarters after the actual winner had won. But that wasn't the point. The little lad was spot on. If I could summon the bloody-mindedness to get over the line, then I too would be a winner. The final minutes weren't pleasant; but I managed them. The finishing photos show my face a sickly shade of blue, but I was grinning as I crossed the line, new life in my exhausted legs, all thanks to the little boy.

Marathons make you miserable, but they also give you the most unlikely and the most indescribable pleasures. The boat and the little boy, the two extremes that sum up that passionate, nonsensical, punishing world of marathon running. A world that I love – a world that is unlocked when you dress up in Lycra, put protective plasters on your nipples and run 26.2 miles in the company of upwards of 30,000 complete strangers. Even when I hate it, I love it still.

I've been running marathons for 14 years now. I've clocked up 25, ranging from 4 hours 20 minutes down to 3 hours 20. I've run in eight different countries and in five different capitals, and no one believes me when I announce that my next marathon will be my last. They're right. It won't be. Life without a marathon looming on the horizon has become unimaginable.

This book is an attempt to explain why – a look back over the pleasures and the pains my addiction has given me. Marathon runners will recognise them one and all; I hope non-marathon runners will want a bit of it too. If you've already run a marathon, I hope you'll be with me on every page; if you haven't, I hope you'll want to run one by the time we reach the finishing line.

Chapter One: 'Start Me Up'
First Steps towards the London Marathon

If you want to annoy a marathon runner, wait till he or she starts to tell you about their latest marathon and then ask, all innocently, 'So how far was that one then?' A marathon is a marathon is a marathon, and a marathon is always just a touch over 26.2 miles: 26 miles and 385 yards to be exact. Or 42.195 km. However you want to express it, it's a fixed distance the world over, and that is both the point and the pointlessness of it.

History tells us that the first marathon runner – though he didn't know it at the time – was Pheidippides, a Greek messenger who was sent from the battlefield at Marathon to tell everyone in Athens about 26 miles away that the Persians had just been defeated. He'd just fought in the Battle of Marathon himself, poor chap, and a marathon straight afterwards was just too much for him. Pheidippides ran the entire distance (presumably with very little crowd support), shouted 'We have won!', keeled over and died. The world's first marathon runner had also set the standard for the world's worst post-marathon celebration.

But it was Pheidippides who ultimately defined the event which featured in the first modern Olympic Games in 1896.

In the 1908 London Olympics, the final 385 yards were added to accommodate the Royals and to give them a better view – or, at least, that's the popular understanding. In May 1921, the International Amateur Athletic Federation set the distance in stone: 26 miles and 385 yards – the distance which has been run around the world ever since.

It was a vague distance in those early Olympic Games, hovering around 40 km, but for the past 90 years it has been immovable – and that's a big part of its charm. The distance is predetermined. It is also absurd. You can't beat 26 miles and 385 yards as a clunky, arbitrary and deliciously random distance, and yet it has become the rigid standard by which long-distance runners measure their prowess.

Generally, it takes a marathon runner to know that a marathon is 26 miles and 385 yards – or even the rather more imprecise 26.2 miles which is more often referred to. And we look at the rest of the world aghast when we discover that they don't share that knowledge. My late grandfather, ex-RAF, was convinced that the wingspan of a Spitfire was the most rudimentary piece of general knowledge on the planet. We marathon runners are rather like that about the exact length of a marathon. But for all we tut, the true marathon runner feels a certain smugness when other people ask the question: 'How far is that marathon?' It sounds condescending, and probably it is, but the fact is that other people simply aren't like us. They haven't joined the club – the best club in the world.

Running a marathon doesn't make you clever, and it almost certainly doesn't make you interesting. In fact, probably quite the opposite is true. But anyone who has ever gone the distance will tell you that running a marathon is your admission ticket to something truly special, something that takes you to the next level of human experience and beyond. And therein lies the bond between marathon runners. As soon as you have run one, you belong to a brotherhood.

Fellow members won't ask you how far you ran. Far more pertinently, they will ask you how quickly you ran it. In their mind will be their own time. The point is that no time stands by itself. Every time needs a point of reference, a point of comparison.

Every time, that is, except your first. And that's what makes your first marathon so very special. It's the only time you will run a marathon wondering simply whether you can finish it. For all the rest, you will be wondering whether you can run faster than you've run before. Only in your very first marathon is it enough to run it for running's sake. Your debut is the marathon that gives you the marker by which all your future races will be judged; the marker you hope will recede as you start to set new standards.

My good fortune was that my first marathon was the London Marathon, arguably the best in the world. London offers one of the greatest marathon experiences imaginable. Many marathons are deadly serious, and so too is London, but London's great distinction is that it is also the biggest street party ever staged.

The first year I did it, one of those interminable Saturday supplement colour pieces nailed it when the writer described the London Marathon as 'part race, part garden party'.

A huge part of the charm is the great atmosphere, the hundreds of thousands of supporters, the almost constant roar of the crowd, the generosity of the man quite literally on the street as he urges you on as if it really matters to him. It's an event which brings out the best in us all, a terrific gathering of selfless spectators egging on tens of thousands of selfish runners. For the runners, even as they raise millions for charity, it's all about their own personal goals on the day. For the spectators, it's all about helping the runners get there. And that's what makes marathon running unique.

Nothing else summons people in quite such numbers for such a mass act of collective altruism, all directed at an endless stream of complete strangers toiling past, in amongst whom, somewhere, is the one person they are truly supporting.

Twenty-five marathons – six in London – have convinced me that it's at the London Marathon that this street-level philanthropy receives its greatest expression, every year, year in, year out. You run through sheer benevolence, and you can get quite drunk on it, the runners responding in kind, which is what makes up the garden-party element.

Musicians of all kinds will set up stall along the route to will you on. You'll get everything from roadside discos to rock bands, from gospel choirs to kettledrums, from brass bands to samba. Every musical hue will be there, beating out every rhythm under the sun – and all so that you might find your own rhythm in your run. It's exotic, it's spontaneous, it's a blast and it's fun – and the runners rise to the occasion, adding their own colour to the most colourful of days.

In amongst the runners will be Teletubbies, rhinos, Elvises, Supermen, people chained together, people tied together. People will run as tins of baked beans, as watches and as cavemen; they will run dressed as a London bus or even an aircraft. And for reasons known only to them, the butchest and hairiest of men will take to the streets in fluffy pink tutus. Everything and anything goes. Disinhibition runs wild as dark dreams and private fantasies are lived out in public.

You wouldn't want to spend too long running behind the chap in the eye-watering mankini, but you can't help but smile as you leave him behind (and no longer have to look at his behind). Why's he doing it? Isn't it enough to run just over 26.2 miles without having your privates dangling round your neck in a strange kind of sling? Clearly not. Along with all the clowns, Postman Pats and other cartoon characters, he's a runner intent on taking it all one step further for the craziest show on the road.

Is it a question of standing out? More likely, it's a question of underlining the inbuilt madness of marathon running. It's like those deeply irritating adverts, usually for furniture superstores, where an overexcited, half-crazed voice tells you of the latest price reductions and then squeals with stomach-churning, smug self-deprecation: 'We must be mad!' Except, of course, they're not mad. They wouldn't be selling you anything at a price which wasn't entirely beneficial to them. Maybe it's only marathon runners who can *genuinely* claim: 'We must be mad!' Presumably the logic goes: I am running an awfully long distance for no reason any sane person would ever understand, so I might as well run it as a Womble.

So much for the garden party, a mix of eccentricity and ostentation in equal measure. But several miles further towards the finish, you've got the business end of the race – and that's the part that attracts me. Down this end is the race in its purest sense, and it's for this that I am there. For some people towards the back, a marathon is about running an absurd distance dressed in an even more absurd costume; for me, keen to close the gap on the front-runners, the pull is that I am running with the greats. The elite athletes will have collected their medals, showered and eaten by the time I finish, but I will still have run the same race as they have.

Football fans don't get to share the pitch with the Beckhams, the Ronaldos and the Pelés. Yet we runners get to share the course with our heroes. It's an unbroken chain which leads from the slowest of the slow right the way through to Paula Radcliffe at the front, setting yet another record. Somewhere between the two extremes is me, generally in the top 10 to 20 per cent of finishers, desperate to get away from those Teletubbies, even more desperate to inch closer to the runners who will make the next day's headlines.

My first marathon – the London Marathon of 1998 – tumbled into my lap by chance, but perhaps I had been seeking it unconsciously for a while. I was reaching *that* age. The age where, if you're not careful, your trousers start to feel just a little bit too tight, the age where you ponder a task and then decide 'Hmmm, I'll do that later'. I was 34; sluggishness had crept in by the back door and was just about to plonk itself down in the armchair of my existence.

A largely sedentary job was partly to blame. As arts editor for a group of newspapers in West Sussex, I was starting to live life just a little vicariously. All the action I saw was on the cinema screen or on the stage in front of me. The journalism training I'd done years before had promised that a career in newspapers gave you 'a ringside seat at life's great events'; eight years into the job, I was starting to realise that I was in danger of becoming a full-time spectator.

The job was demanding, and so too was home life. Our son Adam was just over a year old. He was great fun and rewarded every second you spent in his company; and we were hoping it wouldn't be long before he had some company of his own in the shape of a brother or sister. One way or another, there never seemed to be any time for anything which didn't involve either work or Adam, and if all went according to plan, there would soon be even less time.

I'd run occasionally in my years at university, but never any great distance, never with any real discipline and never with any great heart – and certainly never competitively. Slowly, however, with life's responsibilities stacking up, my thoughts started to turn increasingly to running again, an unspoken longing for that rush of energy you're supposed to get as you hammer out the miles. Mortgage, work and family life constrict you, and so, in some primeval kind of way, you find yourself longing to reclaim a few lost freedoms. In an era when man can no longer dash out of his cave and slay a mammoth, he simply slips on his Lycra and goes for a run.

There's a fantastic birthday card which I have been sent probably a dozen times down the years. It shows a jolly, wonderfully hearty-looking runner, awfully British with his hair slicked back in a 1940s kind of way. A sporty cove if ever there was one, he positively beams at the camera with a smugness that shouts 'Aren't I just a picture of health, don't you know!' Above the photograph, the caption reads: 'After a month of jogging ten miles a day, Phil was feeling terrific. The only problem was that he was 300 miles from home.'

How apt that he should have been called Phil. He's even wearing the same colour of orange running vest I have worn for most of my marathons. Just that look on his face seems to explain it all. Without realising it, I was hankering after Birthday Card Phil's vigorous good health and seemingly boundless energy. As the old lady says in *When Harry Met Sally*, 'I'll have what she's having.'

Work was good; family was great; but I needed something that was me; just me. Which is an easy thing for a bloke to say as he approaches his self-indulgent midlife wallow. Not many dads of young kiddies would get away with it, let alone put it into practice, but fortunately in Fiona, my wife, I have an absolute model of tolerance and forbearance. She knew – and I knew – that I wanted something. I just didn't know quite what. It took a chance conversation to fill in the blank. I happened to be in the right place at the right time, which happened to be the normal place at the normal time: the offices of the *Chichester Observer* where I work, one grey morning in October.

Being arts editor isn't a role that tends to come with too many sporting demands, though I have always been more sporty (it's all relative) than our succession of sports editors – sporty in the sense of actually going out and doing it. My weekly thrash on the badminton court was – and still is – a cornerstone of my life. Bizarrely, you don't see too many sports editors on court, though. They're the ones with the knowledge and the contacts, but they never seem to sample the delights they describe – and for one reason. Sports editors, in my limited experience, tend to be rather on the large side. Not that I am complaining. It was the size of our 1997 incumbent that led to my London Marathon *entrée*.

Our newspaper worked closely with the Macmillan Cancer Relief service at Midhurst, just a few miles up the road from our base in Chichester. For a year we'd run a campaign supporting their bid to raise sufficient money for an additional nurse. I wrote most of the articles as part of a general features role, and they were, strangely, simultaneously both easy and difficult to write. Easy as they touched so many people and so many people had so much to say in support of the fundraising initiative, but difficult because so much of what they had to say was horribly sad. Inevitably, Macmillan's greatest advocates were people who had lost loved ones. It was Macmillan who helped them in the final months as they faced up to impending bereavement – which is why the newspaper was proud to work closely with the charity. Macmillan responded by offering us one of their places in the 1998 London Marathon, as another way to highlight their fundraising efforts.

Our then editor Gary, my badminton partner and close friend, offered the place to our sports editor. Let's call him 'Fred'. Gary felt it was the most appropriate thing to do, not just because he was the sports editor but also because he sensed a good story. Fred was big. Not the largest sports editor we have ever had, but not far off. The idea was that selfless Fred would slim down in preparation, write about it endlessly and then whizz round the London Marathon in a way that was an example to us all, raising several thousand pounds for Macmillan into the bargain

Fred was tempted. It seemed a great idea until one of our features subeditors pointed out the drawback. 'It will kill him,' she said. There was a ripple of nervous laughter. 'No, seriously,' she insisted. 'It will kill him.'

The bubble burst; reality rushed in. Fred, who was already having problems with his knees, consulted his physiotherapist. He learned that when you run, you crash down on your knees and ankles at something like four or five times your body weight, which for Fred would have been an impact approaching 90 stone up to 60 times a minute. You didn't need to be in medicine to work out the implications. You just needed to look at him.

'My knees won't take it,' he told us when he came back from his appointment – a reasonable opt-out which saved face and probably also saved a life. And that's the point at which I chipped in with three momentous words: 'I'll do it.' There was general agreement that the arts editor running a marathon had an appealing whiff of the ridiculous about it, and so the gig was mine. Just as you wouldn't necessarily want to send your sports editor to review the latest in new writing at the National, so you wouldn't want to send your arts editor into the sweaty throng of a mass endurance event – or so the thinking went. Slightly stereotypical thinking, I thought, which seemed to project us arts editors as effete, rather fragile creatures, not strong enough for the exertions of this world. Nonsense, of course. And for me, it was a red rag.

I broke the news to Pamela, Macmillan's fundraising manager and now my marathon mentor. A marathon runner herself, she knew exactly how to go about it and, from that moment, she became a never-ending fount of sweetly dispensed wisdom. Blessed with the most appealing personality, she was bright and breezy; just as importantly, she was also calm and crucial. I didn't move in running circles; I didn't have running contacts; and it wouldn't have been fun simply to read up about it. Pamela was the answer to my every running need.

These days I'm sure all the tips are out there to be found and tested if you scour the Internet enough, but it's no substitute for having someone with you to tell you the dos and don'ts and to bring them to life with genuine, first-hand knowledge. Pamela's gift, amply displayed in her work for the charity, was that she was a born communicator, adept at enthusing and highly skilled at encouraging.

Right from the start, she was insistent that, at the age of 34, the question was never going to be whether or not I could do it. I was generally fit, slight of build and keen. The only question was how quickly I could do it, an argument no first-timer will ever accept until he or she has crossed the finishing line. Nonetheless it was a considerable confidence-booster. After all, I reasoned, Pamela should know. If she was confident, then perhaps I should be so too.

Pamela was crystal clear as to what the first step should be. Get some proper running shoes. She even told me where to get them – the wonderful Alexandra Sports in Portsmouth, a paradise for the kind of anorak I didn't know I was. I wandered in half-expecting the staff to sigh 'My hero!' and swoon when I announced, coat slung nonchalantly over my shoulder, that I was running the London Marathon. But no, they took it disarmingly in their stride, not even batting an eyelid as they motioned me to await my turn at the back of the queue.

The shop is staffed by people who know. It's a place where the romance of marathon running is shoved aside in favour of the basic scientific practicalities. I was seen by the owner, a man with a Sherlock Holmes-like ability to construct a stride, indeed an entire running personality, from the merest glimpse of a foot.

Return customers would present the staff with their used running shoes. The assistant would examine the soles and then pronounce: 'I can see you are a left-handed printer, recently married and now living in a terraced house three storeys high, backing onto a railway line. But tell me, sir, why did you invest quite so heavily in the South African mines?' Or something like that.

They would upend the shoe and read it like a book, pointing out where the runner was wearing the sole down the most, where he was exerting pressure that he shouldn't and quite why the impact wasn't right. All this information would then be computed into a series of suggestions for the most appropriate successor shoe, which would then be road-tested outside the shop. People living in the vicinity had presumably long since ceased to be amused by the surreal sight of besuited blokes and smartly dressed women running up and down in trainers. Alexandra Sports would not sell you anything they were not happy with, and they soon opened up to me a vast world of arcane terminology.

The scientific names of muscles and tendons were tossed around as part of the shop's everyday vocabulary, alongside words such as 'pronate' and the various degrees to which you might or might not do so. They soon told me that I was an over-pronator, which sounded like a compliment. I imagined myself over-pronating over that finish line as I waved to the crowd. Except that it wasn't a compliment at all. It was a polite way of saying – and fortunately they didn't express it quite this way – that you could drive a bus between my knees. Far from being greeted as a visiting Olympian, I was labelled bandy-legged – which meant that I would turn my foot inwards as I ran, a gait likely to lead to all sorts of injuries.

I was the best part of an hour in Alexandra Sports, emerging with a lovely pair of ASICS running shoes, which I swore by – and occasionally at – for most of the next six months. They lifted my instep sufficiently, and they seemed perfect – proof absolute of Pamela's point: decent shoes are the *sine qua non* of running.

A dozen years on, I would temper that. Sheer bloody-mindedness is just as important, and I am sure Pamela would agree. Certainly you won't get anywhere without it, just as you won't get anywhere if you don't spend out on the shoes. I seem to remember that that first pair cost around £65, which seemed a fortune, but the shoes hovered around the £70 mark for years to come – and these days you can get them considerably cheaper on the Internet if you know exactly which ones you want. That's the key, though. Never take a punt on a pair of untested shoes. You need to know that they suit your feet. You need to have run in that model first, ideally in suit and tie outside a sports shop. Buy them untested and you might be lucky. But then again, you might not, and the consequences of getting it wrong can be disastrous.

Even then, it's not plain sailing. Just when you're totally happy with your shoes and go back for your third pair of the same, you will run into that infuriating thing known as progress. Under the banner of striving always to improve your running experience, the big sports shoe companies every now and again ditch some of their most popular models and introduce new improved versions. It's astonishing that they don't hear the howl of protest that erupts up and down the country. To us over-pronators, it effectively means starting again. When that particular model of ASICS disappeared, I was bereft. The successor – in those sprints up and down the road outside the shop – didn't seem to be anywhere near as good.

Under the expert guidance of the sales assistant, I jumped ship, defecting to New Balance with whom I stayed for years, happy as Larry in my 857s, until New Balance foolishly thought they could make a good thing even better. They failed, and so I and my feet started to worship at the temple of Nike, where I have stayed ever since. They too have gone through several different models, much to my consternation, but the latest variety has more or less done the trick for me so far.

Armed – or footed – with the shoes back in 1998, it was now a question of getting down to some serious training, and for this Pamela gave me what every marathon runner will know as 'the schedule', the get-you-round week-by-week plan of action that will overshadow your every weekend from the dark days of winter through to the bright spring day when you finally hit the streets of London.

Alongside it, she gave me a sheet of hieroglyphics which, on closer study, revealed a stick figure pushing against walls and tugging his own legs up behind him, fortunately one at a time. I thought I was back in the realms of Sherlock Holmes. Could these be those famous Dancing Men? But no, they weren't dancing. They were stretching.

Whenever you go out running, so the theory goes, you are supposed to do some stretching beforehand, and before that first marathon I did so religiously. If you are to stay injury-free, it's even more important to do a similar set of stretches after you return, and again I did them dutifully during the early months of 1998, trying to play it very much by the book on my marathon debut.

Very early on, Pamela stressed to me the importance of 'intervals' and 'fartleks', exercises which are designed to increase your speed and stamina. It wasn't until later marathons that I indulged her passion for intervals, more of which later, but for marathon number one I certainly did my best to obey her injunction to 'fartlek', a piece of intensity training nowhere near as antisocial as it sounds.

Like all these things, it can be as simple or as complicated as you want it to be, and I opted to keep it simple, in keeping with what the word actually means. Apparently it's Swedish for 'speed play', and, in essence, it's a way of putting your body under stress. You see two markers on the route ahead – be they gates, telegraph poles, street lamps or whatever – and you run like hell between them. And you do that every now and again as you run along. The idea is that you up the intensity of your endeavours and, in theory, you get your body used to the kind of pressures you will be putting it under come the big day.

Bizarrely, fartleks proved tolerably enjoyable. Unlike intervals, which I didn't dip into until later, they are unstructured, and for me, they seemed to tie in nicely with the whole ethos of running – an off-the-leash surge which is there to be enjoyed. In those early runs, I became reasonably adept (and reasonably strong-willed) in determining the markers for my sporadic sprints, and I am sure they played a key role when it came to increasing my distance, the basic goal of training for a first marathon.

In short, the training has got to get you from not running at all to running 26.2 miles on one glorious day which has got to coincide with the very moment at which you are at your readiest. Fartlekking was one of the ways of getting there.

By October I was running three or four times a week, judging the distance against drives in the car. Within a couple of weeks, I was able to sustain 4 miles in one go, and that's the point at which I started to develop what is known in the business as my 'long run'. For reasons of time and convenience, this will generally be the weekend run – a run which will get longer and longer, an exercise in pure stamina which will take the runner closer and closer to the final marathon distance.

There's a great deal of satisfaction to be had here. Initially, you will consider 3 or 4 miles to be a long run, but week by week, you will stretch it, generally adding around ten per cent to the distance you cover. I can remember the glory of running 4 miles for the first time. Several weeks later, 4 miles was nothing. Every seven days, you are adjusting your expectations upwards. Ten is a major milestone, at which point five is a mere bagatelle, hardly worth getting out of bed for. Train hard and consistently, and the distance racks up sweetly.

People ask how you can possibly run 15 miles, but I've always thought that it is considerably more of an achievement to get from 0 to 5 than it is from 5 to 15. The point is that once you reach five, you are in the swing. You're in the groove and you are up and running. You're past the stage of turning yourself into a runner. You *are* a runner by now. The task ahead is simply to make yourself a more resilient runner.

Even to a novice, it was clear that progress had to be incremental, staged and sensible – and I found myself enjoying it increasingly as I started to range further, exploring more and more of the country roads and paths around our home in Bishop's Waltham.

At times, I've envied the runners I used to see in Portsmouth, further south on the coast, as they strode out along the promenade, the sea an inspiration beside them. Wherever they went, they had street lights to guide them. But I quickly realised that I had the more complete running package at home in the rural heart of Hampshire. There were no lights once I was outside the town, but I could strike out in any direction, a fact which offered endless possibilities. And even when the nearest roads started to seem just a touch too familiar, it always seemed that a new footpath would open up somewhere along the line. White-rabbit-like, I'd dash down it.

Once I had explored the main roads, there was a vast patchwork of paths and tracks to dip into, criss-crossing the countryside in a way which encouraged me to be ever more adventurous. If you kept the pattern of the main roads surrounding you firmly in your mind, it really didn't matter if you didn't know where your track was heading. At some point, you were bound to hit a main road somewhere. I started to see the countryside as little parcels of land to be opened and enjoyed. Even now, a great running delight is coming across a tumbledown footpath sign I've never noticed before.

But it wasn't all straightforward. Rain presented a mixed blessing and, with it, the trauma of chafed nipples, one of the worst running injuries you can suffer. My wife doesn't believe me when I tell her that it is worse than childbirth. But I should know. After all, I was present at the birth of both our children.

Head out into a downpour with unprotected nipples and you'll run into agony unimaginable to those that have been spared. My foolishness early on was to run in an old rugby top. Sodden and heavy, it proved a flesh-ripper of the first order. But even after I graduated to the lighter, specialised running tops, I realised I was still at risk if I didn't slip out the door with a couple of nipple-sized plasters firmly in place. It's not a lesson that needs hammering home. You tend to learn it quickly. Any plasters will do. Just get them on there.

Needless to say, I regaled Pamela with every last detail in a 'this is all your fault' kind of way. Perversely, I liked to tell her how boring I found the training when quite the contrary was true. Countryside running was offering endless challenges, and, suitably protected in the nipple department, I soon discovered that a decent downpour was actually quite refreshing. There is nothing worse than starting out in rain, but if it rains when you are already out there, then the rain can be wonderfully invigorating – all part of the enhanced sensuality which, slightly kinkily, goes hand in hand with running. The rain trickling down the back of your neck can be lovely; the feel of it, caressing; the smell of it, intoxicating.

But, of course, sometimes the great god Pluvius can go far too far. There was one particular incident which became ever more exaggerated in the telling, particularly when it was Pamela I was telling it to. One training run took me out in a downpour which got worse and worse. I was in the middle of nowhere when an old boy slowed beside me in a car I could barely see through the torrents of rain crashing down around me. He wound down a window and, in an elegant voice from a more refined age, politely inquired: 'Can I give you a lift or are you actually doing this for pleasure?' 'For pleasure,' I replied, smiling through gritted teeth.

It was a low point – born of the kindest of motives on his part, but a low point all the same as far as I was concerned. It brought home to me how fundamentally stupid marathon running is – a fact which I have since come to regard as its greatest attraction.

But at least it was goal-orientated, to use the jargon, and it was this which kept me going during that first winter of training. I had no idea how I was going to do, but at least I knew, more or less, where I stood and what I was attempting. Marathon day sat on the horizon, and everything was about the countdown to it.

As it got closer, I was able to tell myself that one of my least appealing character traits was becoming my best friend. With the passing weeks, I was learning that most fundamental of fundamentals: you simply can't run a marathon without a huge degree of stubbornness running right through you. Cut a marathon runner in half, and I am sure you will see the word 'bloody-minded', stick-of-rock-like, running right through his or her core.

Determined is perhaps a kinder word, but call it what you like, as December moved into January and 'Marathon Year' dawned, it seemed to me that total focus was always going to be the greatest weapon in my marathon armoury.

As I increased my distance from 10 miles into the early teens, it was increasingly clear: you can't get away with being wishy-washy when it comes to a marathon. There are no shades of grey. There's no 'Well, I quite fancy it.' Above all, you've got to want it. There's got to be desire. Passion even. You've got to be the slave-driver, Ben Hur-like in your own chariot, whipping your body onwards even when it hurts like hell.

And so it seemed that the training was working: I was hardening up, and with that hardening, confidence started to come. I pushed myself and I started regularly to achieve that rarest of things – a long run which my body didn't rebel against, a long run that I actually enjoyed. I learned to attack 12 miles and then I stepped up to 13, at which point came the encouragement of being very nearly halfway there. General marathon advice was to be able to run 15 miles by the end of January for an April marathon, and I was pleased to achieve it. It was an important psychological marker.

Everyone tells you not even to attempt a marathon if you can't run 15 miles comfortably, and I could sense the reasoning behind it. Even to a novice, 15 seemed the point at which you established your credentials as a marathon runner in the making, the distance at which you proved you were capable of pushing on. Reach 15 and you've shown that you've almost certainly got what it takes for the long run. Training is about building confidence as well as physical stamina – and 15 miles gives you precisely that.

My hope was that I was timing it right in those early weeks of 1998. It became a question of computing distances and dates, and, by January, I was confident enough to devise my own next stage. I decided that for the four months to April I would alternate the long run between 15 and 18, slipping in a couple of 20s before the big day dawned.

Some people will tell you that's far too much. They will argue that those shorter runs, in which you really push yourself, are absolutely key, but I took the view that I wanted to get my body used to distance. I wanted complete familiarity with the stresses and strains that start to show around 15 miles; and once or twice before the big day, I wanted a little foretaste of the even greater stresses which kick in at 20 miles. I wanted to creep ever closer to the abyss and peer over the edge.

It's seemed to me in subsequent marathons that all the training runners do is effectively preparation for the final 7 or 8 miles of the race. Put in the hours, and 18 miles is an achievable, human limit, something you can step up to reasonably comfortably. If you want to go past it, that's when you'll need to go into hyperspace. That's when you'll need that extra-special resilience to draw on.

But just how far you go in training remained the great imponderable, or at least it would have done if it hadn't been for Pamela. Her opinion was clear. Her view – and it's certainly the general view – is that it would be foolish to attempt the full distance before the big day, and for several reasons. The big day would be considerably less big if you had already done the distance. Why try to upstage yourself? Just as importantly, there is absolutely no need. As Pamela kept telling me, the crowds will drag you round the last few miles.

Your lonely 21 or 22 in training will be the equivalent of the full 26.2 once you've got the crowd behind you and are buoyed up by the huge lift that comes with the day itself, Pamela insisted. Get to about 20 miles in training and then trust in the crowd on the day, she urged. Her point was that hundreds of thousands of people cheering you on are worth 6 miles. I started to try to picture it. What would it be like? I just couldn't imagine it, but I tried, and with each attempt, anticipation mounted as I contemplated stepping into the unknown.

How can you possibly know what the cheering will do for you? All you can do is assume that it will do you good – and I clung on to that thought during the nervy final three weeks. Nervy because this is the period during which you are supposed to taper. All the advice is that you mustn't maintain your running intensity until the day itself. Instead, you are supposed to throttle back over the final few weeks, confident in the knowledge that you've got hundreds of miles in the bank which will be your stepping stone to marathon glory on the day.

In the meantime, I was battling pressure on another front – the peculiar business of going public. To justify the charity place, I had to raise in the region of £1,500 for Macmillan, which I did by boring the good people of Chichester with my run, writing articles to go alongside the sponsor forms we printed in the paper.

People rallied to the cause wonderfully. Sponsorship money flowed in; and it was obvious very early on that I was going to exceed my target comfortably. Just as encouraging was the fact that the sponsorship money was almost always accompanied by sweet notes explaining just why it was given. In many cases, the money came from people who knew me and wished me well on that basis; but in many more, it came from people who had lost friends and relatives to cancer and were keen that I should know this as I cashed their cheque. It was humbling. I was becoming part of their refusal to give in, part of their wish to remember. It really did feel that I was running on their behalf, and with that realisation came a sense of privilege. I was going to represent them on the streets of London.

The actress Lesley Joseph was patron of the Macmillan appeal which the newspaper had been supporting, and she wrote me a lovely note of commendation, urging everyone to support me. It meant a great deal. She was graciousness and generosity personified – and utterly typical of the support I received.

But this created a challenge of a different kind. Suddenly, I could see the appeal of anonymity. Here I was writing in the paper about something I had no idea whether or not I could do. How on earth could I face the return to work if I didn't finish the course?

With the marathon a month away, I made my final appeal in the paper, alongside a photograph of me earnestly listening to Pamela's top tips and another of me running dutifully beside her. The headline was 'The final countdown for novice marathon runner', under which I'd written a couple of hundred words trying to put it all into perspective.

One thing I didn't mention in that article was that Fiona was pregnant, with a due date at the end of July. 1998 had become a significant year for all sorts of reasons. Three months after the marathon, I was going to become a dad for the second time.

Chapter Two: 'Streets of Love'
My Debut Marathon – London 1998

From the moment my serious training began in November, my fixed point on the horizon was Sunday, 26 April 1998, my own personal point of no return, the culmination of hundreds of miles' training under Pamela's all-knowing guidance. Poor Pamela. We got on well, but I made her feel nervous. Invariably I overdid the tales of woe, with the result that Pamela was probably more apprehensive than I was as the great day dawned. After all, she felt responsible for me doing it in the first place. I was able to run blithely blaming everyone else for the dumb thing I was about to do. It wasn't my fault. No longer mine to reason why. All I had to do was follow the crowd and run 26.2 miles.

Moreover, I was convinced – and I now recognise this to be an important part of the process – that I was never ever, no, *never*, going to do it again. One marathon was going to be enough. The marathon itch had lurked in my mind for a few years before the chance had arisen, and now I was going to purge myself completely of all mad urges in one insanely long run, after which I would return to normal life. No more getting up stupidly early on a Sunday and running 15 miles. No more nipple plasters. No more sore bits where you really, really don't want to have sore bits. No more stinging eyes as the sweat drips in. No more aches and pains. No, I was going to go back to a life of leisure.

My real world was the one where a Marathon was the much-lamented name for what was now ludicrously called a Snickers; where my only exertion was to reach the bar in the theatre. It was to be a glorious one-off. And that was a big part of my motivation on that slightly overcast April morning. I was going to do it once and I was going to make it count.

We were staying the weekend with my wife's sister and her husband in Tooting – though sadly my sister-in-law Anna wasn't there. She was a couple of hundred yards down the road in the special care baby unit in St George's Hospital, having been admitted horribly early for a baby which threatened to be born fatally premature – a terrible time for her when all she could do was hang on and hope. Days stretched into weeks, and hope started to grow stronger. The happy outcome was that a week after the marathon she gave birth to Callum, a special boy indeed, healthy and to this day a glowing testimony to the wonderful care Anna received; testament too to Anna's remarkable endurance and spirit. But the happy outcome was still in the future as marathon morning broke. Anna's situation was a grim background which helped put everything into perspective. It was only a run, after all. Nothing more than that.

Adding to my motivation was the fact that Linda McCartney had lost her battle against cancer exactly a week earlier. I have been a Beatles obsessive all my life. Given this and the cause I was running for, Linda's death was another spur, another reason to run an unfeasibly long distance – and certainly part of the mental preparation which sees you get your mind in the zone.

Also helping in that respect was the London Marathon registration, another of the areas in which the event is just so damned well organised. Others come close, as I have learned in the years since, but it's London that takes the biscuit, a fact which inspires you with confidence before you even start.

You have to register to run. In other words, you need to pick up your number at the London Marathon exhibition, a great jamboree which I remember most for the inspiring music which plays constantly and for the machine-like competence with which you are processed, packaged and provided with race number and race instructions. After that, you try to find your way through the marathon exhibition, an array of sportswear and shoe firms mixed in with nutritionists and masseurs, all jumbled together with eager representatives from other marathons around the world, keen to nab you to share their own big moment.

Practicalities meant that I registered on the Saturday – the day the marathon exhibition becomes impossibly busy. I panicked and scurried away pretty quickly, fearing it was just too tiring and stressful a place to be the day before a marathon – no fault of the exhibition. It was huge, it was inspiring, it gave you an idea of the scale of the task ahead and it suggested just how well supported you were going to be, but after a few minutes I just wanted to be by myself to contemplate what the morning would bring – 26.2 miles snaking through London on a course I'd heard so many conflicting things about.

Inevitably, if you do well, you will like the course; if you don't, you won't, but it is certainly a course designed to impress, essentially the same course every year, kicking off in Greenwich Park from three separate starts which converge after a few miles. The course then takes you out towards Woolwich and then back towards Greenwich where, just after 6 miles, you pass the National Maritime Museum, so elegant and attractive beside the river. At around 6.5 miles, you pass the Cutty Sark before continuing into Deptford, broadly following the river before turning sharp right at 12 miles to cross the Thames at Tower Bridge, a majestic structure widely regarded as one of the great London Marathon highlights.

Just to its left, enticing you across, is the Tower of London, but once on the north side of the river, you veer right before turning south again into the Docklands where you circle and loop, taking in Canary Wharf, before running back towards the Tower of London. From here, just before the 23-mile mark, you again follow the river, heading west and then curving south past the Embankment at about 25 miles, by which time you begin to sense the finish. As you reach Big Ben, you turn right, away from the river, towards Parliament Square, passing the bottom of Whitehall as you move into Birdcage Walk for the final half a mile. With St James's Park on your right, you run towards Buckingham Palace where a couple of turns will direct you down the Mall for your first sight of the finishing line. With Buckingham Palace behind you now, just a minute stands between you and your finisher's medal.

These were the images I was trying to evoke on the Sunday morning as I travelled to the start. The local trains are free for runners. All you have to do is wave your race number and you're on. Follow the instructions, follow the crowd, follow the marshals and you're there. From Tooting, where I was staying, it's a fair old hike to Greenwich and Blackheath, the recommended tube stops, but while it seemed a pain at the time, yet another thing to think about, I am sure now that it helped, all part of the focusing which culminates in that great moment of release when the gun is fired and off you go.

One of the recommendations for marathon training is to run races, something I never did. I'd read and been told repeatedly that it was a great way to psyche yourself up and get yourself in the right frame of mind. Also that it was good to get used to the idea of running with other people. After all, most runners do the vast majority of their training on their own, churning out those country miles with nothing but the wildlife for company. Marathon day was pretty much the first time I'd seen another runner – the first time running became remotely sociable.

And therein lies one of the great paradoxes of marathon running – the fact that something so solitary and self-centred can also prove, as I discovered that morning, such a bonding experience. Many millions of pounds are raised for charity during a marathon, but I still think there is something self-centred about running even when you are doing it for charity. It is something you do because you want to do it, however much your run will benefit others through the money you raise. Running has always seemed to me an intensely personal thing, and yet huge crowds turn out to watch you do it, all intent on enjoying London's unique blend of street party and elite athletics. Huge intoxication lay ahead – though not of the alcoholic variety.

I'd barely spoken to any other runners until that day, but that morning, suddenly everyone was my mate. Catch someone's eye on the tube, and you're straight into conversation. 'Is this your first?' Stand next to someone at the urinal, and 'Have you done this before?' takes on a different meaning. I remember being struck by the camaraderie, and I continue to notice it to this day. One of the great discoveries of marathon running for the masses is that you run against no one except yourself. The 30,000 other people around you are people you are running with, not against. Run a marathon and you're running a lone race in a huge crowd, all part of the rich fascination that I started to learn and love that day.

On my longer training runs, it had become clear to me just how much marathons are run in the mind, reliant on that bloody-mindedness I was talking about. Consequently, there was something quite forced and determined about my positivity that morning. I was intent on thinking a good race even before I'd started running it. I devised my own little mantra on my way to Greenwich that morning. When I wasn't confessing to being a virgin marathoner to some superfit and slightly intimidating-looking fellow runner, I was muttering to myself 'You can do it, you can do it', my own little hymn that I resorted to on and off throughout the race. Far more important things were happening; Anna was hoping; McCartney was grieving. I needed to keep it in perspective and go out and enjoy it.

I arrived at Greenwich Park at around 8 a.m., with an hour and three-quarters to go until the start. But there were plenty of people there already, and it was quite some prospect as I passed the point of no return, entering the runners-only enclosure where I handed over my labelled luggage to a waiting lorry corresponding to my race number and then settled down to wait. There was an air of nervous expectation overhanging it all; the morning was bright but still slightly chilly; everywhere people were stretching, chatting or queuing for the loo.

Water was available everywhere; tea and coffee were on tap; sports drinks were being dished out. There was everything you needed as you settled down for that final hour or so – everything you needed except sufficient loos. The final 60 minutes passed in what was to become clear to me later as time-honoured marathon fashion, that great queue-for-the-loo ritual which marks marathons everywhere, an essential part of the pre-race warm-up for anyone, anywhere, with 26.2 miles ahead of them.

You've been keeping your hydration up for days; you started the day with a drink; you drank on the train; and you drank on the walk to the start. There's only so much you can take, and so you join the snaking loo queue. Once you reach the cubicle, you do your business and then rejoin the queue, a process you will probably complete – as the minutes tick by – four or five times with ever-diminishing output. The great benefit is that it passes the time – along with whatever else you are passing.

But then, with 10 or 15 minutes remaining before the 'off' at 9.45, it was time to suss out the starting enclosures. A letter on your race number indicates the starting area you will begin from. The faster you predict your finishing time will be, the further to the front you will be placed by the race organisers, a simple tactic which works wonderfully well when it is enforced, just as it is in London. So many of the early yards in other marathons are spent weaving through the wobblers who've started far further forward than their predicted times justified – great for them to steal a march perhaps, but a pain for the quicker runners who've now got to negotiate their way around them. In the London Marathon the organisers get it spot on. At the time, I remember people tutting at the apparent officiousness of it all. It was only in later marathons that I realised how important it is. Strict corralling is ultimately a friend to every single runner.

Of course, the corralling in itself poses a horribly difficult question for a first-time marathoner. Asking you to predict your finishing time seems a terribly unfair question, inviting hubris almost. You've never done it before, yet you are being asked to announce just when you expect to finish.

In reality, it's not too difficult to take a stab at it based on your training, your half-marathon times in particular. I took an average half-marathon time, doubled it and then added a quarter of an hour or so. And then a bit more. More sophisticated methods of calculation are available now, particularly these days with the proliferation of wrist-worn GPS tracking devices, but even without them there are plenty of tables you can resort to, all of which give you a pretty good idea just how you might do in the great unknown ahead. Best of all, perhaps, was simply to follow your instinct. After six months' training, I felt I had a fairly shrewd idea – and I put myself down for somewhere between four and four and a half hours.

Here again, Pamela was wonderfully wise. She was at great pains to point out to me the dangers of fixating on a particular time. Her theory was that you need to have three times in mind: one you would be overjoyed with, one you would be happy with and one that you would consider adequate. In reality, an experienced marathon runner will probably take a more zonal approach, with the range of emotions – over the moon at one end and severely hacked off at the other – shading one into the next over a spectrum.

One way or another, there was plenty to think about as we huddled at the start.

As we waited, I discovered perhaps the thing I love most about marathons, and that's their utterly seductive sense of convergence. Waiting, queuing, wasting time, you see so many people running for different clubs and for different causes, people of so many different nationalities and from so many different walks of life. And yet all of them got up that morning thinking, 'I'm going to run the London Marathon today', and all of them, by whatever means, had made their way here, the only time in the history of the planet that exactly these people will gather together in exactly the same place.

The marathon organisers produce lists of occupations and lists of countries of origin. I like to let my mind be boggled thinking about all the tiny moments and the tiny decisions which have led precisely this group of people to be in this place at this time. Just think of the chain of events which have led to this number of German lawyers lining up alongside that number of French dentists in a field which features this number of English journalists and that number of Spanish accountants. Is it random or is it somehow written in the stars? You suspect it's a quirk of fortune, but you can almost believe there's a hidden hand guiding it all.

Time and again, something quite spiritual rises out of the sweaty mass of humanity which constitutes a marathon, particularly as we gathered at the start that day. I could wax quite lyrical about it, and mentally I started to as I waited. There's something transcendent about a marathon. We've all answered an unheard call. We're lured there to be collectively bigger than the sum of our individualities. Stand at the start of a marathon, and you'll sense it too – a beguiling magnetism about the whole thing which lifts you out of the everyday and lets you glimpse the operating of the universe at a higher level where we are all somehow connected, brought together in a shared consciousness of the task ahead.

And yes, I know that sounds horribly pretentious. But maybe you've just got to be there. On the day, I was welling up at the thought of it. Not many things make me sentimental, but on that morning, I discovered that marathons most certainly do.

It wasn't the morning's only discovery. You'd think that we would all run in the same way. We don't. Far from it. You get the super striders, the low-bodied lopers and everything in between; some people mince, some people prance, others surge; some glide like swans, others are all legs like newborn giraffes; some pump with their arms, some keep their arms stock-still. With some people, you wonder how the mass of their movements can ever combine to create forward thrust. With others, all you can do is marvel at the slick efficiency of it all. Some flail, some ease; some crunch, some coast; some sashay, some flow. Some make it all look incredibly easy; others make it look nigh on impossible. Each to their own, and the great joy is that it is wonderful to see.

No wonder the shoe manufacturers, much as I like to malign them, are constantly pushing forward with their product range, searching for ever-greater degrees of sophistication. It's a wonder they don't give up. How could you possibly ever cater for this lot, charging like rhinos, floating like birds, sprinting like gazelles, hopping like grasshoppers, prowling like tigers, scuttling like mice and heaving like hippos? I soon found myself thinking how exciting it was to be in the thick of it.

It was all decidedly stop-start at the off, though. The gun went. Nothing happened. And nothing continued to happen for the next 30 seconds. We simply stood there shoulder to shoulder. The old hands knew exactly what was happening. We first-timers were bewildered. 'This is going to take much longer than I thought,' I chuntered, throwing in an extra few chants of 'You can do it'. This was something I hadn't anticipated.

Penned in the enclosure for those anticipating a 4 hours to 4 hours 30 finish, we were so far from the start that it was several minutes before the forward motion rippled back to us. Even then, it started out as a shuffle, followed by a standstill, followed by a shuffle, followed by a standstill, a pattern which repeated itself for the first five minutes of my first London Marathon with the start line still nowhere in sight. Finally, the shuffle became steadier; shuffle became walk; walk became trot; the starting arch started to dominate the horizon, and then, almost imperceptibly, trot became run, the transformation completed with the step which took us over the start mat – in my case 11 minutes after the gun, by which time the front-runners had probably completed the first 2 miles.

As I was to discover when my father-in-law joined the fray a few years later even further back, it can be a good 20 minutes before you get over the line – at which point those race leaders would have been 4 miles to the good. Of course you clock your start time from the moment you cross the line, but no wonder I wasn't going to win if I had to give a long-legged Kenyan a 2-mile head start.

But then again, you've got to bear in mind the sheer logistics of it all, the mind-numbing complexity of getting more than 30,000 people simultaneously in motion – people vastly ranging in ability, in expectations and in style. You aren't looking at a complete cross section of humanity, of course.

It's a cross section at the upper end of the fitness spectrum, but even so, there was evidently a great breadth of talent on display, and the London organisers' skill was to get us all up and running as smoothly as possible – something they pulled off brilliantly.

The sky was bright as we finally got underway, a thrilling moment after that initial slowness. A very useful slowness, as it turned out. The received wisdom is that the very worst thing you can do in a marathon is to start off too quickly. The argument goes that with all those miles ahead, you've got to pace yourself – which is fair enough. But unless you're a super-fast runner, most of the big-city marathons will hem you in any way in those early stages.

Even once we'd started, we still came to a couple of shuddering halts – and here the reason was obvious. Scores of runners dashed off to the side for a wee after a few hundred yards. They simply couldn't hold it in any longer, and for reasons only traffic-management experts will understand, their swift side-footing off the course brought us all to a halt. Runners obsessing over time were probably worrying at this point; those of us just enjoying the experience had to view it as part and parcel of the London Marathon's rich mysteries.

The sight of dozens of peeing runners was a timely reminder of all that Pamela had told me. Top up. Top up. Top up every few minutes. Maybe her greatest gift to me as a novice had been to hammer home the crucial importance of hydration. If you feel thirsty, it's too late, she kept saying – words which rang through my head. If you feel thirsty, you are dehydrated. If you are dehydrated, you are in danger. Not necessarily done for, but certainly on the at-risk register.

And so I sipped dutifully from the start as we passed through the leafy residential area which borders Greenwich

Park. Everything seemed very gentle, very guarded, everyone running well within themselves at this point. Spectators had gathered in their front gardens and on the pavements to cheer us on, but suddenly, and slightly strangely, it was all seeming a little low-key. We were passing opulent, attractive houses, but no landmarks at this stage. The only thing approaching a landmark came after 2 or 3 miles, when the various starts merged and the three streams of runners became one continuous flow as we headed towards the Thames. There was plenty of good-natured booing and jeering between the runners as the three races became one, compensation perhaps for the fact that we were in fairly nondescript suburban sprawl and remained so until we reached Greenwich.

Here the Maritime Museum, striking in all its classical elegance to our right, was an early highlight of the day – especially as it seemed to signal that we were making progress.

By now, the crowds were thickening and the noise levels were rising, bands interspersing the spectators, music mixing with the roar as we passed by. Greenwich looked gorgeous on that sunny spring morning, and, just over 6 miles after the start, the Cutty Sark proved exactly the lift I'd been hoping it would be – a lift denied runners in recent years following the fire in 2007. Later marathons showed it boarded up. The 2011 London Marathon bypassed it altogether.

After the Cutty Sark, the route became largely landmark-free once again, but the crowds were reward enough in a stretch which was disappointingly dull in every other respect. I started to pin my hopes on Tower Bridge, just after 12 miles, to lift things once more, as indeed it did. Here, and on both sides of the river, the crowds were intense for one of the day's great moments. Think of the traffic there usually, and here you are running straight across it, but this genuine high was followed by a genuine low. I remember miles 13 to 15 as decidedly dreary. Not a lot distinguished them – a key area where London palls alongside other marathons. The very best courses keep the interest constant, as I was to discover later. London falls short. You just have to rely on the spirit of it all.

By now, the weather had deteriorated significantly, and it was around the halfway mark that we had the second and the heaviest of the three showers that hit us en route. But I loved them – especially when one of the roadside DJs blasted us with 'It's Raining Men'. All you could do was smile. There was goodwill on the day, but even better, there was humour, and the laughs along the way put an extra little spring in our steps.

Time and again, the music chimed in beautifully. Around the halfway mark, 'Honky Tonk Women' by my gods, The Rolling Stones, blared out, always one of my favourites from a band I've idolised for years. It was fabulous to fall into step with an all-time classic; surreal to be one of thousands of runners doing so. You slip into a strange impressionability as you run; you absorb what's going on around you and literally you take it in your stride. As we loped along, the rain, bizarrely, was part of the fun.

It was considerably less enjoyable for Pamela. She was there to support her Macmillan runners, and as the rain came down, all my whingeing was uppermost in her mind. 'Poor Phil,' she kept thinking to herself. 'He hates the rain.' She wasn't to know that I was loving it. I feel rather guilty about that now – and even guiltier when I recall that, selfishly, it never occurred to me just how miserable the downpours were making life at the time for my wife. Fiona had nobly come to support me, despite having a toddler in tow and being now six months pregnant.

Our son, Adam, was very nearly two; our daughter, Laura, was just over three months away from being born. Fiona had a tough day. At the finish, her first chance to change Adam's drenched clothes, she discovered that the spare clothes in her rucksack were even wetter than the clothes he was wearing. The rain dampened the day for thousands in the crowd and probably for many of the runners. For me, at least, it was precisely what the doctor ordered.

One of the benefits was that it helped clear my head for the mind games I was now playing.

I have always found that the great problem with running, certainly the longer distances, is that I just don't know what to think about. Listing various categories sends me round the twist, although it's a technique used by many runners to keep boredom at bay. Actors, actresses, batsmen, bowlers, whatever. I find them difficult to count, even more difficult to remember. And then it becomes all the more infuriating still when I can't remember whether I have already remembered them or not. In the end, it just adds another layer of fretting to the whole thing at a time when, somehow, you need to be relaxing.

Instead, my favoured approach, which I had evolved in training and now started to perfect on the day, was to focus on the significance of the numbers depicted on the mile markers – the only mental gymnastics I can comfortably handle in race circumstances. And this is what I did in London.

The first mile is great because it means you are well under way (and because a round 25 remain). Number two is significant because it is the first even number and means you can start playing with fractions: you've done 1/13th of the race. Number three I like, because if you times it by nine, you've got just slightly more than a marathon (in other words, you've done just over a ninth – well, it's something to cling to). Four is good too, but five is the early highlight. We're getting into round-number territory here, always a treat. 5, 10, 15, 20, 25. I love them. At five, you're just a fraction under a fifth of the way there. Obviously.

Six is a cracker. It means that you've got a round 20 to go. Seven I always enjoy, because the remaining miles have now slipped under 20 and also because you are more than halfway towards the half-marathon. Eight is good – you're just under a third of the way round. Plus it represents 4/13th, a fraction which has a pleasing irreducibility. Nine brings you back to the logic of three – you're just over a third of the way home. Plus there's the bonus that you are just a mile away from the satisfaction of reaching double figures, that great landmark of ten, a figure whose double-digit attraction is enhanced by the fact that the remainder is now just 16, the distance of a not particularly long Sunday run.

And so it goes on, the reasons for enjoying each number ever more strained, ever less obvious. But it was a game that worked for me.

Others say you need to imagine that with each mile in the first half you are adding a block to a big tower you are building that will eventually stretch to 13 storeys high – a tower from which you will then remove a block with each mile of the second half of the marathon until you get back down to ground level again as you finish. I'd far rather be telling myself that 15 is great, because it is the third of those five magical multiples of five which will take you there; that 16 is terrific because you've got the pleasingly round number of ten outstanding; that 17 is another high point because the miles remaining have now dipped into single digits for the first time; that 18 means you are more than two-thirds of the way there with simply a midweek, shortish run left; that 19 is bliss because it's your last teenage mile before you hit the 20s... And so it goes on, ever more desperate, ever more satisfying.

And ever more necessary – if only to guard against thinking about 'the wall' and so being sucked into it. By now – miles 18, 19 and 20 – you are definitely in danger territory. Infamously, the wall is the point at which you've so depleted your body's stored energy that overwhelming fatigue takes over and your energy falls away precipitously. My great fortune was that Pamela had taught me the simplest of ways to protect yourself against it: you drink and then you drink some more.

Just how much you need to drink is one of the things you need to assess as you train, always bearing in mind the simple test that is always available: look at your piddle when you get back home. The experts say that the ideal is a light straw colour, a description which somehow seems rather too romantic for the notion of peering down the pan. 'Light straw' sounds more the kind of thing you might wish for on your kitchen walls. However, that's the guideline. Too much darker and you are dehydrated – a fact which reduces marathon running to a very straightforward task: it's all about delaying the shade change in your wee. Lovely.

My view is that it is inevitable that you will finish dehydrated – a belief which others will say explains why I have never run spectacularly well. But I've drunk to the point where I couldn't comfortably drink any more, and yet I've still finished a couple of dozen colour cards away from light straw. It seems to me that, for us mere mortals at least, hydration on the day is essentially crisis management, an exercise in staving off the crisis – and its effects – until the very last moment.

Certainly Pamela was clear: stay hydrated, and the wall doesn't exist. And she was right. We come back to that natural limit for humans, that 18-mile distance after which you really do have to go the extra mile – and then go it seven more times. Run a marathon and you will see that 18 miles is the moment that separates the hydrated from the dehydrated. It certainly was that day.

At around 16 or 17 miles, I started to see the walkers, those who just couldn't continue running; at around 18 miles, where most people hit the wall if they are going to hit it at all, I saw people pulling up, stretching legs against lampposts, lying squealing on the floor as helpers tugged at their feet. I saw pain. Real pain. And I saw an incentive to keep going, thanking Pamela as I did so. I'd remained sufficiently hydrated, and, as others fell by the wayside, I enjoyed one of those 'There but for the grace of God' moments that spurred me on.

It was difficult not to feel a certain smugness, but I was prepared to forgive myself such unsporting thoughts. I needed to drink deeply on feelings, whatever they were, that would carry me forward. However self-satisfied and uncaring it sounds now, the fact is that I felt emboldened by the distress I saw around me – for the very reason that it wasn't me feeling it.

Pamela had said, 'Sip your water every few minutes and you should be fine,' and events were vindicating her. So many people speak about the wall as if it is really there, some kind of sadistic fixed landmark that you have to launch yourself against in the hope of tumbling through the other side. I learned that morning – exactly as Pamela had said I would – that if you approach the wall in the right way, it need never loom at all, except insofar as you see other people running smack into it; people who have allowed it to grow.

The whole event is set up to hydrate you, with regular water stations plus others dishing out sports drinks. They were generously manned and generously stocked – all part of the remarkable support service which underpins the marathon and keeps it running. Dozens and dozens of volunteers were dishing out tens of thousands of drinks – and always with a smile. It was superbly done, the whole event looking after you every step of the way.

As you approached the drinks station, the helpers were holding out the bottles in anticipation; all you had to do was snatch one, say 'thanks' and glide on into the distance, scrunching a discarded bottle or two as you passed. So many runners just took one swig before slinging the bottle into the gutter, and yet still the supplies kept coming – all part of the reassuring thought, almost every inch of the way, that London wanted you to do well. Marathons are tough, but here the whole organisation was geared up to make it as easy as it possibly could be – and that's also where the huge crowds came into it.

The noise at times was intense, almost overwhelming, particularly in the Docklands area where it seemed to echo, but its net effect was always to urge you on. Helped on by the crowd, no wall on my horizon, I started to focus on the 20-mile marker, so important in my evolving philosophy of cherishing every number for every possible reason. Twenty miles. How good did that sound, and how good did it feel as I passed under that characteristic, balloon-strewn arch which straddles the road every 1,760 yards along the route of the London Marathon?

Beside it, on it and over it were the two digits. Two and zero. It wouldn't be long before I entered uncharted, never-done-before distance. It wouldn't be long before we were leaving Docklands and heading towards the home straight. Just 6 miles to go, I kept telling myself. But what a 6 they were. Running out of the house and knocking off 6 miles is nothing. But it is everything when you are doing a marathon and you've already got 20 miles under your belt.

Tony Blair's press secretary, the marathon-running Alastair Campbell, summed it up beautifully some years later when I had the great pleasure of interviewing him. He was doing a theatre-tour question-and-answer session, mostly I guess about his Downing Street years. On the phone, I was keen to talk to him about marathons. He observed that marathons are in fact two half-marathons put together; it's just that the first half is 20 miles long. Those final 6 miles equal in effort the first 20, he said. He was right.

And here, in London, we weren't particularly helped by the course in the middle stages. We ran through some long stretches where not a lot happened in the early to mid teens, passing through some fairly shabby districts before our reward was the aural lift which came with the Docklands and then the release you enjoy as you are propelled over the cobbles of the Tower of London with just 3 or 4 miles to go, a pleasure denied runners these days for reasons I cannot fathom.

Much was made of how uncomfortable the cobbles were to run on and how dangerous they could be; but the few times I did them, I loved them, and I certainly loved them that day in 1998. They were a landmark on a course which seemed short on landmarks. The cobbles were carpeted, which took away some of the impact, but the main point was that at least they were a feature – and an important one at an important time. This wasn't the end, but at least it was the beginning of the end, as Churchill might have said had he been a marathon runner.

Soon after that, with the Thames on your left, you are into the long, broadly westward final straight, again a point where the crowds are banked steeply, where the noise can be huge and where the roads are wide and comfortable under foot as you steel yourself simply to keep going.

By now, I was wishing I'd written my name on my vest. I was wearing a Macmillan running top, and just occasionally someone would shout at me 'Come on, Macmillan!' I'd glance behind me in fear that I was about to be overtaken by Harold. I was very much the novice. The experienced runners know to emblazon themselves with their name, and then you can play one of the great marathon games – one I have played ever since. Choose the face in the crowd that you want to call out your name, thrust your chest towards them or simply look pained in their direction. The great groundswell of humanity is such that you invariably hit lucky. 'Go on, Phil!' rings out.

And you've just got to hope that it takes you there. Something certainly did that day. The number games, the hydration, the mantra, the crowd, the course: something worked (or perhaps everything did). In recent marathons, I have told myself endlessly that the best way to finish is simply to keep going; and maybe this is where I am finally starting to get a bit deep and meaningful in my marathon running. I tell myself that time is so utterly relentless in its passage that all you've got to do is cling on to it and it will get you there. Think how life has slipped into fifth gear since the children arrived; think how, suddenly, without you remotely realising how, let alone why, you've passed your 30th birthday, then your 40th, and then suddenly you're heading towards your 50th, and there's not a blind thing you can do about it. The years flash by.

These thoughts help me to hang on in there. However slowly you feel you are going, you will get there in the end – for the simple reason that time will pass. All you have to do is somehow keep your feet moving, and time will take care of the rest. Do the training and you're facing maybe three-quarters of an hour, an hour at most, of awfulness. Well, we can all get through that, can't we, if we've got hundreds of thousands of people lining the streets urging us on?

However, on my marathon debut, I was nearly tripped up by something thoroughly unexpected. I was seduced by my first sight of Big Ben in the distance. Stupidly so. I saw Big Ben and I thought I was home. I wasn't. Far from it. There were several miles still to go, the hardest miles, and they suddenly seemed all the harder for the fact that Big Ben had lifted my hopes prematurely.

That first sight was special, but I hadn't realised how easily it can trick you into thinking you are further along than you are – and that's when I had my marathon debut low point. I'd been feeling increasingly tired, but basically OK, still surviving on the wide-eyed wonder of the novice runner, lapping up every experience and trying to take it in, convinced that this would be my one and only marathon and that I was going to make it count.

Perhaps Big Ben was simply the trigger for something which would have happened anyway, but I suddenly felt I couldn't run any more. I tried to hold on, but my run became a walk – just for two or three paces. I'd reached the point at which my body rebelled. But fortunately, after three and a half hours of running, my body simply refused to walk. The two or three steps sent my legs flailing into a kind of spasm. The only way out of it was to start running again. The whole thing lasted perhaps ten seconds at most, but it was a turning point.

It helped that by now the Thames was so close. We were following it, almost flowing along it. And it helped that at last we were back in landmark territory. Finally, after those nondescript central sections, we were ticking off recognisable places as we passed, getting ever closer to the turn into Parliament Square. We passed the Embankment tube station, and everything was getting reassuringly familiar; Big Ben was getting so huge in front of us by now that I just *knew* it wasn't deceiving us; and the noise of the crowd was growing ever stronger as we approached it and turned right, away from the river.

The 25-mile marker had come and gone. There was less than a mile to go, and all I had to do was keep going as we moved into Birdcage Walk, knowing that just the other side of St James's Park to the right, hidden by the trees, was the finishing line.

But now it started to seem horribly, painfully long again. Once more I was thinking that I was there when I wasn't. Birdcage Walk seemed to stretch for miles; we just didn't seem to be moving along it, but we were, and then we were turning right, Buckingham Palace now resplendent to our left. And I steeled myself to see the finish in the Mall.

Except I didn't see it. There was still another turn to go. And then there it was in the distance, drawing all of us in as we screwed that final effort out of our legs, pushing ourselves forward towards the finish, the noise of the crowd now reaching a peak.

And yet the finishing line didn't seem to be coming any closer. I saw it too soon. Was it going to do a Big Ben on me? But no, it was getting bigger, and then suddenly it was exerting a force all of its own, pulling me towards it and over the line – the point at which the tears started to fall. I realise now that they are inevitable, a natural reaction to the effort finally ceasing. Back then, though, they took me by surprise. I saw my time as I crossed the line. I stopped, I wobbled and I cried, a gentlemanly tear or two.

I swayed as my body absorbed the news that I was finally going to let it stop, and I dabbed my eyes after 26.2 miles of grind, all directed at that one moment – that lovely, indescribable, you've-just-got-to-be-there moment of finishing. Other activities may throw up something similar, but I can't believe anything beats that surge of emotion which chokes you as you complete a marathon – especially when it is your first.

And even then, the London Marathon organisation was making my every moment as simple as possible. I inched forward and I wobbled some more – the point at which a rock-steady hand shot out from nowhere and held me under the elbow. They are eagle-eyed, these marshals. They know what to look for. They can spot a runner about to keel over, and they do what they need to do. And then, when I was steady, I did what I had been doing for hours: I followed the crowd. I wrapped myself in a space blanket because suddenly I knew – I don't know how – that I would shiver uncontrollably without it; and I leaned forward as the medal was placed around my neck. It was the final proof, as if my feet could possibly have doubted it: I had become a marathon runner.

A few minutes later, when it started to sink in, I discovered that I was far too happy to feel tired. I managed to find Fiona and Adam relatively quickly at the end, and there is a lovely photograph of me cradling Adam in Parliament Square. Everywhere around, the sun now out, runners were relaxing on any available patch of greenery. Some were stretched out, eyes closed, satisfaction written across their faces. Others were talking animatedly with friends and family, reliving the key moments. The atmosphere was superb, a general air of fulfilment hovering above thousands of exhausted runners. We paused to soak it all up before repairing to the Macmillan reception where there were food and medical attention to be had. It was beautifully organised but, unable to find Pamela, we didn't linger.

It was far more enjoyable to savour the world outside, particularly as we could see thousands of runners still running, still streaming past. There was no sense of 'Hey, look, I beat this lot'. It was simply a delicious feeling of camaraderie. We were looking at them at about 25.5 miles, and I knew exactly what they had been through, exactly what they were thinking. We were all in it together, gloriously so, whatever our respective finishing times.

As I wrote in the paper that week: 'In what other race can you come in two hours and three minutes after the winner and still be stupidly, eternally thrilled? Oh boy, oh what a day. Just over four hours of grind and then a lifetime of inane, self-satisfied grinning.'

Chapter Three: 'Not Fade Away'
A Country Slog - Chichester 2001, 2002

You walk a little taller when you become a marathon runner. How could you not? Train properly, as I like to think I did (well, more or less), and your first marathon will dominate your life for half a year, like exams, only worse. It sits on the horizon, slowly inching closer, and all you can do is wonder whether you are doing enough; whether you're deluding yourself even to think that you might be able to do it. And that's precisely why it's such a glorious feeling when you finally manage it. It probably also explains how quickly you recover.

There had been a wall in my first marathon, but not the one that legendarily cripples runners at 18 miles. It had been the wall of emotion I ran into as I crossed that line. The finishing photo was straight up in the hall at home.

If you've ever completed a marathon, you'll know not to underestimate your achievement. You've not saved a life, split an atom or pushed back the frontiers of human endeavour, but you've pushed your own endeavour painfully beyond what you believed to be its breaking point. In terms of your own existence, you've gone places you've never been before, and that's why swift recovery is so satisfying. You've displayed stamina you barely dared hope for, and now you've sprung back into place, showing a resilience born of the underlying fitness you've acquired over the past few months.

That night I wrote it all down, anxious not to lose any of those memories, keen to relive all those impressions, and the next day at work – there was no way I wasn't going into work on the Monday – I was ready to recount it all once again at the merest hint of interest on anyone's part. In fairness, everyone was genuinely interested, but after a while I realised that most people were more than happy to settle for the edited highlights. There was really no need to part with all the gruesome detail. Not everyone wanted to hear that the insides of the tops of my thighs had been rubbed raw by my shorts – discomfort which had merged with the more generalised discomfort of the race itself.

But at least my nipples were intact, and I was mighty glad of that. Some friends, hearing of my early tussle with the agony of chafed nipples, had given me a good-luck present of Harry Potter plasters, a little bit of magic which certainly worked for me. Over 26.2 miles, even those of us blissfully free of man boobs will still shred our nipples if we don't take precautions. The sweat, the fabric of your running top and the rain will all combine to reduce you to nipple misery. I certainly felt for the runners, and there were plenty of them, who hadn't realised just how important a couple of plasters might be. There was no mistaking them. Their running vests were stained with two ragged columns of blood, like some kind of kinky stigmata.

Fortunately I was saved that, but I did wake up on the Monday to the dawning realisation that in the night someone had injected concrete into my thighs. When I stood up, it shifted agonisingly. I eased myself into the bath, which brought some relief, but all movement that day had to be preprogrammed and absolutely essential. This was the dreaded lactic acid build-up, and stairs were a particular problem. I'd stand at the top thinking it would probably be less painful to throw myself down. But the weird thing was that there was actually something slightly pleasant about the pain. Not for a moment could I forget that I had run a marathon the day before; nor indeed could any of my colleagues.

Experience has since taught me the huge importance of keeping walking at the end of a marathon. Once you're washed and changed, keep moving still. Walk several miles, and you'll feel the benefit in the morning. And if it does hurt in the morning, then you need more of the same. Just keep walking. Walk and walk. My only evidence is my own experience, but I'm convinced that walking really is the best antidote to the effects of running. Unfortunately, I didn't know that in 1998. I barely strayed from the office, and I probably made my discomfort even worse. The one saving grace for colleagues bored with my tales was that by now they could definitely move more quickly than I could.

Smug just wasn't the word for it, though, as I penned my piece for that week's newspaper. I'd finished in 4 hours 11 minutes, a time I now shudder at the thought of. What on earth had I been doing? Did I stop for a pub lunch en route? Did I sit in the park and read the paper for half an hour halfway round? But no, at the time, I was delighted. It wasn't until weeks later that I even started to think how nice it would have been to knock those 11 minutes off. That's the great thing about your debut marathon. Just to finish is enough. Whatever the time. And to cap it all, I had comfortably exceeded my fundraising target for Macmillan. I'd been convinced I was taking a great risk over the whole thing; but, in the event, everything came up trumps.

In hindsight, of course, there was precious little risk at all. I was fit, I was 34, I wanted to do it, I was given superb guidance by Pamela, and I had plenty of family support at a great moment of opportunity – just a few months later, we would become parents for the second time.

And, above all, I had got one thing blissfully right. I had taken the whole thing incredibly seriously. It wouldn't have been in my nature to have done otherwise. A marathon is a huge undertaking. The only way to complete it is to treat it with the utmost respect, and I did so.

I noted with a mix of dismay and vindication a few years later when a celebrity runner, proclaiming her lack of preparation, simply launched into the London Marathon, apparently without knowing, or even asking, how long a marathon race was. She reached about 18 miles, that natural human limit, before collapsing. A newspaper article ripped into her the following day – and rightly so. It reflected on the huge disservice she would have done marathon running by dropping dead. Had she done so, it would have been entirely her own fault. Her crime was to disrespect the marathon and, with it, every single one of her fellow runners, all the men and women from all walks of life who had put in month after month of preparation, running mile after mile in readiness for the big day. The celebrity had attempted to belittle us all. The marathon didn't have the least qualm in showing her emphatically just who was boss.

In the newspaper following my London debut, I waxed lyrical about the day, lauding everyone and everything, signing off with the words, 'So what about next year? I don't think so. One marathon seems very special. Two just sounds like a small number.' It was out of my system. Laura was born in the August following the April marathon. I didn't want to run another marathon; and even if I had wanted to, I would have counted it unreasonable to head off for all those hours of training. Fiona would have let me. It would never have occurred to her to stop me, but I wouldn't let me because I knew my place was with my family at this critical time. Not that there was even any great sense of sacrifice on my part. I'd done a marathon. As simple as that.

But clearly something was niggling away in the unvoiced recesses of my mind over the next couple of years. Not high-level niggling, but niggling all the same. And so it was that in July 2001, more than three years after my first London Marathon, I converted my 'very special' number into a 'very small' one with a spur-of-the-moment run which broke all the rules.

By now, Laura was nearly three; Adam was five years and two months; and the difficult days of having two really tiny children were starting to slip into memory. Of course, Fiona had borne the brunt, as any mother always does, however much of a new man you try to be. But by 2001, life on the home front was easing to the extent that I started to contemplate quite openly what could be next in the running stakes. Life seemed manageable again; possibilities were opening up, one of them right on my doorstep at work.

For years, Chichester had boasted an annual event, inaugurated by the Royal Military Police, in which servicemen were joined by members of the public on a long trek out into the countryside, up onto the South Downs and back down and round to complete a big circle. It became known as the Chichester March. Inevitably, it started to attract runners.

When I covered it for the newspaper one year in the 1990s, turning out to work – oh horror of horrors – on a Sunday morning, I arrived so ludicrously early that it was the runners I found myself interviewing. Generally, they were on the wrong end of a bit of unspoken disapproval. There was a feeling among some of the march diehards that running around the course somehow really wasn't in the spirit of the whole thing. But it certainly impressed me. It's perfectly possible that meeting the front-runners that morning was one of the keys which eventually unlocked my own marathon aspirations. In hindsight, there was something inspiring about them, arriving back far too soon, looking tired but satisfied. There was something in what they'd achieved which appealed to me.

Gradually, over the years, the running element had grown, and by 2001 it sat comfortably alongside the marching element in an event which had changed character. The Royal Military Police stepped back from the march, taking with them much of the services interest which had defined and driven the early years. By 2001, with the runners getting more numerous, the day had sprung its own marathon on the back of a few changes to the route to bring it up to the marathon distance. Or nearly. It was advertised as a marathon – otherwise I wouldn't have gone near it. But, confusingly, the event was promoted as a '42 km All Terrain Run', in other words almost a couple of hundred metres short of a marathon. But I decided I could add that distance in myself somewhere along the line. Everything else was in its favour. It was in the city in which I worked, and I couldn't think of any reason not to have a go.

You couldn't wish for a marathon more different to 'the London', as we runners like to call it. In the capital, you had massive support on a fast, flat course, bringing together tens of thousands of runners in front of hundreds of thousands of spectators; in Chichester, just looking at the route, it was obvious that you had ahead of you a hilly ordeal, mostly in the middle of nowhere with only the occasional other runner for company. The course rapidly left the city behind to head out onto the South Downs. At least 90 per cent of it was going to be out in the country. A good proportion was going to be on decent roads, but a substantial part of it was clearly going to be on trails and tracks. The whole event was as low key as 'the London' was high profile – and that suited my purpose.

Making a mockery of just about every piece of marathon wisdom I'd ever acquired, I decided to give it a go on the back of virtually no training whatsoever. And, yes, I know that does make my criticism of that celebrity just now sound rather hollow. It was the kind of rashness which really ought to have left me collapsed in a ditch halfway round; but at least, I reasoned, I did already have a marathon under my belt, even if it had been three years before.

My initial approach was that I would treat the day as a training run, that I would run the first hour and see what happened. I did a test run on the Thursday before the race on the Sunday, running for 1 hour 28 minutes and guessing my distance to be around 10 or 11 miles. The important thing was that the run had gone well.

I consequently broadened my ambitions for the Sunday, deciding that I would aim for a half-marathon and then walk the rest. 'You can do it' had been my mantra for London. For Chichester, it was 'Let's see how it goes'. The impact on the family was minimal, just half a day away. There was no reason not to try.

The route was essentially a large loop to the north and north-east of the city, taking us out from Chichester, up through the Goodwood estate, past Goodwood Racecourse, down into the village of East Dean and then up into the woods and onto the South Downs Way, before curving back down south-westwards towards Chichester again. The outline was easy enough to grasp, but once we were out there, we would never really know just how far round we were. In London, the runners always had a good idea. On the Chichester route, no distances were marked. I realised I was just going to have to try to assess distance in terms of how I was feeling.

The marathon set off at 8 a.m., as I recall, well before the walkers were unleashed on the same route, and, after all the planning and preparation which had gone into London, it was rather nice simply to drive to the nearest car park and walk the couple of hundred yards across Oaklands Park to the start, just north of the Festival Theatre, next to Chichester Rugby Football Club. A few marquees had been set up as the walk/race headquarters, and it was all very relaxed, with plenty of people I knew manning the tents. I'd signed up for the race during the week, and the remaining formalities on the morning were quickly dealt with.

With ten minutes to go, worried about the missing 195 metres, I walked away from the start line; with three minutes to go, I ran towards it, timing it to perfection to cross the line as the gun went off. I'd done the little extra which would turn – to my satisfaction, at least – a 42-km run into a marathon, and off I went, one of several dozen runners heading out under clear blue skies, still with just a hint of chill in the air.

Just as in London, it was great simply to get going; interesting too to see which route the marathon was going to take us on as we headed northwards out of the city before veering across towards the former Westhampnett airfield, which so famously became the Goodwood motor-racing circuit in the years after the war. We were on historic turf as we clipped the corner of the site before crossing the road to head towards Goodwood House itself, seat for centuries of the Dukes of Richmond. Running past the house, we headed up the celebrated Goodwood hill climb, now a central part of the annual Goodwood Festival of Speed. The Festival website bills it as a 'challenging white-knuckled 1.16-mile course', which 'starts as a tree-lined run through the southern corner of the Goodwood estate' and then 'turns to sweep past the front of Goodwood House before climbing a steep and narrow estate road bordered by flint walls and dense woodland groves towards Goodwood's equine racecourse on top of the magnificent South Downs'.

Magnificent indeed, but on foot it wasn't quite so white-knuckled. Instead, it was a slog; long, slow and draining, but, coming just 40 minutes into the race, it was manageable enough, bringing us to the top of the first of the day's four climbs, emerging on the high ground next to Goodwood racecourse, elegantly positioned to enjoy stunning views across the Downs. Not that we paused to enjoy the views. Instead, we ran beyond the course and then darted down a country track to run sharply downhill on a tough, rutted, stony footpath through the woods northwards into the beautiful village of East Dean.

Against the clear early-morning sky, it looked ravishing, full of archetypal Sussex appeal and, for me, full of happy Sussex memories. It was here that the poet and playwright

Christopher Fry lived for many years, and one of the great pleasures of my job was occasionally going to see him, always a treat as I stepped back into another world full of charm and pleasantries long since lost to modern-day living.

'Have you come here by motor car?' he would ask with a twinkle, and I would always wonder whether the archaism was deliberate, before concluding that it wasn't. Christopher really did live in a world where cars were motor cars. I smiled to myself as I ran through the village, just a few yards from where he was doubtless sipping tea from a bone china cup. 'No, I came here on foot this morning,' I chuckled to myself in tribute to quite the most endearing man I have ever met.

But there was no time to pause for thought as the route took us on and out of the village, a flattish road taking us eastwards towards a left-hand turning which led steeply upwards through the woods to the top of the South Downs where we joined the South Downs Way. The ascent was a struggle, particularly as the risk of tripping seemed high, but it was more than worth it. There was something about the air at the top. You could almost feel it cleanse your lungs as you breathed it. Again it struck me: you couldn't possibly conceive a marathon more different to London.

As so often happens after a long climb, I accelerated once I was finally on the flat. It's as if the ascent had somehow coiled up my legs, unleashing me to spring forward once the climb stopped, and it was certainly with renewed energy that I hared off eastwards on our section of the splendid walking route which runs 100 miles from Eastbourne to Winchester. We were on the South Downs Way for probably 3 or 4 miles, and I had an excellent half an hour to start with up there, largely by falling into the slipstream of someone running at more or less my pace. I'd like to think I helped him keep going, but I doubt it. When two hours were up, I remarked how quickly the time had flown since the start. His only answer was 'Yes!' Conversation clearly wasn't on his agenda. We separated soon afterwards. The London camaraderie wasn't much in evidence out on those lonely hills.

Maybe that was why my high started to evaporate, and soon afterwards I endured a tough quarter of an hour, struggling for the lack of landmarks, struggling for the lack of company. I was lucky if I could see more than a couple of runners ahead of me, so thinned out were we by now, and my struggle was compounded by the fact that suddenly a solitary runner came running towards us the other way. I started to think we were going to turn around at some point and that he was miles ahead – a depressing thought. Even worse was the niggling worry that somehow I had gone wrong. I hadn't, as it turned out, so heaven knows what he was doing. He had a number on. He was part of the race. Unless I just dreamt him. Who knows?

Tiredness was certainly taking hold. This was far further than I had run since London and on terrain I had never attempted before. Even during my 'London training' I had mostly kept to roads; this was now mile upon mile of track, often uneven, often stony and just occasionally slippy. It was much more forgiving on the knees than tarmac, but in my tiredness I started to feel that I couldn't trust it. Again, I started to worry about tripping.

Fortunately help was at hand, and from an unlikely source. A checkpoint suddenly loomed, unheralded, just as we were about to leave the heights and head back down through the woods. High on the Downs, I was suddenly being offered water by a former Mayor of Chichester. I knew her reasonably well, and it felt more than a touch surreal to see her again in such circumstances. But a friendly face is always a boost, particularly when she offered me welcome confirmation that we were comfortably past the halfway mark. I knew it. We had to be. But it was great to hear someone say it.

And that's where the mind took over. I enjoyed an excellent three-quarters of an hour after that. Feel good, and you'll run well. For those 45 minutes, I enjoyed the almost spiritual lift that running can give runners but so rarely gives me. I could feel the rhythm of my run and I could feel that the rhythm was good. I wasn't aware of speaking, but I could hear myself saying 'good running' every now and then, which made me run even better. Mind games, indeed, and the games got even better during a lovely stretch which took us back down off the Downs. It felt like the beginning of the end. Just to cap it all, there was a hint of spitting, refreshing rain and the temperature was perfect.

The long downhill stretch took us right back into East Dean, just a few miles north of Chichester as the crow flies. There, at the checkpoint, a rather vague woman said that we had either 8 or 10 miles to go, she wasn't quite sure. I remember thinking that she might have thought it an idea to find out – a rather ungracious reaction given that she was kindly dishing out water.

Soon afterwards, still in East Dean, we passed a table groaning with choccies and flavoured drinks for sale. I imagine it was intended for the walkers who would be coming along several hours later with pocketfuls of cash. But just the sight of it was enough to undo me. I was starting to get hungry – or rather I was starting to think I was. I saw a Bounty, and that was it. I wanted it. But I had no money. It had never occurred to me to bring any. When you run, you take as little with you as you can possibly get away with. A fine principle, but the damage was done. Hunger – or maybe just the thought of it – took hold. My problem was that I had no idea how to deal with it.

Maybe eating would have been the wrong thing to do. Given a choice between running hungry and running full, give me running hungry every time. I've never experienced it but I've always assumed that a full stomach must be one of the worst discomforts on a racecourse. You need to be lean and a bit mean. Hunger keeps you going. A full tummy would stop you in your tracks – or so I've always assumed.

But that day, it was hunger – or the illusion of it – that was nearly my undoing. I was tired, and there was nothing robust about my thinking. I was showing my inexperience and, with it, a lack of control. I should have nipped the thought in the bud. Instead I let it grow, and that was the big mistake. I made things difficult for myself.

At least we were clearly heading towards Chichester now. Unfortunately there was one very sharp ascent to go. After East Dean, the course cut across a field which rose vertically before us as we headed back towards the plateau where the Goodwood racecourse stands, high above Chichester. It was the low point of the day. Tiredness was kicking in strongly, hunger was hammering, and I was reduced to a disjointed run-walk-shuffle with the summit still hundreds of yards above me.

All I could do was cling on to the thought that what goes up must come down, and sure enough, eventually, we came out close to the racecourse – and the realisation that almost everything would be downhill from now on. More encouraging was the fact that we got our first glimpse of the walkers. They had set out on their trek several hours after us and were now 5 or so miles into their circuit. The runners – and we were very thinly dispersed by now – knew exactly what the walkers had in front of them. We also had the huge satisfaction of having put it behind us.

From the racecourse road, the last little ascent was to the top of the Trundle, an Iron Age hill fort on Saint Roche's Hill just north of Chichester, for a fantastic if fairly blowy view towards the city. Beyond it was the sea, and beyond that was the Isle of Wight in the far distance. Just in front of us was the joy of the final checkpoint, this time manned by two former mayors. One of them asked me how I was. I told her I was starving, to which she offered moral rather than actual sustenance – welcome news that there were just 3 miles to go.

From the heights, Chalkpit Lane sliced wonderfully straight through the chalk of the lower Downs in an invitingly direct line to the city below. At last, after all the hours of where-am-I uncertainty, the goal lay ahead, and so I trotted on with surprising vigour. Big Ben-like on the horizon, the spire of Chichester Cathedral seemed to grow with every step, a lovely sign of getting oh so close, until the road dipped and the cathedral disappeared from view.

But then suddenly, with the cathedral gone and only fields in front of me, I ran again into that sapping sense of not having the foggiest idea where I was. We really could have been anywhere. I walked for five minutes or so, conscious that I was probably losing the chance of beating my London Marathon time, but I was tired. And maybe deep down I didn't want to beat my previous time for the simple reason that this was a run done without training. Subconsciously, perhaps, I wanted to believe that all that training first time round had actually counted for something.

Eventually, we rejoined the road by which we had left Chichester. Knowing where I was, I broke into a strong run again for the last half-mile and felt quite choked as I crossed the finishing line. It was sad not to have anyone to meet me. But I felt good. I felt strong and loose-muscled. I glanced at my watch as I finished. I had completed the course in 4 hours 13 minutes 43 seconds, two minutes slower than my London debut three years before. And I was home in time for lunch, wondering more and more just what it was – if anything – I had accomplished.

Any other day I'd have struggled to run 10 or 12 miles, and yet suddenly I had done a marathon. And I had done it on no training at all. My knees hurt and my ankles ached, but no more so than the last time. My only conclusion was that I was reasonably fit and unreasonably pig-headed. But I still couldn't work it out. Perhaps I had kept going because the run was for real in a way that training never can be. Perhaps I'd kept going because I already had a marathon to my credit and knew I could do it. Perhaps also I'd benefitted from the low-key nature of this particular marathon. There had been no pressure. Almost nobody had known I was doing it, in sharp contrast to the London Marathon, which I had repeatedly mentioned in the newspaper in order to bring in the sponsorship I had needed to justify my place. By contrast, here was an instance where the absence of a sense of occasion had actually been a help during the run – even if it was somewhat deflating afterwards.

The terrain had been tough. There had been four steep climbs. And yet I had found it much, much easier than the flat London course with its endless streets and huge, cheering crowds. Maybe it was the fact of just deciding to get up and do it – a return to the kind of freedom that running really ought to be about. In all these ways, the pressure had been off.

But the downsides were that suddenly I had done two marathons rather than one, and that the second had been completed with no build-up whatsoever, leaving a downbeat sense of 'Well, what was that all about then?' I wasn't remotely on a high. Instead, I felt disappointed. Ultimately, it was an anticlimactic experience, one which underlined the extent to which a marathon needs a build-up and just how much it needs an audience. You need to feel that you have earned it; you also need to feel that you have been urged on to finish.

I returned to the Chichester Marathon in 2002 for an almost identical experience, completing the course in 4 hours 10 minutes. In July 2004, I went back again for what should have been my hat-trick of Chichester marathons. Except that was the year of the marathon that wasn't. Again, it was generally referred to as the Chichester Marathon. Without the M word, I wouldn't have shown up. Officially, it was still a '42 km All Terrain Run'. But I knew the score on that one. Once again, making up the missing 195 metres, I gave myself a three-minute run-up before the start.

But within a couple of hours, I was mystified to find myself much further around the course than I ought to have been. At the end, I was given a certificate to confirm that I had completed the City Of Chichester International Challenge 42 km All Terrain Run, but nothing about it seemed right. I came in fifth with a time of 3 hours 19 minutes, and I knew that something was seriously up. How likely was it that I would knock nearly 50 minutes off my first London time on an up-and-down course such as this?

As the poor chap wrote out my certificate, I grumpily told him: 'That was never a marathon, you know.' He confessed that 'some lads' had been caught changing the arrows up in the woods.

Maybe that was true. But I felt sceptical. As acts of vandalism go, it rang false. You can't imagine a bunch of ne'er-do-wells getting tanked up in the city and then walking miles to the middle of nowhere simply to change the direction markers on a cross-country marathon. Hee, hee! What a lark! If that had really been the case, we would probably still be running it now. A random act of vandalism was hardly likely to have shortened the course. More likely it would have dispersed us to the four winds. Or perhaps they were philanthropic vandals, worried for our feet, knees and hips. But somehow I doubted it.

I didn't know the course well enough to work out where the route had been changed, but that was hardly the point. The worst thing race organisers can do is to lose the trust of the runners in their charge, and that's what happened in Chichester in 2004. Or so it seemed to me.

Significantly, the event has since abandoned its pretentions to be a marathon – though you've only got to look at the Internet to see that plenty of runners still refer to it as the Chichester Marathon or the Chichester Marathon Challenge. They need to be careful. Marathon is far too important a word to be abused in this way. It can be claimed only when the course is well marked, well protected and exactly 26 miles 385 yards (or 42 kilometres 195 metres) long. The plus side was some fantastic scenery, but that's little compensation for those who ran along to the increasingly depressing realisation that they weren't running a marathon at all. Maybe the organisers have made all sorts of improvements in the years that have followed, I don't know. But there's no getting away from the fact that in 2004, it was a good 4 or 5 miles short, maybe even more.

Somehow, it seemed, for me at least, that satisfaction and long-distance running in and around Chichester weren't destined to go hand in hand.

Chapter Four: 'Street Fighting Man'
Fitting in with Family – London 2002, 2003

In hindsight, it's obvious that the Chichester Marathon in 2001 did serve one purpose at least. Effectively it cleared the way for another tilt at the London Marathon, which I returned to in 2002. And, just to double the motivation after the purposelessness of Chichester, I decided to do it for the MS Society, a charity dear to my family.

In 1982, my parents created from scratch the Gosport & Fareham branch of the MS Society, in part a response to all the difficulties my mum's sister, Diana, had faced. An MS sufferer from her late teens, Di started to show the signs of the disease in the late 1960s and early 1970s, that is, at a time when little seemed to be known about MS. When diagnosis came, it was harshly delivered, with little explanation and no backup – so different to all the support that is available now.

Fortunately, my mum, a nurse, was able to make a genuine difference; and my elderly grandparents, to the limit of their abilities, adapted their bungalow to Di's every need. Sadly, however, her condition deteriorated rapidly. I can still hear my grandmother saying, 'It's a wicked disease.' Within a few years, Di was wheelchair-bound, and there she stayed, knowing no remission until her death at the age of 43 in 1991. Within a couple of months, my grandparents had also passed away. But by then, the Gosport & Fareham branch of the MS Society was flourishing, scores of people relishing the companionship, comfort and sheer common sense it was able to provide.

When I managed to get a place in the 2002 London Marathon, I resolved to use that place to raise money for the branch. I thought of the aimlessness and emptiness that had sunk any sense of achievement in my Chichester run. London 2002 was going to be different.

But first I had to get there, and that meant a return to training – something I hadn't seriously done for four years now. The Chichester Marathon was under my belt, but I had no intention of approaching London with the levity with which I had approached Chichester. For London, I was going to be back in training in earnest. The last time I had done that, Adam had been nearly two and Laura just a bump. Now, in the autumn of 2001, Adam was five and a half and Laura was three and a quarter. These two VIPs had to be factored into the equation, and I am convinced that they are to blame for the strange addiction I developed around this time to running in the dark.

These days, work is much more flexible. I have taken the opportunity to make it so, championing the notion of working from home a couple of days a week, saving many boring and, indeed, expensive hours on the motorway, and making the whole thing so much more manageable into the bargain. Back then, though, things were much more rigid. By the time I'd got home, helped with the tea, done my bit towards kiddie bath time and enjoyed the bedtime story routine, it had been dark for hours. If I wanted to get my run in, there was no alternative but to head off out there into the dark. The surprising discovery was that it was hugely enjoyable.

I was hooked. Within a few hundred yards I'd left the town behind me and was heading off down country lanes, criss-crossing rural routes and relishing a newfound freedom. Work couldn't reach me, and nor could home. Recklessly and irresponsibly, I refused to carry a mobile. It's only very recently that I have consented to possess one at all – though, much to Fiona's annoyance, I don't take it running. Foolish and selfish, I know, but it would be an intrusion. This was me on my own, out there running, grabbing a bit of life that was mine, all mine, all mine.

Older and just possibly a fraction wiser, I generally avoid running in the dark these days, but back then, I'd head off as if in answer to some kind of call. The wolves were howling. The drums were beating. I was summoned, and no one was getting in the way.

It was strange how quickly my eyes became accustomed to the darkness; after ten minutes or so, I could quite persuade myself that near-total obscurity was actually a kind of half-light. I never had a moment's fear for my safety. In fact, I managed to persuade myself that I was safer in the darkness. During the day, you might not hear a car heading towards you the other side of a narrow bend. But at night, in addition to various reflective strips on my clothing, I had an extra protection. I might miss the noise of the engine, but there was no way I could miss the headlights glowing in the darkness, throwing up all sorts of shadows around me. It gave me plenty of time to retreat into the hedgerows, well out of the way. The last thing I wanted to do was spook an oncoming driver. As for me, I was spooked by nothing, and I was having a ball.

It became addictive – an alternative, murky existence in which every stride was an email deleted, every yard a phone call answered. All the people who'd pushed me during the day were being pushed back in a darkness which put me beyond their reach. It started to seem the perfect antidote to work. The benefits were huge. For years, I'd suffered from insomnia, and while I didn't particularly notice it recede the first time I trained for the London Marathon, this time round it vanished altogether. The early months of 2001 marked the start of the year-round running I've pursued pretty much ever since. It's no coincidence that my insomnia, though it comes and goes, has never returned to its pre-2001 levels.

Equally, I found my asthma easier to deal with. As a child, I'd occasionally been quite debilitated by it, and it had flared up from time to time ever since. But with the introduction of running as a fixed and regular part of my life, the asthma seemed so much more under control. The cold night air was cleansing. Away from work and in my own bubble, I was breathing the deepest I had ever breathed.

In hindsight, a late-evening run, darting wherever I wanted in the obscurity, created a need every bit as much as it satisfied one. It became addictive, but part of that addiction, I started to realise, was the simple fact that I always felt better for a run. Opt out of a run, and I knew I would regret it. Go for it, and somehow I felt back in touch with myself.

It was almost like a rebalancing, a re-synching at a time in my life when perhaps the demands were at their greatest. It was me jumping off the treadmill, I'd tell myself as I darted down blind alleys, and I started to become quite pretentious and pompous about it. It seemed to me that I was somehow realigning my existence, tightening up my life and refocusing – all of which sounds terrifically self-centred. But I am convinced that it was self-centredness with a purpose. My me-time made me much more generous in my everyone-else time. It was as simple as that. Or so I liked to tell myself.

In those early days of fatherhood, it was quite difficult to make the regular transition between taking myself seriously as a respectable journalist and being a dad wiping bottoms and getting regularly puked on. In some ways, the running was part of handling that transition, and it seemed to me that if I got a regular run in, then in so many ways I was able to be both a better dad and a better worker. I like to think I never lost sight of where my real responsibilities lay, but I genuinely believed that I fulfilled those responsibilities all the more effectively once I'd burned off some energy in the darkness. It seemed a reasonable pay-off. For a few hours off the leash, I was much more focused when I got back.

Fiona wasn't necessarily ecstatic at my absences, but she recognised the equation and the benefits it brought. In fact, it was often Fiona who encouraged me to go out on those rare occasions when I wavered. As she puts it, she likes me better when I've been for a run.

Besides, as the 2002 London Marathon dawned, she started to realise that there was just something about the men in her life. This was the year I gained the most unexpected and the most welcome of running mates, Fiona's father, Michael, and I am delighted to take the credit for tipping him over the edge.

Michael had been extremely supportive and encouraging before my debut marathon, but only, I thought, out of healthy respect for any level of sporting endeavour which takes you out of your comfort zone. A skilled cyclist in his younger days, Michael had always had the sporting bug, and through his cycling he probably knew far more than I did about pushing yourself to the limit and beyond. Little did I know that he had been contemplating a marathon of his own.

Unknown to me, Michael had for many years seen the marathon as a great achievement, envying anyone who managed to complete the course. He later admitted that he had posted a ballot application to run the London in 1998, the year in which I had made my own marathon debut. How lovely it would have been to be novice marathon runners together. Sadly, however, he had been unsuccessful in the ballot, much to the relief of Stella – Fiona's mother – who pointed out that he had never run in any race whatsoever up to that point. But my London finishing photos niggled away at him to the extent that he decided to mark his 70th year in 2002 by having another attempt at getting into the London Marathon.

Thus he embarked on what was to become a remarkable sequence of ballot rejections that has lasted to this day. Anyone else would take the hint and conclude that London really didn't want him, but not Michael. He wanted London, and he got it, finding a different way into the race which bypassed the main entry ballot. After the initial rejection from the London Marathon organisers, he made an application for one of six places that were offered by *The Times* newspaper. Just after Christmas 2001, he was told that he could have a place provided that he ran for charity.

After all the trauma of grandson Callum's arrival in this world, Michael opted for Tommy's, a charity which supports premature babies. This left him 16 weeks to do some training and to try to raise as much sponsorship as possible. Michael was up and running, and I couldn't have been more pleased.

All sorts of reasons militate against us running together, not least the fact that Fiona's parents live in Colchester, 140 miles away from our home in Hampshire. Even more significantly, Michael and I run at a very different pace, not surprisingly given that there are 31 years between us. But I welcomed him warmly into the running fold for so many reasons. We'd always got on well, but maybe this was the point at which the usual father-in-law/son-in-law relationship developed into the firm friendship we now enjoy.

I'd got together with Fiona in 1986 towards the end of our modern languages degrees at Oxford, the university Michael had also attended, completing his doctorate there just before Fiona was born. His encouragement was central to my decision to return there – with Fiona in 1987 – to embark on my own doctoral research. A university librarian, Michael was well versed in research at that level. He knew what was required, and it was helpful to have someone within the family who had been there before. I completed my PhD – or DPhil, as Oxford prefers to call it – in 1990, confident that an Oxford doctorate would do wonders for my approval ratings as far as Michael was concerned.

And now the boot was on the other foot. Just as Michael had blazed the academic trail for me to follow, so now he was dipping into my world of marathons – much to my delight. It was a vindication as much as anything else; proof – to my mind – that running stupidly long distances wasn't necessarily a daft thing to do. Of course, I loved the bizarreness of it anyway, but if two of us within the family were at it, then somehow it was legitimised. It helped that it was no longer just me doing it.

Just as importantly, it gave me someone to swap ideas with, someone to share the enthusiasm with. I wasn't a club runner; I was fitting in running whenever I could. Now, in Michael, I suddenly had someone to chew the running cud with. For Michael's first marathon, I enjoyed dispensing my own wisdom and experience, much as Pamela had done for me four years before, and this helped my own confidence grow. But, in reality, it was an instant rapport of running equals, the link not forged by any superior knowledge on my part, but by a meeting of two rather stubborn (OK, very stubborn) people united in a common cause. The pleasure of the relationship was that he now 'understood', just as I 'understood', and the value of that is incalculable.

London 2002 was my hypochondria marathon. I took co-codamol, paracetamol and a couple of ibuprofen before starting. I also, for no particular reason, took the diarrhoea medicine Arret; ironic really, given that arret-ing was the very last thing I wanted to do. The problem was that my deformities were catching up with me. My knees were a mess; stiff, aching and awkward. As the race approached, I ran into trouble. My big dream was to run the marathon in under four hours, and, in the final few weeks, I could see that dream evaporating. It was gutting. Grumpy became my middle name.

For London first time round, my bandy-leggedness had been negated simply by well-chosen running shoes.

Alexandra Sports had directed me to the best possible match to compensate against my tendency to roll my foot inwards, and it had been enough.

But six weeks before the London Marathon of 2002, I did a three-hour 20-mile run and discovered – perhaps because my imperfection and its consequences had worsened – that 20 miles was now the limit of my shoes/knees without prosthetics, those artificial devices or extensions which replace or correct a missing or malfunctioning body part. I was rolling my foot/leg inwards as I ran, which didn't simply twist my knee; it was also wastefully inefficient. Nature was failing; science needed to step in.

I saw a physio who massaged my legs, showed me some exercises and told me which prosthetics to order – a pair of shaped plastic pieces which sit in the shoe just under the arch of the foot to prevent it from rolling over and inwards. He was confident they would do the trick, and suddenly there was hope. But the first time I wore them, after two weeks without a run, I quickly developed some spectacular blisters just where they rubbed, particularly on my left foot. The skin flopped with fluid. A pin seemed the only option – unwise, I know, but at least it brought some relief – until the fluid built up again. Frankly, my foot looked awful.

Fortunately, by the time race day dawned, the healing had started, but one way or another the final weeks of my training had been poor, erratic and sore. My knees still ached and were occasionally sharply painful, and I had no idea what I might be about to open up on the soles of my feet. Confidence ran out the door. Fear took ever-greater hold, and sleeplessness was my nightly companion. You need everything to come right if you are to run a good race. Absolutely everything. My 2002 London Marathon bid was punctured below the waterline before I even started, I moaned. And then moaned some more.

On the morning of the marathon, my knees were still tender. I worried whether they could possibly withstand the endless pounding of 26.2 miles, and I let the worry go round and round in my mind. I just wanted to get out there and get started, but at the same time I was dreading it.

But at least there was the extra companionship to look forward to. The night before the marathon, Michael and my mother-in-law, Stella, stayed in the same hotel as Fiona and I did, just by Charing Cross Station, perfectly situated for the early-morning train to Greenwich for the start.

The children stayed with my parents in Gosport for the weekend, and while Fiona and her mum took in shops and museums on the Saturday afternoon, Michael and I enjoyed four hours of total inertia in the hotel room, flicking through endless TV channels, reserving for each the attention span of a flea as we resolutely refused to do anything likely to expend any energy. We wrapped ourselves in cotton wool for an afternoon of utter idleness. Towards the end, even channel-hopping became too energetic as we whiled away the hours watching some obscure sport on an even more obscure channel. Whenever we've done a marathon since, Saturday-afternoon indolence has been a vital warm-up to our Sunday-morning exertions.

Adding to the pleasure on the Sunday, of course, was the fact that I now had someone to travel to the start with. This really was going to be a family marathon, and Michael and I lapped up the atmosphere before going our separate ways to our respective start points. We were starting several hundred yards apart. His aim was to finish, mine was to break four hours.

After a minute's silence for the Queen Mother, who had died two weeks before the race, we got underway in warm and pleasant conditions. Soon the miles were slipping past, and with them my fears. My knees were holding up remarkably well. So far. They were bruised and tender, but they weren't holding me back – to my huge relief. More miles came and went, and still no major discomfort.

I passed the halfway point after 1 hour 51 minutes, a time which horrifies me now but which at the time seemed fine. It was 14 minutes short of the time it took the men's winner to complete the entire course, but for an also-ran like me, it was perfectly acceptable. Even better, things continued to go well for the next 4 or 5 miles. But then suddenly I started to wonder if I hadn't gone off too quickly at the start. It wasn't knee-related, but I was starting to flag, a problem not helped by the fact that by now I was going through some of the dullest sections of the course.

Here, however, the crowd really started to come into its own. I started playing the name game in earnest. My name was on my chest this time round, and I wanted everyone to shout it out. The really valuable support comes from the people who take the next step. They don't just call out your name. They catch your eye. By this stage, I wanted the personal touch, and I was rewarded with some lovely, encouraging smiles.

My race became a tactical search for encouragement. All the way along there were children standing with their hands outstretched, wanting you to touch them as you went by. I tried to indulge them. They were there for us, after all. The least we could do was let them touch a real athlete. Either that or touch me. Just as welcome were the outstretched hands bearing sweeties – jelly babies and the like. I soon learned to avoid the sweets still in wrappers. More hygienic, yes, but hardly practical in the circumstances. I took what I could, and it did me good.

I reached the 20-mile marker in a time of 2:51, which is when I started to panic a little. My prospects of coming in inside four hours were starting to drift away. Slowly but surely, I was starting to feel ghastly. I was now markedly slowing, and the miles became a haze, with confusion creeping in. I remember thinking that I would later curse myself for hobbling so slowly, but then, thoroughly losing the plot, I found myself turning on an imagined future self and saying, 'Well, you bloody try it then!' Between two mile markers in the early 20s I wasn't sure for a while which mile I was on – which was shockingly bad given how little else there was to think about. How hard can it be to keep one number in your head?

Fortunately, walking wasn't an option. It was easier to keep trying to run, however badly. I was trying to drink more, thinking I hadn't drunk enough. At least I now knew not to get overexcited at the first sight of Big Ben. There was still a long way to go. Slowly, very slowly, I chipped into it. Twenty-four miles came and went and so did twenty-five. It is astonishing to read that Paula Radcliffe did her 25th mile in 5 minutes 5 seconds that day. Mine was double that and more. But there was good news too. I forced myself into some calculations, and clearly sub-four was back on. There was a voice inside my head now telling me not to blow it, that this was my golden chance. A voice kept telling me, 'Come on, you don't want to have to do it again.'

Once again, I started picking out people to shout my name. And the people were responding, little angels in the crowd locking on to those of us on our last legs and desperate. Then, suddenly, it was all starting to happen quicker than I had thought it would. Big Ben came and went. And then we were on Birdcage Walk, running towards a big sign saying '800 metres'. I thought, *How am I supposed to know how far that is?* Confusion was taking hold again. All I knew was that Birdcage Walk seemed to stretch forever. But then I turned and turned again to catch my first sight of the finish line.

I had about five minutes in hand on four hours. And then I was listening to the guy over the tannoy urging everyone on to a sub-four finish. It had taken me 2 minutes 37 seconds to get over the start line, so I knew that even if the big clock over the finishing line said four hours, I would achieve my aim. The tannoy man was shouting, 'Less than four hours! How good does that feel! Come on! Come on!' He was fantastic. He drained the last drop out of me. He reeled me in to the end of the race.

I got over the line and ran slap bang into a great wave of exhaustion that took my legs out from under me. I staggered and wobbled, and from nowhere a rock-solid hand – once again – was suddenly under my elbow, steadying me and keeping me moving. The frightening thing was that I was hyperventilating, a horrible panting noise that I couldn't control. I feared I was going to suffocate.

I wanted (being very well brought up) to thank the guy who steadied me, because without him I would have been flat on the ground. He had intervened in the very nick of time. I so wanted to thank him, but I couldn't talk through my foghorn-sounding breathing. And when I did say something, I'm sure it didn't make sense. He was steadying me still as I collected my medal.

I guess the way I felt simply underlines the huge emotional investment we make when we run a marathon. Crossing the finishing line is a trauma in itself. Just seeing it can be too. Stella later told me she saw a runner turn the corner for her first sight of the finish and promptly collapse. The shock of finally seeing the thing she'd craved was all too much for her, and sadly she was stretchered away, recording after her name those tragic three letters: DNF. Did not finish. So close and yet so very, very far.

I had made it home, though. I was barely in one piece, but I was home all the same – and for me, it was a landmark result, the first time I'd entered the exalted ranks of the sub-four runners.

2002 was also a landmark year for the event. For the first time, the ChampionChip in your shoe was activated as you passed the start line and not just as you passed the finish line. It meant that you had an actual running, or chip, time, rather than the useless 'gun time', which hadn't accounted for how long it took you to get over the start. Marathons were going electronic, and technology was taking over. All the results were on *The Times* website that night.

My official time was recorded as 3:56:24 – just over 14.5 minutes better than my first London Marathon in 1998, an improvement which brought a significant step-up in my finishing position. I came in 11,016th out of about 33,000 finishers. In 1998 I had been 16,005th. An improvement of just under 15 minutes moved me up around 5,000 places. In other words, I was now approaching the race's peak finishing time.

All that remained to do at the time, however, was to stagger to the family meeting point where Fiona awaited, having seen me three times on the course – which would have been a huge boost if I had managed to see her. I now had the prospect of a trip to the MS reception, which involved crossing the marathon course at about 25.5 miles. The wait was endless as we joined the thousands trying to find a way through, but it was worth it.

When we finally got to the reception, there were very few runners to be seen. Many must have given up trying to get across the road in their fragile state – which meant all the more attention for me. There was no queue for the massage. In fact, I had a masseuse on each leg and one on my back. The only problem was that I could hardly hear a thing – one of the weirder post-marathon episodes I have ever experienced. I started to panic, asking the masseuses what was happening. In my supersensitive state, I was starting to get frightened. One of the girls suggested it was the pounding for all those hours; another said it was the result of prolonged exposure to the crowd noise; I couldn't hear what the third one said. I've certainly never experienced anything like it since, but it was a suitable ending to my hypochondria marathon.

Fortunately, however, something rather cheerier was steadily approaching on the horizon. Michael. He made it home in 6 hours 36 minutes. Not the time he'd wanted, but few runners ever actually do the time they want. The fact was that he'd done it. He'd completed the course. It was a glorious double. And for me, it was a chance to ask him a question I had been burning to ask.

I'd completed in time enough to freshen up and wait for him at the finish. It was fairly quiet by then, and, with my medal still around my neck, I was able to go back into the enclosure and catch him just after he'd crossed the line. There was something I needed to know.

We'd both completed doctorates at Oxford University. Receiving the degree was a moment I thought nothing could eclipse, until my first marathon. 'Which was the better moment?' I asked the newly finished Michael as he looked around, slightly bewildered. 'The DPhil or the marathon?' 'The marathon' was his instant answer. *Welcome to the club*, I thought. Forget the brains, forget the poncy degree. We'd both missed our vocation. Now we'd found it. Two 'academics' had turned into 'athletes', Michael at 69, me four years previously at 34.

London 2003 was a similar run, this time finishing in 3:53:38 – around three minutes quicker than in 2002, but a time accompanied by disappointment. Having cracked 4:00, I'd wanted to crack 3:50. But it was not to be. Even so, I had moved up to 8,540th out of 33,000 finishers – which again illustrated just how thickly people were finishing at that point. I was just under three minutes quicker but around 2,500 places further up the field. I was getting there. I'd halved my 1998 finishing position by coming in 18 minutes quicker.

Once again, Michael was running, this time on a charity place, having failed again to get a ballot place. I was delighted he was there, not least because his presence meant all the more family support. I was flagging at 17 miles, which is when I saw Fiona's brother Alistair. He took my picture and shouted 'How are you?', to which, not at my most articulate, I replied '******* knackered', to which he replied, 'You look it.' But the conversation helped. Ten minutes or so later, I was feeling better and more in control. There is something very significant in being asked directly how you are and being able to give such a colourful answer. It's as if it gets something out of your system and allows you to move on, almost like spitting out a poison. Not nice for the spectators, but it was from there that I started to improve.

And once again, I was marvelling at the London crowd. Loads of people were shouting out my name, as if they had some sixth sense, unerringly finding those of us that really needed it. Again, I was looking for that eye contact. There was a glorious moment when a chap roared at me, 'Come on, Phil, dig deep, dig deep, you can do it!' It was really special. I go tingly even now just thinking about it. It says so much that massed humanity can roar you on and yet, the icing on the cake, you can still get that sublime individual connection.

But after the race, there was one particular individual connection I enjoyed even more. This was the day that Paula Radcliffe knocked almost two minutes off her own world record to come in at a sensational 2:15:25. The pleasure was immense for all of us who followed.

Radcliffe is simply the most gracious and graceful of athletes. In interview, she always comes across so well; generous and sporting in the very best sense of the word. She's one of those rare heroes who never alienate. We share in her disappointments and we share in her glories. She's never surly in defeat; she's never arrogant in her triumphs. She's a running genius – and her 2003 London Marathon was an astonishing achievement which stands to this day. No one else is coming remotely near it. And I was there.

Technically, of course, Radcliffe was running a different race to me, but I wasn't prepared to let a technicality like that stand in my way. As far as I was concerned, I was a tiny, tiny part of a race which saw her rewrite the history books. And that is one of the many thrills of the London Marathon.

Chapter Five: 'Harlem Shuffle'
Biting the Big Apple - New York 2003

I haven't done a single marathon I regret. Even the ones I hated are ones I love in memory, stinkers which are somehow transformed by hindsight into worthy efforts. In the end, it all comes back to that old saying that has always seemed so barking mad: whatever doesn't kill you, makes you stronger. If I start to look at my marathons as parts of my running's rich tapestry, then a pattern does start to emerge, the rotters becoming somehow leavened by the wonder runs – runs in which the pleasure isn't in the perversity of it all, but simply in the sheer joy of running. The going has frequently got tough, but in amongst the troughs are unbeatable highs, none higher than the New York City Marathon of 2003, a fantastic experience in surely the world's most exhilarating city.

New York was the marathon that brought it home to me that, when I say I love running, what I actually mean is that I love marathons. Mine is a very specific obsession. I have to concede that I am unusual. Hundreds of thousands of runners know that the best way to improve is to run races across all sorts of different distances, safe in the knowledge that each discipline will benefit every other one in the long run, if you'll pardon the pun. The running magazines tell you endlessly to mix it up, just for the enjoyment of it all as much as anything else – but it's advice I've never been tempted to follow.

Rightly or wrongly, probably wrongly, I've never been able to psyche myself up for any race other than a marathon. Other runners will reckon I've pointlessly limited my horizons; my belief is that I've focused on the only running horizon that inspires me. The big M – the only race I want, the only race that stirs me, and none comes more stirring than the New York City Marathon.

It was meant to be. No one had told me how heavily oversubscribed the New York City Marathon was. I simply applied and got a place, but my jaw did drop when I looked online on the appointed day and trawled through the thousands and thousands of rejections. For some reason, they publish the whole lot – presumably to make the rejected feel somehow less rejected. The other effect, of course, is that it sends those that are actually accepted into orbit. Rejected, rejected, rejected, rejected, accepted, rejected, rejected, rejected. Hang on. Whose name was next to 'accepted'? Mine!

And the timing couldn't possibly have been better. Just three weeks before the race, I celebrated my 40th birthday, a landmark which suddenly seemed slightly more palatable for the prospect of the New York City Marathon following so soon in its wake. Is there any male who hasn't gulped in horror at the ghastly thought of turning 40, a day which couldn't possibly ever be just another day? For years – well, 40 to be precise – it had hung there, immovable and depressing, like a final farewell to youth and a 'come on in' to cardigans, dribbling and dotage. It seemed the stopping-off point between a world of endless possibility and a world of 'No, I never did quite get round to that'; whatever marathon I ran after 11 October 2003, I would be running as a 'veteran', a word which made me shudder with its images of upright, overpolished, ancient cars farting along at 5 miles an hour while queues of traffic snaked endlessly behind them.

But suddenly New York hove into view – and it seemed that some kind of afterlife might actually be possible. Having cracked four hours in London, I now wanted to crack 3:50. The New York City Marathon was the perfect birthday present, one which suggested that there might just be a future worth having.

I was straight on to the MS Society. They were offering places to people willing to commit to raising certain amounts in sponsorship. I told them I had a place already, and they promptly added me to their team. We were called the MS Superstars. How fantastic was that. What a great team to be part of, and what a great place to go and run.

Fiona and I had had a couple of days in New York a few years before, and I had instantly fallen head over heels in love with the place. I'd asked the taxi driver at the airport how long it would take to get to the city centre. 'Anything between forty-five minutes and the rest of your life' was his gloriously New York answer. That was it. In that moment, I was hooked, and over the next couple of days I became increasingly enchanted by the mad, bad brashness and excitement of the whole place, the stunning beauty and the awful ugliness which sit side by side in the least restful, most intoxicating city I had ever seen. How fabulous would it be to see it on foot, slowly and in the company of 35,000 other runners? How fabulous indeed. So much more fabulous than I could ever have hoped.

In *Desert Island Discs*, having chosen your eight records, you're allowed to take only one with you to your desert island. In *Desert Island Marathons*, my choice would have to be New York, for the sheer thrill of it, for all the poignancy of running it just two years after 9/11 and for the pinch-yourself unbelievability of a magnificent course through all five boroughs of a magnificent city. Kicking off on Staten Island, you run into Brooklyn before clipping Queens and then heading into Manhattan for a loop which takes you briefly into the Bronx before heading back into Manhattan for a Central Park finish. In prospect, it seemed running simply couldn't come any better than this.

The organisers haven't gone all-out for speed. Apparently they could have come up with a quicker course if they had wanted. But these are people with huge pride in their city. They don't want you just to whizz through it. They want you to set foot in its every borough – and that's the course they came up with. Moreover, New Yorkers want to be there to see you do it. The crowds were phenomenal.

By now Adam and Laura were seven and five; it was term-time; there was no way I could drag them out to New York. Instead, I went out with my mum, Juliette, flying out on the Friday before the marathon on the Sunday.

As always with a big-city marathon, the build-up begins at the registration. It's when the juices start to flow, and the New York registration was suitably inspiring. You signed in at the Jacob Javits Convention Center, which certainly gave you an idea of the scale of the whole event. The centre was huge, and there were hundreds of people milling around. However, the queue to register was moving all the time and we were processed very efficiently. It was all very friendly as well. You were given your number and a microchip. You then scanned the chip and looked to see whether your number and name came up on the screen. If they did, you were ready to roll. Next, you got the chance to buy a bus ticket ($12) to the start – not quite your usual ticket, simply a sticker that they attached to your running number. And then you were done, free to wander out into the marathon exhibition to soak up the atmosphere before heading out into the New York evening. This was 31 October – and the Big Apple was in Halloween party mood. Scores of people were in Halloween costumes, dressed as horned devils, or as scary, green-faced witches. New York was fun that Friday night.

Saturday morning was phase two in the marathon build-up. I was keen to get a feel for the finish, and so we walked to Central Park where it would all come to an end, just a few minutes from the hotel. Already it was clear that it was going to be a hot day. There were plenty of joggers around and also groups of dog-walkers. The atmosphere was relaxed and tranquil, with the park resplendent in all its autumn glory, the leaves every shade of yellow, orange and red – a gorgeous oasis right in the heart of the crazy rush of the big bad city.

The finishing area is in the south-eastern corner of the park and on the Saturday it was also the finishing area for the Friendship Run, a 4-mile leisurely trot from the United Nations building. Maybe I should have done it. It was open to all international competitors in the marathon, but actually it was rather nice to be a spectator. Again, it was very relaxed. There were lorries full of waiting goodie bags, huge piles of drinks bottles, music playing and people strolling around.

The arrival of the Friendship runners was heralded by sirens and by police on motorbikes, and then came the runners themselves, coming in by country by country, all very colourful and impressive. Playing over the loudspeakers was 'Shattered' by The Rolling Stones – which shouldn't have been appropriate so early in the day after just 4 miles, but maybe it was. It was getting worryingly warm by now and quite a few people were looking fairly sweaty. But it was lovely to watch it, a little foretaste of the big day itself.

It made me realise just how relaxing the day before a marathon needs to be, and so we relaxed in style on board the Circle Line boat trip around Manhattan Island – a spectacular trip which takes you past the densely packed skyscrapers of the financial district at the southern end of Manhattan and up to the rocks and woods at the northernmost tip. The guide offered a particular welcome to the marathon runners among us, adding that we were all more entertaining on the Monday after the race, creeping around gingerly, going downstairs barefoot and backwards.

On a more sombre note, he said that on September 11, just two years earlier, his boat was about to go out when the attacks started. They saw the smoke and then the flames. The boat was evacuated and then became part of the fleet getting people off Manhattan. His boat transported around 5,000 people away from New York City's central island that day.

Back in the present, race preparation continued on the Saturday evening when mum and I dropped into the MS runners' and supporters' reception at the Paramount Hotel. We arranged for mum to meet up with them the next morning so she could go with them to the MS cheering point on First Avenue. It was all falling into place. All that remained now was the usual near-sleepless night ahead, made all the worse by jet lag.

I was asleep by 9.30 p.m., but awoke at about 1 a.m. and couldn't get back to sleep. I lay there waiting for the 4.30 wake-up call. I was up and in my running kit by about 4.35 a.m. and then waited some more before leaving the hotel at 5.20 a.m. for the great odyssey of getting to the start – an undertaking almost as great as the marathon itself.

The New York City Marathon, as I have said, starts from Staten Island, south of Manhattan Island, and the easiest way to get there is to catch a bus from central Manhattan. The marathon buses were leaving between 5 and 7 a.m. from the New York City Library on Fifth Avenue, and at 5.30 a.m., more or less the only people around were runners. On the way I got chatting to a chap from Memphis, Tennessee, who was on his sixth marathon, and then to an English guy who'd been living for the past few years in Indianapolis, now doing his first marathon in quite some years. I enjoyed the chance to swap notes and tips on the bus. The race-day camaraderie was starting early.

We got to Staten Island at about ten to six, which seemed ludicrously early for the 10.10 a.m. marathon start. But there was no choice but to be there early. The Verrazano-Narrows Bridge, over which we'd just driven, is the first thing you run over. It closes to traffic at 7.30 a.m. on marathon morning. And so hours stretched ahead.

Our waiting area was in the grounds of Fort Wadsworth, a former United States military installation now maintained by the National Park Service. Some people lay down in the big field. Many of them simply fell asleep. But I was too psyched up. By now it was light and there was a good atmosphere building with a jazz band playing, soon to be replaced by a brilliant blues band from California called Blues Barbecue.

For breakfast I nibbled some bagels and had a yoghurt drink and a power bar. I also had coffee and took on a decent amount of water, but mostly I just lay on the grass and enjoyed the music – when I wasn't waiting in queues for the loo. I also visited what was quaintly billed as the world's longest urinal – a long, downhill, open trough which must have had a Niagara-like flow in its lower reaches.

Organisation was good, and time passed relatively quickly. Before long, we began to think about moving into the starting area, which was broken down into sections according to your bib number, though no one took too much notice. I joined the race queue at about ten o'clock and we soon started to move forward, easing slowly up and out onto the approach to the Verrazano-Narrows Bridge. It was a beautiful day, very warm with very blue skies. Crowning it all was Frank Sinatra, presumably not in person, singing 'New York, New York' in the background. Perfect motivation, which pumped us up nicely.

When the gun went off, initially we didn't move. I thought we'd be there for ages but then the familiar slow shuffle started. And then everyone broke into a trot and I was across the line in just over two minutes – the ideal start. Even better was the fact that the bridge was very wide and there was no bunching whatsoever. This was perfect race thinking, enabling the maximum number of people to get off to precisely the kind of start they wanted. The bridge was huge and imposing, easily absorbing the tens of thousands of runners now pouring onto it.

I was able to get straight into my game plan, starting to pick up a succession of eight-minute miles, which was very much my aim. I was running against a previous best time of 3:53 in London earlier that year, and eight-minute miles were key to my plan of attack. Much more than ever before, I'd planned the race, knew what I needed to do and intended to do it – even if that meant giving much freer rein than ever before to the time-obsessed anorak just waiting to come out of my closet. I had to think in minutes, I had to think in miles and I had to get my calculations right.

The runners spilled out across the various levels of the bridge, and soon I was in one of the enclosed levels, which seemed a shame at first. I thought initially that it would have been better to be out on the top, but actually it was great in terms of atmosphere. It was mostly open at the sides so you lost little in terms of looking at the view, but every now and again, where the sides were more solid, everyone compensated by whooping loudly with great echoing effect.

To our left was the lower Manhattan skyline with the twin towers of the World Trade Center so sorely missed. Ten years before, when Fiona and I had visited New York, we'd marvelled at the towers, astonished at their immensity and solidity. We spent hours at the top of one of them, wandering around, enjoying the view and relishing the sheer thrill of visiting buildings which redefined the word massive. Their absence now was shocking.

Also visible to our left was the Statue of Liberty, instantly recognisable and so much a symbol of the city and all that it stood for. Just to see it made me tingle. I knew we were in for an exciting day. In the foreground, just below the bridge, a couple of boats were squirting a multicoloured tribute to the runners – jets of red, white and blue water. Very impressive and all part of the fun.

One sad moment came when a guy took a tumble just half a mile in. He was writhing on the ground, clutching his knee in agony. He'd clearly fallen very heavily. I hoped his race wasn't over, but I suspected it was. He would have done very well to come back from that. Maybe he'd been clipped by another runner; maybe he'd just taken his eye off the ball. Poor chap. I really felt for him that morning. He was one of us, and he could have been any one of us. He'd put in months of training. He'd been looking forward to it all and planning it for weeks. And then that happened.

For the rest of us, it was a timely reminder of the need to concentrate. There are greater dangers when there is bunching; but whatever the conditions, you have always got to be race aware. And even then, there will be times when sheer misfortune will get you and there is nothing you can do.

The first mile marker came just before the end of the bridge, which underlines just what an impressive structure it is – a bridge so long that it was one of the first structures ever built to have to take into account the earth's curvature. From there we ran into Brooklyn, which proved one of the big treats of the run. First we were on a kind of freeway and then pulled off it onto a slip road, at the top of which were the first roadside spectators of the day, setting the tone for the entire event with their enthusiastic shouts of 'Welcome to Brooklyn!'

After that, we were soon into the populated areas; wide, leafy avenues lined by attractive brick or coloured houses several storeys high and all looking very smart. The main shopping areas were great too, and here the crowds were impressive and very vocal. There were lots of 'Go, man!' shouts all the way, a terrific, totally intoxicating atmosphere which was typical of the entire course from this point onwards. They don't just shout 'Come on' and your name. They give it the full works: 'You can do it, go man, Phil baby!' or 'Go, Phil, go!' And, yes, I was milking the shouts a fair amount. It was all part of the fun and the indescribable thrill of running the New York City Marathon. I had to keep saying it to myself: I am running the New York City Marathon. And still I couldn't quite believe it.

Uplifting and poignant was the fact that along the course we passed probably a dozen fire stations, each with a fire engine on show, mostly with the firefighters sitting on top, sometimes with the ladder extended, firefighters straddling it. All very moving in the light of September 11, so recent and so raw a memory that year. It was as if the firefighters were turning out to applaud the city which had applauded them when they responded in its days of need. I felt proud and privileged to be there with them in their city. How could I not be inspired?

Looking at the map earlier, I'd thought that the race wouldn't really take off until we were on Manhattan, the central island borough and the bit that we all conventionally think of as New York. But the 12 and a bit miles of Brooklyn were fantastic; mostly neat and attractive, always colourful and lively, and wonderfully enhanced by the bright sunshine of an increasingly warm day. Thank goodness for that, I remember thinking. Pamela, who'd trained me for my first London, had told me tales of the weather extremes you can get in New York on the first weekend in November. One year it might be freezing, another absolutely boiling. Just for sheer comfort's sake in those early stages, I was pleased that we were inching towards the hot end of the scale.

I was clocking up my eight-minute miles and occasionally thinking that I was going too fast and would regret it later, but at the same time I was thinking I should just make merry while I could and get the miles in the bank while the going was good. It seemed a balancing act and I tilted it in favour of enjoying present exhilaration. The euphoria was enormous: I wanted to exploit it; and I wanted to amass distance at a time when I felt I was running well. Let the future take care of itself.

The considerations and calculations that usually fill my head in a marathon started to slip just a little into the background. Or rather, they started to become part of the bigger picture. I'd been determined to cling to them, but it wasn't long before sheer enjoyment of the day started to seem an equally important imperative. Why hammer myself about minutes and miles when everything around me is so damned interesting? There was a constant sensation of 'Am I really doing this?' as I passed through Brooklyn. Nor yet can I believe that I also ran through Queens, Manhattan and the Bronx on that glorious day. It was a blissful run, every street a new discovery.

As I look back on it now, I can see that so much of what you take to be tiredness in another place on another day is simply lack of stimulation. I think of those long boring sections early and mid-race in London – boring partly, no doubt, because they seem so familiar and so un-exotic to a Brit. On my sunny Sunday morning in Brooklyn, on the other hand, there was endless stimulation, pushing further and further back the inevitable moment when genuine tiredness really would start to take its toll.

And so the miles mounted, each new eight-minute mile a pleasure and a relief. I even started to feel expectation grow within me. Having cracked 4:00 in London, cracking 3:50 was the target now. I wanted 3:40-something. 3:40-anything was the aim – territory I had never before entered. My half-marathon time left me with just over two hours to achieve it in. A few quick calculations confirmed that the 3:40s were looking within my grasp, and just the thought of them proved a spur as the miles ticked by.

The 2 miles of Queens, the third borough of the day, consisted largely of industrial-type buildings, but, uninspiring as they were, they were definitely a staging post, all part of the progress towards the Queensboro Bridge which was to take us over the East River onto Manhattan Island for the first time.

The bridge is so huge that it starts a long way back on land. More importantly, it starts with the 15-mile marker, which I reached in 2:01. From the rare occasions I had paid much attention to my training schedule, I knew that I was supposed to be reaching 15 in 2:05 if I was going to do a sub-3:45 marathon. In training I had managed it a couple of times, but then only by about half a minute. Now I'd smashed it.

It sounds terribly anal now, of course, but anyone who has ever pushed themselves in a marathon will know: these things matter, and they matter hugely. You need to know how you are doing; you need to assess; you need to adjust. You need to keep the focus and, to do that, you need to find an approach that is right for you. So much marathon talk is far too dogmatic, far too prescriptive, neglecting the fact that for the most part it simply isn't an exact science. Far from it. It's all about reaching conclusions that suit you and then modifying them whenever experience suggests you should do so.

By now, I was starting to think of myself as a reasonably experienced marathon runner, and with that went the need to use that experience to my advantage. As I ran, I thought back to Pamela's point about having three finishing times in mind. Her argument was that fixating on one particular time is potentially the road to disappointment, too absolute an approach over such a long distance. You need to be able to adjust your expectations on the hoof, as it were. What might seem achievable at the start might very quickly seem impossible once you start to factor in the real-life running conditions.

But in New York quite the opposite was happening: the dream was starting to seem ever more likely. Things were starting to slip into place. My times were confirming that the 3:40s – that inviting ten-minute time zone – were there for the taking. I had achieved comfortably my fastest 15 miles ever; confidence was coursing through my legs.

Even better was the fact that we were now on Manhattan, where the reception was stunning. Soon after the bridge, we veered right to head north on First Avenue, a deliciously wide and straight stretch, wonderfully packed on either side with massive, roaring crowds. I positively tingled. My feet almost left the ground.

New York City Marathon folklore tells you that this is the danger stretch where many runners, pumped up by the sheer excitement of reaching Manhattan and buoyed up by the stupendous crowds at this point, simply go much too fast and rapidly burn out. It is the most seductive and encouraging stretch, I learned later, and it has wrecked many a runner, seducing them into forgetting that there are still 10 miles to go.

I'm glad I didn't know this at the time. All I remember is the glory of it on a glorious day, and also the fact that I knew that the MS reception point, with mum waiting, would be at around 17 miles, just a mile ahead. For some reason, as I approached the marker, I was convinced the group would be on the right, and then I realised that I had no reason for thinking that. And so I started scanning both sides, fearing that I had already missed them. But soon enough, just after the 17-mile marker (which came up a predictable eight minutes after the 16th), there they were – on the left.

I'd been carrying a very light, one-use-only disposable camera from the start, hoping to catch a few moments along the way, but mostly forgetting I had it to hand. But with the chance to ditch it coming up soon, I had rapidly used up the last shots on the Queensboro Bridge and on First Avenue. I veered across to the cheering group and thrust the camera into mum's hands before she'd even seen me. I was well ahead of the time I'd said I'd be there. I didn't consider stopping because the going was still too good to believe and still those eight-minute miles kept coming. Besides, seeing cheery, friendly faces was yet another boost, and I had to make it count.

First Avenue was massive, wide, noisy, invigorating and very straight. As with so much of the route, there was space in abundance, with absolutely no need for that debilitating weaving in and out that you get in London, though perhaps that was because by now I was so much further ahead of my corresponding London position. At this point, though, I was trying not to work out finishing times. I was just preserving and nurturing the rising feeling that I was going to do my best time ever.

In fact, on the Queensboro Bridge I had been mentally – and very presumptuously – writing the piece for the paper: 'Phil Hewitt raced to his sixth and fastest marathon in a sweltering New York City on Sunday.' Oops. Count no chickens. Take nothing for granted, I told myself, but not too harshly.

Confidence and enjoyment were running hand in hand, carrying me with them – especially when the 18-mile marker came up, always a favourite figure in my number games and particularly welcome now. Here the officials were handing out sachets of power gel, the energising fix that's supposed to revive flagging feet.

We were well into the so-called 'wall' territory by now and I did wonder whether I was going to be able to keep my pace up – so I took a couple of sachets. I reckon it must have done me some good. By 19 miles we were in Harlem, another name rich in resonance. It seemed pleasant enough, nice buildings, each decorated with characteristic retractable wrought-iron staircases on the outside. I was still running well; the sun was out; the crowds were strong; I was having a ball.

At about 19.5 miles, leaving Manhattan to enter the Bronx, we went over the Harlem River, across the Willis Avenue Bridge, a shortish span with a hard, iron-grid surface at a couple of points which the organisers had thoughtfully covered with a very soft, plush red carpet. It took us into the fifth of the five boroughs of New York City, but we ran through it for barely a mile, the crowd as loud as ever, thousands of people lining the streets to cheer us on.

The 20-mile marker came just inside the Bronx and felt crucial. A couple of weekends before I'd done a 20-mile run in 2:43. I thought at the time that I'd be delighted to do that in New York. In fact, I hit the marker at 2:42. Six miles left, and they surely wouldn't take an hour, so the possibility of 3:30-something suddenly opened up. And even if those final 6 miles did take an hour, I would still be comfortably in the low 3:40s, which I'd have happily settled for. Even now, I was calculating. Enjoying everything and everyone, but never letting the numbers slip from my mind.

As we clipped the Bronx, we veered momentarily north and then west before heading back south-west again, over the Madison Avenue Bridge onto Manhattan Island once more. Just at the start of the bridge there was a gospel choir, which simply radiated happiness. I can picture them now, beautifully turned out, singing in perfect harmony but with such joy across their faces. I had a little tear at that point, I don't mind admitting.

Just after the bridge, just inside Manhattan, was the 21-mile marker, and I was annoyed to clock my only ten-minute mile of the day. My response was to run the 22nd mile in just over seven minutes, which even now I find highly surprising. It was my second-fastest mile of the day. Later I wondered if I had muddled up the timings in my head, but I doubt it. I was thinking unusually clearly for a marathon at this point. There I was at 22 miles and inside three hours – progress beyond my dreams – as we passed back through Harlem, heading south now along Fifth Avenue towards Central Park.

It wasn't long before we touched the park's north-eastern corner, definitely the beginning of the home stretch. Fortunately the guy I had been speaking to on the coach that morning had reconnoitred the finish the day before. He warned me against feeling you're home once you see Central Park because there are still well over 3 miles to go, and it was useful advice. For a start, it's ages before you actually enter the park. You run alongside it first for at least a mile – the point at which tiredness finally started to kick in for me.

By now I was positively courting support, willing people to shout out my name. Even so, I still didn't let my pace drop significantly, perhaps a reflection of the fact that the crowds, so strong throughout, were getting noisier still – a sure sign that the home stretch was beckoning. And indeed it was. Just before the 24th mile, we finally made the turn into Central Park, the point at which I started sucking on the other power gel sachet I'd grabbed – raspberry, I think.

I'd been drinking water and Gatorade sports drink throughout, pouring the cups they distribute into the plastic bottle I'd had from the start. With the heat, I had been very aware of the possibility of dehydration and so sipped regularly throughout, missing out on very few of the drinks stations. I must have got it just about right because I didn't need a single wee – and certainly wouldn't have stopped if I had.

I was flagging just a touch by 24 miles, but just being in Central Park was a boost, especially on such a beautiful autumn day. Once you're in the park, the terrific thing is that the route is fairly gently downhill for the mile and a half or so to the south-eastern corner from which you exit, and that definitely helped me to stay reasonably in touch with my eight-minute miling.

As I left the park at its south-eastern corner, I saw a glorious sign saying 'one mile to go', just as we turned right to run along the road which skirts the bottom end of the park. At the end of it, we re-entered the park, this time by the south-western corner. Along the bottom of the park, it was just one long roar from the crowd – terrific motivation spurring us on.

Then there was the '800 metres to go' sign and then I was back in the park, the roar rising all the time. Then came the 26-mile marker, a fantastic sight – but precisely the moment I had my only serious downer of the day, the overwhelming feeling that I was going to be sick. The gel had been just too thick and too rich. I knew I would make it over the line but I was sure the first thing I would do on finishing would be to throw it all up. I am delighted to say that I didn't, but for those last few hundred metres, the nausea was awful.

But at least I was nearly there. I was thinking that I ought to be 3:30-something by now, and when I looked up at the finish line, I saw the clock change to 3:38. Crucially, that was elapsed time from the start, not my actual running time. I'd taken just over two minutes to cross the start and so I noted my time as 3:36 as I finished – a fantastic feeling. I had a time to my name which simply wasn't the kind of time I ran. It didn't seem like mine.

My five previous marathons (three Londons and two Chichesters) had been, in time order, 4:13, 4:11, 4:10, 3:56 and 3:53. I'd been hoping for 3:40-something. In fact, I had waltzed through the 3:40s entirely and out the other side, recording a confirmed finishing time of 3:35:45. It was an astonishing result in my own terms and heralded my longest-ever period of being pleased with a time.

For weeks afterwards, I wondered whether there was any point ever doing a marathon again. It was the closest I had ever come to complete satisfaction – a time I couldn't ever see myself beating, 18 minutes faster than anything I had ever done before. And it felt wonderfully, blissfully good.

I had produced a controlled run, thanks largely to running with an exceptionally steady pack. I must have passed quite a few people and quite a few others must have passed me, but my overall impression was that I simply matched the general pace.

I started hyperventilating after the finish, but I kept walking and it didn't last long, being replaced by a confusion which I hadn't felt to any great extent during the race itself. I had to keep working out when four hours would have elapsed just to keep checking that I really had done it. Meanwhile, I was being processed. First of all you get handed a space blanket and then someone secures it with a sticker and then you get your medal placed around your neck. A glorious moment. A medal from the New York City Marathon. And what a day. What a wonderful course. Five boroughs, five bridges and the most stunning support for virtually the whole length of the run.

Writing in my marathon diary the day after, I was perhaps a little harsh: 'I hate to say it, but it makes the London Marathon pale into insignificance – probably largely for the fact that New York is foreign and thousands of miles away.' But somehow the support had just seemed so much greater in New York: so many fire crews, the gospel choirs, so many faces. It was the place and the exhilaration of being there that got me around so quickly.

I had been far too busy thinking 'Can I really be here?' to bother about getting tired. If the course can take your mind off tiredness, then you're bound to succeed. Plus the conditions were perfect. How things can change. In London 2002 I had come in blue in the face, in a state of near collapse and absolutely shattered, yet 21 minutes slower in considerably cooler conditions. I was starting to realise that I thrive on warm marathons. I have since learned that I am useless in comparison in the cold and wet.

Early on in New York, the heat had been a problem every time we went into an east-west shady street from a sun-drenched north-south avenue. I was so dripping in sweat that I felt chilly until we were out in the sun again. But overall, the sun had just made everything look all the more colourful and all the more beautiful on an absolutely sparkling day.

The icing on the cake had been just how friendly the people were as they dished out space blankets and medals. They all said congratulations and really seemed to mean it. A bit less impressive was the time it took for my bag to be found on the van at the end, and then there was a long walk to get out of the marathon finishers' enclosure. But in that moment, I would have happily forgiven New York anything. Besides, walking was definitely the right thing to do. I'd felt a bit wobbly while waiting for my bag, but all in all I was feeling fine, helped on by complete strangers saying congratulations to me, all the way back to our hotel, half a mile or so south of Central Park.

I freshened up and then headed out again, bumping into mum in the lobby just as she was about to go up. I bought a phonecard (how dated does that sound!), phoned Fiona and was amazed to find that she knew more about my time than I did. She'd been tracking me on the Internet, as had my dad and Michael, now a marathoner himself of course. She told me my time was 3:35:45 and knew that I'd taken just over two minutes to cross the start. She'd been worried when my quarter-marathon time flashed up – worried that I was going too quickly. The website had even thrown up a couple of predicted finishing times for me, one for 3:43 and the other accurate to within seconds. These days, we take this kind of thing in our stride. Back in 2003, it seemed positively space age.

I was on a high. I wanted to dash back into the action and so left mum in the hotel for an hour and a half during which I wallowed in the whole experience of it all. I was very glad I did. I wanted to soak up every moment. I watched the runners going along the road at the bottom of Central Park and then made my way to the finish, determined to swim in the gush of post-race sentimentality which was threatening to engulf me.

The grandstands were pretty thinly peopled by now so it was no problem getting right up close to the finishing line where I watched a fantastic woman on the tannoy who seemed to sum up the whole spirit of the day. She kept shouting: 'And here's Bill (or whoever)! Bill's going to make it! And so's Susan! And here's Jane. Jane's going to do it!' Or 'Rita's just done it. Dex has just done it. Brad's going to do it. And here's Leroy! Come on, bring him home. Bring him in. It's getting cold. He's tired. Bring him home!'

Even now, when I think about it, I go a little misty-eyed. She was oozing goodwill in her relentless, fantastically good-humoured patter – an image of the day I will always retain. She was generosity on legs, a mother hen urging all her chicks home. It mattered to her as if she knew us all. For me, she'll always be the lasting symbol of the welcome that New York City gave us all.

This was marathon running at its absolute best. Everyone was welcomed over the line as a winner, and that's what makes marathons (the good ones, at least!) so intoxicating and so addictive. There you are, flogging yourself on a course, your whole horizon reduced to the road ahead as you try to remember distances, calculate times and see your way through. It's the solipsistic 'me, me, me' of marathon running.

But in a race such as New York – and to a very large extent London too – your narrow focus is balanced by the broader focus of hundreds of thousands of spectators who see the wider perspective, coming together to witness the mass spectacle of all those individual battles out on the course, all part of one monumental effort on the part of everyone.

It's that gorgeously seductive spiritual side to the whole marathon experience once again, that wonderful thing that makes humans human, that generosity of spirit which makes mankind en masse gather together and urge us on. It's that great kindness – embodied by the woman on the tannoy – that brings us runners home. Days really don't come much better than this – and in a sense, I've never let it go.

It's become an annual ritual – easier of late – to watch the New York City Marathon on TV. In the early years, it meant hanging on to some flaky streaming from a cloudy website, sound and pictures never quite in synch. Now we've got satellite TV, it's as if I'm there. Each year I watch it, refreshing my memory of the streets on which I ran; each year, the memories get better. It really was one of the greatest days of my life.

I have never seriously considered trying to do it again. My New York experience was too perfect to risk tarnishing it by trying – and undoubtedly failing – to recreate it. Everything was just too good for it ever to be so good again.

Chapter Six: 'In Another Land'
Why the Course Counts - Paris 2004

If 'Fred', our sports editor back in 1997, had been lean and mean, would I ever have run a marathon? I'd like to think so. I'd just have come to it rather later.

By the time I'd run New York, however, I was a marathon regular and even fancied that I was some kind of role model at home. It seems to me crucial that you don't just preach to your children the benefits of regular exercise. You need to put it all into practice. Just as you need to create a home environment where books are everywhere and often open, you need to create a home life in which exercise is simply there, where it isn't an event if someone does something energetic, where it's simply part of your weekly existence.

I try to do the right things. I try to pronounce the 't's on the ends of words; I try to avoid rising inflections; and I try not to swear. I try to be as rude as possible about the Conservative Party at every opportunity; and I also like to think that I have always projected The Beatles and The Stones as the great pinnacles of man's achievement, the highest high points of our civilisation, never to be surpassed.

But, above all, I like to think I've set an example to my children that exercise is vital – though I can't honestly say that that's the reason I go out running. By 2004, running had become such a central part of my life that it was always going to be there, existing in its own right as something to be treated with reverence. How I sneered and sniffed, a few years later, at the comedy film *Run, Fatboy, Run*, which the rest of the family enjoyed – and which I secretly enjoyed too. But it was a film which committed a crime, allowing its hero to run a marathon on the back of the poorest of training regimes imaginable. This was reckless, I chuntered. This wasn't the way marathons are run, and it wasn't helpful – even in popular culture – to portray them this way. You don't undertake marathons lightly, I moaned – 'pompous' my middle name as I conveniently overlooked my own version of *Fatboy* in Chichester in 2001.

Oh yes, I was a serious runner, and I was facing the kind of problems only a serious runner will face, not the least of which was 'Where next?' *How on earth do you follow New York?* I wondered. The answer, as it turned out, was simple. You go to Paris.

Some marathons have just got to be done, lifetime highlights that should be obligatory for anyone capable of putting one foot in front of the other. Paris is one such marathon. I have run it three times now and have happy memories of all of them, even my most recent Paris when I recorded my slowest time on the course. So what? How could you ever be disappointed about anything you do in Paris?

For me, London had been all about the excitement of the debut; New York had been all about the thrill of New York itself; but in Paris, the thrill was all about the course, the thing that keeps you going and makes Paris such a memorable running experience. Like New York, Paris is very generous with its sights, and what sights they are.

However, the attraction begins much earlier than that. One of the great advantages of the Paris Marathon is that it is so easy to get a place. The London Marathon application process was – and probably still is – one of its biggest drawbacks. In years gone by, I would trail the sports shops vainly trying to find a London Marathon application form, an ordeal fortunately considerably simplified now. In recent years, at long last, London has finally moved across to online application, but even now you endure a long, long wait to discover the outcome.

Paris, on the other hand, was an absolute doddle. Sign up while there are places still available, and you are instantly confirmed as a runner. French bureaucracy isn't known for its simplicity, but here Paris was streets ahead of London. Adding to the appeal was the fact that I was approaching it from a position of strength. I went into my first Paris on the back of a couple of good marathons. I was on a roll.

Also key to the anticipated fun was that this was going to be a sociable marathon. I travelled out to Paris with my good friend Marc, a running enthusiast whom I knew through work in Chichester. Marc lives in Brighton, which is as far east of Chichester as I live west, and consequently we have only rarely enjoyed the chance to run together. Instead, we have shared countless run-related conversations over a Chichester coffee, and it was during one such coffee that we hatched the Paris plan.

Also joining us was Michael. Michael was itching for his first overseas marathon; Marc was on marathon number two; and I, as ever, was looking for new marathon experiences. But first, urged on by Marc in those early months of 2004, I knew that I had to up my marathon training. My 18-minute improvement in New York was massive, and I knew I was going to have to find something else in my armoury if I was to improve once again. That something, it pained me to admit, was the ordeal known as intervals.

Intervals seemed the key to making it all happen – a dip into the draining, knackering world of intensity training I'd flirted with when I did those fartleks for my first-ever marathon. They had been free and easy, and I'd occasionally gone back to them in the intervening years. But I had always avoided intervals, finding plenty of reasons to steer clear of them. In truth, one reason had generally been enough. I hate them.

Even through that hatred, though, I have to admit that they are – or should be – central to serious marathon running. And, sadly, if I wanted to build on my New York improvement, there was no getting away from them this time.

Intervals are supposed to give you two things. They increase your overall running speed, but also, just as importantly, they give you the strength to carry on when you are starting to flag. They are about overall pace, but they are also about end-of-race endurance. Intervals are there to help you keep going when stopping is all you crave. How do they manage it? I haven't a clue, save they attune your body to greater demands.

Intervals presumably come in all shapes and sizes, but the only one I know – as explained by Marc – is that you chalk a line on a straight stretch of road and then run absolutely flat out for, say, 40 seconds, timing yourself as you positively bust a gut to achieve maximum distance in that time. And then you stop, topple over and chalk a finish line on the road. This is the marker by which you will subsequently test yourself. Whatever the distance, if you have run it properly, you will have run it at a blood-vessel-bursting 100 per cent of your potential. The challenge now is to run that distance repeatedly at 75 per cent of your potential, a speed which should still be significantly above your natural running speed.

I've long harboured the suspicion that the maths doesn't quite add up, but Marc's system is that you add 25 per cent of your initial time to your subsequent running times as you redo the distance in multiples of four, ideally building up to 16 intervals in all. If your full pace was 40 seconds, you now need to complete that distance repeatedly at 40 seconds plus 25 per cent of 40, which even I can work out is 50 seconds in total. It should still feel like you are pushing yourself, particularly as you push towards 16 repetitions.

Then, when you've done however many you are doing, the big test is to repeat the distance in the original 40 seconds. I always aim to do so in 38 or 39 – which presumably, the purists will say, means that I was holding something back for the very first one, which is absolutely not the idea. It's got to be flat out to start, flat out to finish and severely pushed in the middle. Equal that initial burst and you can count your intervals a success: you've taken a key step towards running at an overall quicker pace and you've told your body that you're more than willing to push it when the time comes to shove.

Be a good boy or girl and intervals will form one of your four weekly training sessions. The intervals, plus the sheer weight of regular training runs, will help you increase the number of miles you do as you head towards the big day.

In recent years, I have inflicted intervals on my son's football team, telling them – and genuinely believing – that they are the means by which they will acquire essential stamina towards the end of the game. Some of the players are gracious enough to admit that the off-season intervals have actually made a difference. The year 2004 had, therefore, seen me practise what I would one day preach. It was the year I played it by the book more than I had ever done before or have ever done since. It seemed like a way of trying to take control of the day before it dawned, and in that respect it was a confidence-booster I wished I'd drawn on before.

Michael and I converged at Waterloo station. We wandered through to the Eurostar lounge where we soon found Marc, his partner and his young daughter. The added bonus, as far as I was concerned, was that Marc had family in Paris. Michael had booked a hotel, but I stayed with Marc and his folks, just about ten minutes' walk from the Arc de Triomphe. Their flat was brilliantly located for getting to the start. It was all set up perfectly.

As always, I slept really badly the night before, but I knew that it didn't really matter. The time 3:27 kept coming into my head all night. *Is it possible?* I wondered. I set the alarm for 6 a.m., but I needn't have bothered. I was wide awake by then, as I had been for most of the night, and soon afterwards Marc was wandering around too. We looked out the window. It was pouring with rain and very windy – not at all what we wanted. The forecast the day before had been for mild weather, some sun and no wind. That happy state seemed a long way off just after 6 a.m.

Marc and I passed the time with some stretching exercises, which were actually good fun. He was excellent at explaining the point of the exercises, something I hadn't really grasped before. It was all about loosening you up and toning you up, and under his expert guidance I did indeed feel somehow much more pumped and primed. There was a definite element of getting in the zone – of yet another element slipping into place. Stretching prepares a runner's body, but it also prepares his or her mind. During the stretches, rather than thinking as I so often had before a marathon that it would be good just to get going, I found myself positively looking forward to the off – an important difference. The right mind frame for the day was starting to emerge.

And then, at about ten past eight, Marc and I set off. Gently continuing our limbering-up process, we jogged the ten minutes or so to the Arc de Triomphe, joining the crowds of people who had presumably been hanging around for ages. It was a highly civilised way to prepare for a marathon and we both felt relaxed and up for it. It was coolish, but bright, with increasingly big patches of blue in the sky. The weather was improving with every passing minute. Fortunately, it seemed the French weather forecasters had got it exactly right, and we'd be running in ideal conditions.

Not quite matching the conditions was the organisation. Marc was in the yellow band for those wanting to do 3:15 and I was in the blue band for those aiming at 3:30, but the reality was light years away from the neatly cordoned-off time sections the organisers had promised. It was a scrum. The problem was that the entrances into the time zones were tiny gaps in high barriers right at the back of each section. Rather than slipping in at the back and moving forward within the zone, most people, understandably, were forcing their way along the pavement outside the zone and then clambering over the barriers once they had got as far forward as they could. The zones were fairly tightly packed at the back, but from the mid-section to the front, the crush in each was awful.

Marc abandoned all hope of entering the yellow section. It was all we could do to get into the blue section, where we stood squeezed shoulder-to-shoulder and genuinely worried. Any significant surge from the back, or anyone toppling, and it could have been nasty. At times, my feet were off the ground. Rather inappropriately, perhaps, I kept thinking about all those Middle Eastern holy sites where hundreds of pilgrims get crushed as a seemingly regular occurrence. Shove tens of thousands of people together in cramped conditions, and disasters do happen. I was getting nervous.

Making it all the more unpleasant was the fact that plenty of bodies around us were already pretty whiffy. Even worse was the fact that the chap next to me, who probably couldn't have raised his hands above his waist if he had wanted to, was quietly pissing into his water bottle. Scores of other people were doing the same, or peeing straight down onto the road, which was covered in discarded, increasingly wee-soaked plastic ponchos, dished out the day before to keep us warm at the start. It seemed a treacherous combination. The upper-body crush held you rigidly in place while your feet skidded on urine. This really was mankind at his most unappealing. If we could have hopped, we would have been hopping mad. Any serenity had long since gone, replaced by increasing anxiety.

Fortunately we weren't there long. I didn't hear the gun but I heard the roar and soon we were moving forward. People weren't breaking into a run until they got to the start, but all the same things moved reasonably quickly and I was delighted that we were over the line in three minutes, joining the thousands of runners who were already pouring down the Champs-Élysées for that 'difficult' first kilometre.

The 'difficulty' was noted in the official course map, handed out at the registration the day before. Like most of the half a dozen or so 'difficult' sections identified on the route, the difficulty here came from the fact that it was downhill, offering the temptation to set off at too quick a pace and so get into a draining rhythm too soon. I'm not sure that it really was too much of a danger in the event. It was just nice to get going, and it was great to be setting off with Marc. The crush dissipated. The Champs-Élysées, so wide and inviting, soon saw to that, and so we trotted along, bemoaning the awfulness of the organisation so far.

The crowds along the Champs-Élysées were excellent and highly vocal as we continued towards the Jardins des Champs-Élysées, through which we were soon passing. It wasn't long before we reached the first kilometre marker, just before Place de la Concorde, and that was a good feeling. We really were underway now, and I was pleased to see that the first kilometre came up after almost exactly five minutes – all part of the adjustment I was having to make, as this wasn't a marathon in miles; it was my first in kilometres, and that in itself called for a significant amount of new thinking. There weren't 26.2 of them, but the even more bonkers figure of 42.195. There was no point thinking in eight-minute miles when I was suddenly moving in kilometres. I needed to find an equivalent.

Marc had told me about a website you can use to create a wristband printed with the times you need to do each kilometre in for a specific overall finishing time. I'd printed out a wristband for a 3:30 finish. Every kilometre had to be just a few seconds short of five minutes to achieve it.

The downside was that this didn't allow for slowing, but I calculated that if I ran the first half of the marathon with the aim of having five minutes in hand at the midpoint, then I could allow those five minutes to evaporate over the second half and still achieve my aim. Marc had created his own wristband, which took account of last-half slowing and also of a steady start which then accelerated – all far too complicated for me. Mine was the simpler task. I just kept thinking in fives.

The maths was easy, and I started to enjoy my first experience of running in kilometres. Of course there are many more of them stretching ahead than there are miles, but at least they stack up quickly. Somehow you seem to be into your stride much more promptly.

Given the choice between fewer miles that just won't budge and many more kilometres that fall away quickly, the choice is an easy one. Just think in fives, I told myself, quickly slipping into the kind of time-obsessed focus which simply has to be at the core of a decent marathon run. It sounds desperately anal and terribly anoraky, but the point is a simple one: if you want to do a good time, you need to know how you are doing as you go along. There is no alternative. You've got to log times, you've got to calculate possible outcomes, you've got to stay on top of your run. And for me on that sunny morning in Paris, that meant totting up the fives.

But obsessing about time was, of course, no bar to enjoying the sights on a route which was superlative from the start, one which brought home to me, with almost every pace, just how important the quality of a route is when it comes to overall marathon success.

There can be few grander or more splendid boulevards than the Champs-Élysées, with the sights beyond it so perfectly aligned. There is a magnificent neatness to the Parisian thinking which lined up the Arc de Triomphe with the tip of the obelisk which crowns the Place de la Concorde on a straight line, which then travels the entire length of the Tuileries gardens to hit the little Arc de Triomphe dead centre and, just beyond that, meet the pinnacle of the Louvre's great glass pyramid – a straight line which unites *grand boulevard* with military triumph and links the ultra-modern with the most beautiful of big-city oases.

If you want inspiring, then Paris has got inspiring – and the Paris Marathon, to its eternal credit, was happy to deliver it in spades.

Running round the Place de la Concorde – usually dominated by cars – was great, but Marc and I both took it very wide because the runners were still fairly tightly packed and we were wanting to get ahead. Needlessly we added metres to our overall distance. As Pamela used to tell me, the only thing on a marathon route which is exactly marathon distance is the blue line you are supposed to follow. We were conscious that we had already strayed off it much too much.

More worrying still was the fact that, already, the crowds lining the route were getting sparser. Out in Greenwich in the London Marathon, they can be a little thin, but that's a long way from the centre. This was central Paris right at the start, and as we joined the Rue de Rivoli, running alongside the Tuileries, there were just two people standing in one long section. The *rue*, with various sights off it, including the Louvre itself, was looking terrific as the sun broke through, but very soon the roadside support was in short supply.

Marc had wanted to reach the 3-km marker in 14 minutes. We reached the second in 10 and then the third in 15, which suited me – though I was starting to be conscious of the need to get some time in hand. It didn't suit Marc at all so I encouraged him to run on. It had been great to start with him, but I didn't want to feel I was holding him back. Suddenly, I was on my own, a relief in the nicest way. I wanted Marc to get the time he wanted. Besides, there was plenty to enjoy.

I'd lived for a year just outside Paris in 1984, underemployed as a teaching assistant at a huge comprehensive school in Creil. I had oodles of spare time and I used to come into Paris two or three times a week simply to stroll, always finding somewhere new to explore but often coming back to the Rue de Rivoli, always so full of life, always so quintessentially Parisian with its buzz of boutiques and big-capital chic.

And I loved it now as I ran along, slowly feeling my pace increase as the kilometres slipped by. We passed the Hôtel de Ville on our right as we headed eastwards from the city centre towards the Place de la Bastille, by which time it was clear that every other mile was going to be marked. Briefly it threw me, but the kilometres equation was too convenient for me to jump ship. We were so steeped in all things Paris by now that it would have seemed disrespectful to start thinking in miles. *Vive la différence*, as they say in England.

It has to be said, though, that the distance markers were a disappointment compared to the huge overhead jamboree-type affairs you get in London. In Paris they were just roadside numbers with a little line, awfully easy to miss, but at least they mounted up steadily and it didn't seem long before I reached the 10-km marker – which was finally a marker worth writing home about, a big up-and-over-the-road style celebration which was also the first point at which the microchips in our shoes became effective.

There was the familiar high-pitched peeping sound as thousands of feet flew over, recording thousands of individual times. For those who had registered, it also sent text messages to friends and family. More importantly, for the runners themselves, it brought a genuine sense of progress.

On the refreshments front, things were a bit sparse, but the Place de la Bastille, once we got there, more than made up for it – tables of water bottles interspersed with tables groaning with fresh fruit, big plates of raisins and big bowls of sugar. The Gallic gastronomic approach contrasted sharply with Anglo-Saxon restraint back in London. The French heaped it high.

The fresh fruit was oranges and half-bananas, the bananas still in their skins, which meant that at about half a dozen points along the way you were running through a couple of hundred metres of banana skins. What on earth were they trying to do to us? We could have been the biggest pile-up in history. But I took advantage. I ate four large handfuls of raisins at equidistant points along the way, and they were good – nourishing without being heavy.

It was here that the landscape was about to change dramatically and enjoyably. Soon after the 10-km marker, you approach the Château de Vincennes, a big, brooding, forbidding-looking castle sitting in extensive woods, and those woods – the Bois de Vincennes – would be the route for the next 10 km. Lovely they were too.

I was feeling good. At 7 km I had about a minute and a quarter in hand on my five-minute kilometres. Running through the woods helped me add to it, though by now I was needing a wee. A quick sidestep behind a tree meant a minor setback, but I was relieved – in another sense – to start reclaiming lost time pretty much straightaway.

After 10 km of big city, it was refreshing to be in amongst all the greenery. Time in hand started to increase rapidly over the next few kilometres, helped by gorgeous running conditions. There were just isolated groups of supporters along this stretch, nothing to compare with London, but then this was very different to London – a genuine country run a quarter of the way into a big-city marathon. It felt more like a Sunday morning training run which just happened to be in the company of 30,000 other runners. It was a happy, straightforward trot.

Towards the end we were running along the southern edge of the Bois, heading westwards back towards the city with some attractive town houses on our left. The route at this point was undulating gently, and it was around the 20-km point that I passed a blind runner (*coureur non-voyant* written on her back), handcuffed to her seeing guide. They'd been doing an impressive pace – and I couldn't help but marvel at the trust she was putting in her companion. To stride out without seeing is bravery indeed.

I hit the half-marathon (21.1k) nearly five minutes ahead of my half-marathon split for New York. And believe me, these things matter. I was ahead of my game and was starting to feel confident, particularly as I was still building up time in hand on the five-minute kilometres I needed to do. After a few more kilometres, I found I was something like six and a half minutes to the good – riches indeed. I really started to believe that I was looking good to crack 3:30.

Quite suddenly, the surroundings had changed again. Within moments, we were back in the familiar Paris street scenes after all those kilometres of woodland. Once again, the streets were lined with shops and bars, everywhere Parisians coolly sipping their *cafés*, dragging on their *Gauloises* and wondering what on earth all these sweaty runners were up to. Not too many Parisians were out on the pavements to egg us on. But somehow it didn't matter. Just seeing Paris going about the business of being Paris was incentive enough. The city looked lovely – even if the locals weren't exactly making us the centre of their day.

After this, we were back at the Place de la Bastille and heading down to the Seine for another of the day's great highlights, several kilometres running alongside the river. We came out on the riverbank more or less opposite the Île de la Cité and soon I could see the top of Notre Dame. The sun was out, it was a lovely day, it wasn't too hot and I wasn't feeling tired. The sights along the way did the rest. The course was glorious, and I was having a great time.

After a while, still on the north bank of the Seine, we came into what the official course map calls '*les quatre tunnels de la voie Georges-Pompidou*', another of the stretches which the map identifies as a danger spot. It certainly was for Princess Diana. The tunnel by the Pont de l'Alma was the one in which she was fatally injured, and it felt strange – though not disrespectful – to be running through it. It looked so familiar from all the pictures.

The tunnels were effectively underpasses, dipping under the main routes which headed north-south across the river as we headed generally east-west. I'd expected the four tunnels to look the same, but each was subtly different in character, not least for the fact that by now the crowds – at last – were building all the time. The tunnels took us towards the 30-km marker, and the map had warned us to take them carefully and certainly not to accelerate on the descents. In the event, they were fine. It was good to know that there were four and good to count them off, especially as I could feel the atmosphere rising as we emerged from each into the sunshine. This was one of the places where the atmosphere was at its best, helped in my case by knowing that Marc's family were waiting for us around the 30-km marker.

All the while – and if you are a runner, you will know that you simply have to do this – I was comparing my time to my New York time six months before. In New York I reached the 15-mile marker in 2:01. In Paris, I passed the 16-mile marker in 2:02, a mile more in just a minute more. When you can log such facts as you run along, it's impossible to overestimate just how much they can help you. Success breeds success on a marathon route. If you can prove to yourself that you are doing well, then invariably you will do even better. I was feeling good. At 20 miles, I was eight minutes ahead of my New York time – and I am sure that keeping a close eye on comparative times had a lot to do with it. Over marathon distance, you've got to cling to anything that will sustain your pace.

Around the 30-km marker there were some fine views of the Eiffel Tower, and there I grabbed a power gel sachet (fortunately vanilla, a flavour I liked). It was the first I had seen of the gels, though there had been plenty of discarded sachets on the road at various points. I don't know how I missed them. I had started out with a bottle of sports drink that I had made up, but after that I was solely on water and started to worry that I wasn't replacing salts. I sucked on the power gel occasionally over the next few miles, always being careful to wash it down with fluid. I am sure it made a difference.

Eventually the race turned away from the river and up towards the Bois de Boulogne, and here it was great to see the kilometres creeping into the mid-30s. By the time

I reached 34 km I was thinking in terms of a run from Wickham roundabout to home, just 5 miles remaining, perfectly manageable, nothing you would get too excited about. It was all about reducing that deficit to manageable proportions and until about 35 km, those kilometre markers had come up pretty nicely.

But it was here that tiredness started to kick in and take hold. I think 36 was OK and perhaps also 37, but thereafter I was struggling. Maybe it was the lack of salts earlier on. I kept thinking: only another couple of kilometres and then it will be the 40-km marker and I will be virtually there, with just two more to go. But in those final five or so kilometres, it felt that each kilometre was at least a mile. And this was where I was lucky to have maintained my time in hand.

Those minutes in hand gave me exactly the cushion I needed – just! I was haemorrhaging nearly a minute a kilometre at this point, and it was a huge struggle. The difficulty was that the Bois de Boulogne was vaguely pleasant but completely uninteresting, with nobody there to watch – a very flat final stretch, flat in height but also flat in atmosphere, which probably accounted for much of the discomfort I felt.

There just wasn't any buzz. And worst of all, it felt as if the organisers had fallen short on the overall distance they needed and so decided to make it up any old how in the Bois. There was one point where you ran around a lake, which wouldn't have been so bad if you hadn't been able to see runners much further ahead, already on the other side. All a bit dispiriting.

The atmosphere was zero. There were a few people around in the Bois but they were just doing their usual Sunday-morning thing. There were even a few joggers going past us in the opposite direction. I couldn't help wondering if they felt they were missing out on something.

And so the Bois seemed to go on forever. One little delight, though, came out of the blue – a stall, at around 40 km, advertising the Marathon de Vannes, at which they were offering wine and what looked like cider, plus cheese, brioches and all sorts of food. I doubt there were many takers. For some reason a swig of cider and a lump of cheese really didn't seem too good an idea at this point. But the bizarreness of it – as surreal as the stretches of banana skins – did at least elicit a weary chuckle. They certainly do things differently in France.

The chuckle was just about all I could manage by now. A degree of disorientation was starting to creep in. I was trying to work out the miles and kilometres remaining but it was all just too much to think about. I was chasing thoughts but incapable of grasping them, a really curious sensation. I could feel myself starting to get confused and my thoughts on time in hand, so clear previously, were now all over the place. Suddenly I just couldn't do the maths any more.

This blasted Bois de Boulogne, a place I'd hoped was going to be a lovely little marathon pre-finale, a chance to take stock and catch my breath before the flourish of the finish, never seemed to end. I was hating it. I'd entered a zone where I simply couldn't picture my way to the finishing line. We were running around all over the place. The distance was stacking up, but there was not the slightest hint that we were ever going to leave the Bois, and I knew that this wasn't where the finish lay.

How strange that the Bois de Vincennes had been such a pleasure, such an inspiration, whereas now the Bois de Boulogne was draining the life out of me. The 40-km mark came and then, eventually, painfully slowly, 41 km, and yet still we were in the Bois. The finish had never seemed so near and yet so far. The reality is that I should have studied the map more closely – an unforgivable omission for a runner who was fairly seasoned by now. If I had studied it, I would have seen that you don't leave the Bois until the very end of the race itself.

But then there was a minor miracle on the route to the Arc de Triomphe. Marc's family suddenly materialised, there on my left shouting out for me. I hadn't for a moment thought I'd see them again before the end, but, map in hand, they'd cut across Paris quickly, and there they were. I veered over and touched an outstretched hand. It did the trick. It refocused me. They later said that I wasn't looking very 'with it' at that point, which was probably putting it mildly, but their presence did me a huge favour. Never mind that I had met them for the first time the day before. They were there for me, and it made an enormous difference.

I was suddenly much more aware of what I was doing, who I was and why I was doing it. And so I plodded on. I kept thinking about walking and knew I wouldn't. I don't think I had the energy to make the decision to stop running. Besides, the atmosphere was starting to mount.

Marc's family had been standing just where the crowds were beginning to build again. I knew it had to be a good sign. Several people in the crowd had been shouting out *'Allez! Allez! Allez! Les derniers 400 metres!'* and I accepted it as if they really knew. I was annoyed a hundred or so metres later when someone else shouted out *'Allez! Les derniers 400 metres!'* And just after that someone shouted out *'Allez! Les derniers 500 metres!'*

But then, the great miracle happened. We left the Bois. All of a sudden there was the first sight of the Arc de Triomphe as we turned the corner onto Avenue Foch. In front of the Arc was the straight stretch up to the finish, with the 42-km marker hovering just a couple of hundred metres in front of the finishing line.

And so I made it to the end. People were finishing thickly at this point. I was in much more of a crowd than I had been in New York. As I approached the line, I could see the clock turning 3:30 and so I knew – given the time it had taken me to get over the start – that I was home and dry, well within my target.

I started hyperventilating within moments of finishing. In London you are conscious of marshals looking out for you, but there was no such luxury in Paris. I just kept walking and my horribly noisy breathing soon subsided as I walked towards the medals. The marshals didn't triumphantly place your medal around your neck as they did in New York. They just gave it to you in a cellophane packet. And then you were handed a big blue plastic disposable raincoat, almost impossible to put on when you are exhausted. I had my head coming out of an armhole for a moment.

No, there was no great feeling of being looked after, but I found myself recovering and very soon – surprisingly soon – feeling good. They were dishing out water and fruit, and I grabbed a bottle. I contemplated eating, but briefly I felt my stomach tighten and so decided against. Instead I contemplated the run I had just completed.

Those minutes in hand had done the business. I came in at 3:27:34. I had run a good race, and just as importantly, I had *thought* a good race. I had two and a half minutes remaining on my time in hand, and that was what took me under the all-important 3:30. Just as importantly, I'd knocked just over eight minutes off my New York time.

The satisfaction was double. I was able to tell myself that this was the race where I had come of age, in the sense that this was the race where I had used my head, drawing on past times and past experiences to see me through.

The second part of the satisfaction was that it been so wonderful a course. Support from spectators had averaged out as moderate, finishing strongly but in places sparse to non-existent. But that didn't matter. This had been Paris on a beautiful day, on a fast, flat course which offered everything from the Arc de Triomphe and back again, taking in the Place de la Concorde, the Rue de Rivoli, the Hôtel de Ville, the Place de la Bastille, the Château and the Bois de Vincennes, a gorgeous stretch of the Seine and glimpses of Notre Dame and the Eiffel Tower. The Bois de Boulogne had been dull at the end, but really I couldn't have asked for more on a course purpose-built for the kind of stimulation a marathon runner thrives on.

New York had been perhaps the better overall experience, but possibly, just possibly – I really can't decide – the course in Paris just shades the course in New York. Or maybe not. Best simply to say that both are outstanding examples of what a big-city marathon really ought to offer. New York could so easily have been followed by grim anticlimax. In the event, it was capped and crowned by Paris.

The day was now beautifully sunny and I followed the crowds towards the runners' exit, where the organisation returned to the level which had characterised the start of the race. There were huge barriers across the road and a great press of runners, some a bit unsteady, trying to get through the narrowest of escapes into the tightly packed crowd of well-wishers on the other side.

It was stupid to be subjected to this, particularly as the crowds outside, so eager to greet their own runner, weren't giving an inch. In defence of the organisers, it would have worked if everyone had been sensible, but the point is that crowds aren't sensible, and the organisers had completely failed to factor that in. It was a complete farce.

Eventually I made it out and was walking towards the Arc de Triomphe – a magnificent sight at the end of a magnificent day. Feeling pleased with myself, and knowing that the feeling wouldn't last long, I wandered back to the flat. Just outside, I found Marc. He'd finished ten minutes ahead of me and already he wasn't happy with his time. He was doing his second marathon, having done 3:36 in London the year before. His Paris 3:17 was a time I have never achieved, but he was annoyed, convinced he should have done 3:15.

When you're running well, you're never going to be truly satisfied, and slowly, my own dissatisfaction started to grow. I'm not blaming Marc in the least for this. It was the most natural of reactions. Everything had been so much in my favour. *Surely I should have done better than 3:27,* I thought. But common sense reasserted itself, and I told myself to enjoy the moment.

Those early-morning stretches as the rain hammered down outside seemed an eternity ago now as we returned to our starting point. Marc's family were there, and I told them again and again how they had saved my day in the Bois de Boulogne. Of course, I would have finished without them, but I couldn't help wondering just how much more of my time in hand I would have eaten up if it hadn't been for their presence at that crucial moment. After all those hundreds of miles in training, strangely, such is running, I could quite believe that in the end it all came down to that moment in the Bois.

After a very welcome meal with Marc and his family in the flat, I returned to the finish to find Michael, who finished, soon after I got there, with a time of 5:34 – an hour quicker than his debut London two years before. Fortunately the crush had eased by then, and he emerged looking great, delighted to be hailed by name over the finishing line by the guy on the PA – a suitable tribute to a run born of a stamina which I honestly don't think I could ever aspire to.

Running round in three and a half hours is one thing, but being out there for five and a half is an achievement of quite a different order – one I genuinely marvel at. Michael certainly wouldn't see it that way, but for me his achievement is in the amount of time he sustains the effort, simply keeping going in a race in which most people are pulling away from him. His marathons are a study in concentration which leaves me lost in admiration. He will say he's horribly slow; for me, that's missing the point. Don't weigh up the speed. Simply admire the endurance.

Three of us had set out on the Eurostar from Waterloo the day before. Each of us had achieved something, and we each enjoyed each other's success as much as we did our own. I couldn't run a marathon in 3:17, as Marc had done; and I certainly couldn't keep running for 5 hours 34 minutes, as Michael had done. And yet, for me, it was 'job done' too, my first day as a sub-3:30 marathon runner. *La vie* was definitely *belle*.

Chapter Seven: 'Plundered My Soul'
Misjudging a Marathon – Amsterdam 2004

One of the most genuinely bizarre aspects of running a marathon is that you celebrate it by stopping. Not just stopping on the finishing line, but you actually stop running for a few weeks. To an extent, it becomes a habit. You step off the conveyor belt – a necessary response, if only to underline the fact that the marathon was an end point in itself. You build up to it, you count the number of runs left until you are running for real and then suddenly you cast aside your trainers as a mark of respect. Mission accomplished, you pause before the next one.

Partly, and more obviously, it's also a question of recharging depleted batteries. By then you are ready for a rest, but subliminally it has always seemed to me that something slightly darker is happening.

You are waiting for withdrawal symptoms to set in. You've been so focused on the big day for weeks that it's good to remind yourself of the emptiness which comes when you just don't run. To start with, it's great. You enjoy those extra hours in bed at the weekend; during the week, you look out into the darkness and rain and you think, 'Huh, I'm glad I'm not going out in that.' But beneath the superficial laziness, just waiting to break through, something much more primal is gathering momentum, something you are allowing yourself to discover anew: the fact that you actually want to run. Rest, and you will refresh your hunger, sharpen it and refocus it.

For the weeks before the marathon, you run because you have to run, because you've mapped out a training schedule, however idiosyncratic, and you are trying to keep to it – if only because keeping to it will be a big part of your confidence on the day. All of which obscures the fact that running is actually something you want to do. Moreover, it's something which your body is expecting you to do. Desist for a while, and it won't be long before your mind starts to long for it and your body starts to crave it.

You sense the pressure building up, and you let it build up a bit more, knowing that the moment of release will be all the sweeter. I usually manage to hold off for a couple of weeks, which probably sounds a ludicrously short break, but by then the cracks in what I like to consider my usual sunny demeanour have started to show. Mr Grumpy moves in and takes up residence. Fiona is convinced she can tell whether or not I have had a run, and she can certainly tell when I need one.

It's not quite cold turkey, more what the Aussie cricketers used to like to call mental disintegration before they started succumbing to it themselves. You start to feel fat, and no matter how much the feeling flies in the face of all evidence, it's a feeling which grows as you feel increasingly de-energised, lardy and slothful. When the children were small, my yardstick was that I needed a run when I started hearing myself say too frequently, 'Adam, will you fetch this?'; 'Adam, will you fetch that?' If I've had a run, I simply get up and fetch it myself. Time and again, it seems the only way to replenish energy is to expend it. As the French say, *l'appétit vient en mangeant*. So it is with running.

And so it is with missing a run. Even when I've really, really not wanted to go for a run, I've forced myself, knowing the satisfaction of having gone will be worth its weight in gold compared to the self-flagellating grumpiness of not having gone. Once running has got hold of you, all you can do is obey; once marathons have got hold of you, all you can do is decide which one next.

On the back of Paris, I thought I would turn my attention to Amsterdam. After London and New York, I had already felt I was getting the hang of these big cities. And I wanted more. Amsterdam was an obvious one to try, another database marathon which is easy to get into. Just as with Paris, you pick your moment, you whip out your credit card and within seconds you've got an email confirmation: you're in. I was now in the habit of running a spring and an autumn marathon, occasionally throwing in an extra one. Amsterdam on Sunday, 17 October was to be my autumn treat for 2004, another notch on my growing list of countries conquered.

It would be a hectic weekend, flying out on the Saturday morning and heading back on the Sunday after the race. With the children at school, there was no way we could turn it into a family break, and I wasn't keen to use up holiday allowance without them. We decided that I would go off alone, not something I particularly relished, but the marathon bug was strong, and I felt I was getting stronger. I had eaten into my finishing time over successive marathons, and I wanted to eat some more.

A huge part of the attraction was also that Amsterdam in the autumn would be the perfect complement to Paris in the springtime: another legendarily beautiful city at an attractive time of year. The Venice of the North, with its characteristic architecture reflecting in those endlessly alluring canals, strongly appealed to me. Throw in the gorgeous colours of the season, and I was hoping to come close to my New York experience of a year before.

Cost, too, was a factor. It was barely an hour's flight from Southampton Airport, just a few miles up the road from home. In fact, it was so close that, in one of those appealing quirks of European timekeeping, you actually arrive home – regaining the hour – at pretty much the time you took off.

In short, it was a marathon which ticked all the boxes: close enough, but still exotic; no great disruption to family life, but still a chance to go on a plane (always a big plus in my book) to a beautiful city which was relatively cheap to get to.

And when I studied the course, I soon saw another reason to lap it up. The marathon starts and ends in the city's Olympic Stadium. How inspiring was that going to be? What a prospect. First New York and then Paris had underlined the importance of picking an inspiring course. The thought of running on an Olympic track had me drooling. And then, in between, when tiredness set in, just how inspiring were those canals going to be? As marathons go, it looked ideal.

I was psyched up and confident as I flew off on that Saturday morning in October 2004. Soon after arrival, I discovered to my delight that registration was just a few minutes from the Olympic Stadium. Disappointingly, the stadium turned out to be a fairly ugly building from the outside, but the glimpse of the track I got through the main entrance looked enticing. A historic running track was bound to put a spring in our step, I told myself.

But then things started to go wrong. I've always prided myself on having an excellent sense of direction, but after registering, I struggled for a couple of hours to locate my hotel. I found a street plan but I couldn't see the road anywhere. I wandered into a hotel and asked. The guy replied, 'That's almost in Belgium' – which wasn't exactly what I wanted to hear. Eventually I found it, but a preparation which involved a flight and getting lost wasn't good. Nor was a poor night's sleep – even though I kept telling myself that the night before a marathon wasn't the night that mattered.

I was finally asleep when the alarm went off at 6.20 a.m., which was far too early. I can't imagine why I set it for that time, save to say it's possibly some kind of Pavlovian conditioning. If you're doing a marathon, you get up stupidly early – really stupidly in this case, given that the marathon started at 11 a.m., which was far too late – an hour and a quarter after London and two and a quarter hours after Paris. I lay on the bed for a couple of hours, had a light breakfast and idly waited for the time to pass. Instead of mounting excitement, I felt a deepening gloom for no reason I could fathom.

Finally, I left the hotel at about ten to nine and joined a train, which was already full of marathon runners. It took a quarter of an hour to get to the marathon stop and then five minutes to walk to the sports hall which served as marathon HQ.

In keeping with Paris, this was a marathon which ended where it started. I dumped my bag in a big hall divided into sections according to your running number – all very straightforward. I queued for the loo several times, largely to waste time and then, to my annoyance, I started to get worried about being hungry. I bought a biscuit and a coffee. 11 a.m. was a bad time to start. You really don't want to be running right through a time of day when your body might reasonably be expecting to get fed, but there was no way round it. For a 9 a.m. start, you want to be having a light breakfast soon after six. For an 11 a.m. start, it was all much more difficult to compute, and I suspect I got it wrong.

The other problem was that the later start gave us all far too much time to think about it, and the more I thought about it, the less appealing the whole prospect became. I glanced outside the sports hall at the dark grey skies. The temperature had dropped significantly from the day before. The morning was overcast and threatening to deteriorate. The air was chilled. It had been raining heavily when I woke up, and it looked as if the rain would return any second.

The sensible thing, partly to get in the mood, would have been to wait around outside, and plenty of people did, but I didn't fancy it, hanging back instead in the relative warmth of the sports hall – a decision which probably nibbled away at my confidence even more.

Finally I emerged at about 10.40 to join the crowds wandering towards the start, a few minutes' walk away. Some people were jogging gently, which seemed daft. *Surely the first kilometre or so is going to be warm-up enough*, I thought miserably. But, of course, they were doing the right thing. I was shivering and hunching up; they were loosening and starting to focus. I was beginning to dread; they were starting to synch body and mind.

Inside the stadium the atmosphere was good, which lifted my spirits a little as we assembled for the off. A choir was singing on a huge, temporary stage, and there was a reasonable number of supporters in the stands which rose up above us all the way round. I walked around the outside of the track and found the pink starting zone, the colour corresponding to the time I had said I hoped I'd finish in – 3 hours to 3 hours 30 minutes, the third group back from the front. The organisation was good, which is always an early comfort, and slowly I found myself being sucked into the zone, both mentally and physically. There was quite a buzz.

The fact that we were standing on an Olympic track definitely added to the sense of occasion, but it was noticeable that people were looking cold already. People were jumping up and down on the spot in an effort to keep warm. Runners were reluctant to discard their bin bags and extra layers. I was among the many who left it to the last couple of minutes to cast aside sweatshirt and extra T-shirt, flinging them into the trackside piles which generally get donated to the homeless at these events.

Just as in Paris, I didn't hear whatever it was that started the run, but suddenly we surged forward, stopped and then surged again in the time-honoured big-city marathon way. I was over the line in about 40 seconds, which I was delighted with. This wasn't a marathon remotely on the London, Paris or New York scale. It was much smaller and, on a more forgiving day, it would have been much more manageable. But at least we were away, and with no hold-ups or significant bunching, it was all looking more promising.

After a couple of hundred metres of track, we left the stadium and disgorged onto the streets where it was suddenly all just a fraction tighter, or so it seemed – an impression which lasted just a few minutes as the wide avenues opened up ahead of us.

This was my second marathon in kilometres and once again I came armed with a wristband, having printed out one which promised to get me around in 3:20. After New York and Paris, I was feeling ambitious. It meant having to keep my wits about me. The 3:30 wristband which had been such a success in Paris demanded five-minute kilometres. For the 3:20 schedule, I had to be doing kilometres in about 4:45, not such an easy figure to multiply in your head.

But, of course, it was more complicated than that. Wristband times don't allow for the inevitable slowing across the second half of the race. I calculated that, just as in Paris, I needed to have five minutes in hand at the halfway mark, but I knew that working that into multiples of 4:45 was never going to be easy.

From the stadium, we launched into a big, rectangular route, which, bizarrely, after 7 kilometres, took us back into the stadium. The fourth and long top side of the rectangle was a couple of kilometres through the Vondelpark, a picturesque run through a lovely autumnal open space. Conditions were damp from the overnight rain, and a glance at the skies suggested it was only a matter of minutes before more rain hammered down. More worryingly, even after 5 or 6 kilometres, I didn't feel that I had remotely warmed up. I wasn't into my stride, and inside I felt cold. Rather than slipping into an expansive forward flow, I was hunched and uptight.

But at least this stretch of the course served a useful purpose, I told myself. After Paris, I had learned my lesson and had mugged up on the route, no easy task in a city I didn't really know. But one thing I had noted, and which had stuck, was that the last couple of kilometres of the rectangle were a dress rehearsal for the actual marathon finish. We'd be back along here a couple of hours later. I tried to remind myself how much that kind of knowledge ought to be of benefit.

Even so, it did seem rather pointless when we were back in the stadium after just 7 kilometres. *Have they really got nothing else to show us?* I wondered. You can take familiarisation too far, I chuntered – something I seemed to be doing rather a lot that morning.

But my timing was still good. I was back where I started after about 33 minutes – still nicely in touch with the 4:45 minutes-per-kilometre schedule I was hoping to run to. Plus this time, having covered just one end of the track on our way out, we were going to complete a full circuit. I expected a lift from the loop. It didn't come. Instead, there was the worrying thought that somehow we were counting our chickens rather too early.

We ran over the finish with around 35 km still to go. On another day, in other circumstances, I can quite see myself thinking this was a brilliant idea, the ideal way to spur you on, giving you every opportunity to visualise the finish before the final approach. But not that day. Instead of inspiring, it felt dangerously presumptuous. Instead of rousing, it simply brought home to me how far there was to go – a thought I certainly wouldn't have been thinking if I had been running 7 kilometres away on virgin territory at that moment. What works one day, won't work on another, and I started to let negative thinking creep in.

Outside, it was back onto fairly large avenues with the runners starting to thin appreciably, genuine breathing space in a race which had never been too cramped anyway.

And then things suddenly looked up at about 9 km when I made what I thought was a wonderful discovery. I found the *Runners World* 3:15 pacers, two guys running along with 3:15 on their vests and each trailing a pink balloon. It was the first time I had ever seen a pacer, though I knew they existed, and these were the ones for me. Their promise, which they radiated with every strong, confident step, was that they would get you home in the time they had blazoned all over them. All you had to do was keep up with them. *Brilliant*, I thought, and I stayed with them very comfortably for the next 10 km. I wanted to do 3:20. All I had to do was follow them, and they would get me there well inside it.

In that instant, those pacers represented, as far as I was concerned, an end to thinking. They could do it all for me. I'd just catch their slipstream.

At around the 13-km mark, we reached the River Amstel, and this was probably the most pleasant part of the route, down the western side of the river for a couple of kilometres, across a bridge and then back up the eastern side. Fairly early on, across the water, we heard the sirens from the other side and saw the outriders for the front-runners. One guy sped past, probably less than a hundred metres away. There was a longish gap and then a big group of runners, superfit and strong, stormed through. Even from a distance, it was obvious that they were thundering.

On my side of the river, it was also going nicely, if rather less quickly. Running alongside the river was lovely, and it all felt very manageable. It reminded me, just a little, of that lovely Bois de Vincennes stretch you get in Paris – much more rural for a few kilometres before you head back into the bustle of the big city. This was country running, the rain was holding off, and I was feeling strong. The pacers were looking very comfortable, just as it was their job to, and effectively I handed everything over to them.

Crossing the river was a great moment, a real feeling of progress, especially as we were now the ones looking across at thousands of runners several kilometres behind. Oh yes, life was beautiful at that point.

And then, oh so suddenly, it all went wrong. The drinks stations were bargy, hectic, hassly affairs with nothing terribly gentlemanly about the way runners cut in and jostled for drinks. Earlier I had missed out completely on a Gatorade sports drink station because I simply couldn't get through the big blokes around me. There was an aggressiveness about the runners I'd never experienced anywhere before – or since.

Another problem was that the sports drinks were in paper cups, which were awkward to handle. I knew by now how important it is to have a proper sports top to your bottle, one you can suck on without taking in any air. At the 2002 London Marathon, I'd gulped on an open cup – absolutely the wrong thing to do. I got a lungful of fluid and feared I was going to drown in the middle of a big-city marathon. It was the most horrible feeling. The discomfort lasted several hundred metres and the shock even longer. Consequently, I was always careful to use a proper sports bottle with a teat-type top.

But the jostle at the Amsterdam drinks stations meant that I missed out too many, and when I did stop, the fact that they were using cups rather than pouches for the Gatorade meant I simply wasn't taking in enough fluids. At the 20-km drinks station, I knew I needed a substantial intake of sports drink, but I got shoved in the process, gulped too quickly and took in too much air – not as much as I took in at London, but more than enough to signal what was probably the day's first significant discomfort. Soon after followed the major discomfort.

When I moved on from the drinks station, the pink balloons were about 50 metres away, not too far, but that was that. I never got near them again. I passed the halfway mark at just under 1:38, by a good three or four minutes my fastest ever half-marathon – not that that was a cause for rejoicing. If I had been several minutes slower, I might well have kept control. But suddenly, at about 21 or 22 km, the whole thing just seemed to collapse on me.

It sounds stupid, but I was suddenly conscious that I was very slight and weak in a field of big, big blokes – not the kind of marathon runner I was used to. It was almost certainly all in my mind and not a true reflection of the actual field, but I felt out of place and miserably inadequate. I'd tried to keep up with the big boys and now felt myself fast coming a cropper. If there had been any sand around, they would have kicked it in my face.

The very best runners are pretty skinny, but they were well to the front by now. Instead – and as usual – I was running with the pack, but this time a very muscle-bound pack in a very male field. It was probably all in the mind, but I didn't just run puny, I felt puny – all part of a loss of confidence which, sadly, was the only thing about me that was actually gathering pace. I was disintegrating mentally. I felt out of my league. Everyone seemed huge, and so I started to fade, losing it in the mind long before I lost it on the road.

We continued on the riverbank for another couple of kilometres and then cut through a grassy embankment for a kilometre or so, but by then I was struggling. Seriously struggling. I had an orange gel and got a bit of a lift from that, but people were starting to stream past me in a worrying way. And as they looked bigger, so I felt smaller.

Soon we were running through a nondescript industrial suburb, which I later recognised as the area in which my hotel was located. It was a grim, uninspiring landscape, with nothing to look at except business units and warehouses, and with nothing to think about except the knowledge of so many kilometres stretching ahead. In a good marathon, the kilometres tumble away after the halfway mark, but in Amsterdam, it felt as if they were still stacking up. It was miserable, and now I endured a couple of kilometres convinced that I was going to get cramp, a worry heightened by the fact that my slowing meant I was feeling ever colder.

A new low point was a depressing section where you slog up one side of a dual carriageway simply to turn at a roundabout and head back down the other side – a couple of kilometres of pointlessness, the product of wretched planning on the part of the marathon organisers. It was demoralising to see all the runners heading back the other way several kilometres ahead, and even when it was me coming back on the other side (which can be a boost in a marathon), all I could see was hundreds of runners who would soon be overtaking me.

They were all looking great. I felt ghastly. I had a very brief walk at this point but felt much worse for it and so just plodded on through yet more industrial suburb, dour and uninviting, offering nothing to lift the spirit. For kilometre after kilometre, Amsterdam was unimaginably dull. And not a canal in sight.

All the boxes were starting to be un-ticked. I was fed up, I was cold, the rain was starting and the route was doing nothing for me. So much for the Venice of the North. This was a city intent on showing off only its warehouses and lorry parks. It was crushingly boring, and slowly I let it crush me.

When things started to pick up, it was too late. After about 32 or 33 km, we broke out beside a canal for the first time in far too long, but by then the mental damage had been done. I had lost it. All hope of a 3:20 finish had evaporated – and therein lay the danger. It wasn't just the dream that was lost, but the will to participate. I was always going to finish, but I had nothing left to give. Fear of cramp had receded, but my thighs felt like lead, and with fatigue came the usual confusion. I was struggling to work out how many miles were left and muddling them up with kilometres.

Reaching 20 miles is always a good point, because that last six is a manageable distance to think about, but I didn't have the energy to calculate what 20 miles would be in kilometres. Not that that would have helped. You'd have to be pretty alert to run in both measurements. I could barely cope with one.

Self-pity set in. Just after 35 km, with 7 km to go, you reach the edge of the city centre once again and go past the Music Theatre, from where you soon go over a pretty bridge. In places now the crowds, which had been sparse throughout the boring bits and not that great in the other bits, weren't too bad, but not having anyone out there cheering for me was dispiriting. I was on my own in a race I wasn't enjoying, battling against kilometres which were refusing to budge. I'd never felt more miserable on a racecourse – especially when somebody pulled the plug and the rain hammered down, cold and unforgiving.

I walked for a few minutes, trotted on, and then walked for a couple of minutes more. There was a runner with a St

Neots vest who seemed to have run a parallel race to me. I saw him struggle at about 20 km and then he headed on. But then I found him again and overtook him. Then he would overtake me and so it would go on. His presence was a help in some ways, giving me a reason to carry on. In hindsight I wish I had teamed up with him, but you don't think of these things at the time and I don't know how he would have reacted. However, he did at least give me something to focus on in the final few kilometres.

Eventually we got back to the Vondelpark, which meant we were on the final stretch, but even then it was impossible to keep running. I walked for several minutes, the rain lashing my face, so cold as to be painful. I knew I had blown the whole damned thing by then, and I'd gone past caring. Looking back, it's very easy to be critical of yourself and wonder why you stopped when surely it was easier to carry on, but the problem is that it is just so difficult to keep going once you've set a target only to watch it drift irretrievably out of your reach.

Those pink balloons had long since floated away, and I'd long since discarded my wristband. After about 37 km, hopelessly, helplessly behind schedule, I chucked it into an Amsterdam gutter in disgust. It was all the wristband's fault. It could hardly be mine. If I hadn't been so hung up on doing 3:20, I could have done 3:30, and now even that was running away from me. Run well, and wristbands will help. Run badly, and they're a reminder of mounting failure. I was sure I could hear it laughing. Down the drain it went, and I threatened to follow.

My target was probably unrealistic from the start. I'd been hoping to leap from a previous best of 3:27 to hit 3:20, but as I wobbled in Amsterdam, I started to think that not even favourable conditions on the day would have been enough. It was the kind of leap that required the kind of speed work I'd never wanted to do. I wondered if I was approaching the point where general fitness ceased to be enough and serious speed training had to take over.

And that's the moment my marathon imploded – the moment I was pushed one crucial place further back. Not that the position mattered one bit by then; far more important was the person who had overtaken me. You'll never guess what he had on his head. Oh. OK. You've guessed it. A beautifully ornate model yacht, fully rigged and sailing serenely through the rain, which was now falling heavily. I expect he'd carved it himself while we waited at the starting line.

This was a fast, serious race, and at the start I remember thinking that I had never stood among so many lean, superfit-looking blokes. There was absolutely no hint of fun run about this one, and yet I was passed by the nearest thing to a fun runner that Amsterdam threw up. What a prat. Me, not him. Just the sight of him was enough. I was beyond misery and almost beyond continuing. My problem was that I was in wholly uncharted territory for me – a marathon that was going seriously wrong. And I didn't know how to cope. The only possibility was somehow simply to keep going.

Slowly I reached 40 km and started to look out for 41 km. It never seemed to come. I was out of the park heading along what had been the fourth side of the rectangle earlier on, and it seemed the 41-km marker was never going to arrive. I saw it the first time round, but this time I completely missed it. I sagged into a dejected walk again. I probably walked for almost a kilometre in total over the whole race, and that is bad. Really bad.

But a policeman by the roadside shouted 'Run, run, you are almost there!' I managed a sickly smile and said to him, 'I will run if you will', and he did, for 50 metres or so, a sweet gesture. But then he stopped and said in a lovely, thick Dutch accent, 'I will stop here. I am wearing my bicycling booties!' It was an exquisite moment – just enough to get me home.

Soon people were shouting that the stadium was just around the corner, and it was. That was when I realised that I had completely missed the 41-km marker. I turned the corner and the stadium loomed massive before my eyes. I had barely the strength to run but I trotted into the arena once again. We were suddenly on the track, running round and the finish slew into view. But even that was an anticlimax. I usually can't help but shed a tear on crossing a marathon finish line, but this time I just felt monumentally depressed.

My only consolation – and it counted for little – was that I had rallied just a fraction in the final few hundred metres. I had glanced at my watch and had seen how perilously close I was to slipping into the 3:40s. That would have been the final humiliation. I had dredged up something from somewhere, put on a spurt and finished just 20 seconds inside what would have been the ultimate defeat. Even so, I felt horribly flat at the end, as if the whole thing had been pointless.

For every high, there's a low. For every cloud with a silver lining, there's one with a big, black duffle coat. For every moment of elation, there's a moment of abject misery. For every Paris, there's an Amsterdam.

Marathon number nine was in many ways the most disappointing of any I have ever done. I came in 1,669th out of 4,498 recorded finishers, completing the course in

3:39:33, which at the time was my third-fastest marathon, but that wasn't the real significance of my finishing time. Amsterdam entered my record books as the first time I had done a serious marathon slower than the previous one. I can find lots of reasons for the failure, though it is probably better to call them excuses. Basically, I fluffed it – almost certainly by setting off too fast. And probably by never being truly up for it in the first place.

When the post-race reaction set in, I started to shiver uncontrollably. I could see plenty of other runners suffering the same fate. Some had even succumbed before the end. For the last few kilometres, there were noticeable numbers of people pulling up and stretching their leg muscles, clearly fighting off cramp. There was a good number of runners standing by the roadside looking bemused. Like me, their eyes had lit up at the thought of a traditionally fast course but in the long run they simply didn't have the legs. I tried to cling to the thought that clearly I wasn't alone in all that I was suffering, and it was a thought which brought a kind of consolation. Whatever my miscalculations, I had plenty of company in the pain stakes.

Another factor was that support had been poor and there had been none personal to me. Another was that I had walked around far too much the day before. Another factor? Another excuse, more like. In hindsight, from the start, the whole thing just hadn't felt right.

Dejectedly, I made my way back to the sports hall, picked up my stuff and resolved to go straight back to the hotel. It was raining icily and heavily, and I'd had enough. But then something started to change in my thinking.

I knew without a shadow of doubt that this wasn't a race I would ever contemplate doing again, but I knew too that my experience of the day wasn't done yet. I baulked at the thought of simply walking away. I knew that it would add to the sense of defeat. But more insistently, something told me that a key part of the experience still awaited me, and so I headed back to the Olympic Stadium to watch the finishers.

I am glad I did. What was crystallising was the need to show and share a little solidarity. I'd had an awful time with that ghastly, icy rain for the final half an hour, but those runners still out there had now endured an hour and a half of it. I wanted to show them that I cared. It was as simple as that. I would have hated to be out there still. From that thought it was a short step to wanting to show support towards those that were.

I put on all the clothes I had in my rucksack and ventured out of the changing area to find that the rain at last was easing. I smiled for the first time since finishing. Those still on the course hadn't deserved the weather they had been enduring. None of us had. I made my way into the stadium, and, finally, it was then that I had some of the emotions I usually feel on finishing – except that this time I was having them for my fellow runners.

They were now coming in 60 to 75 minutes after me, and they were absolutely streaming in, hundreds and hundreds of them. And I felt for them. At last I had my post-marathon tear – a selfless one for a change. 'Well done!' I shouted. 'Come on, come on, come on!' I thought of that wonderful woman on the tannoy in New York. 'Come on, Bill, you can do it! Come on, bring him home!' I wanted to be that woman. I wanted to be the one who helped them all in out of the rain, stoked the fire, brought them a steaming mug of hot chocolate and ran their bath. Metaphorically speaking, that is.

From the stands, I looked down at the recent finishers below me, emerging from the enclosure in their orange throwaway macs. I could see how cold and exhausted they looked. Scores of runners slumped against walls. Others, more canny perhaps, went straight into stretching exercises. Wherever you looked, there was distress. I stood high in the stands, but in spirit I was down there with them. We'd run it together, and that was all that mattered. It didn't matter that I was way off my target time. All that mattered was the marathon effort which had got us all home. Forget the PB. It was just about being there.

Chapter Eight: 'Out of Time'
Slipping and Sliding –
Steyning and the Isle of Wight 2005

After running smoothly in my previous marathons, I'd run into a wall in Amsterdam, and inevitably it was tough coping with my first stinker, a run which was effectively a step backwards. And this is where the slightly (OK, the very) obsessional side of marathon running takes over. The fact is that those extra minutes really did matter – something that non-runners will never quite grasp. Most people have no idea what constitutes a good marathon time; more particularly, they won't know (and why should they?) what constitutes a good marathon for you. You've run an absurdly long distance; what does it matter if you end up five or ten minutes either way? Oh, but it does, and it matters hugely, and it matters more and more, the more you think about it.

Amsterdam brought home to me one of the curiosities of running. You would expect your fastest marathons to be your hardest marathons, the ones where you have strained every last sinew for those extra few seconds that will take you over the line to a new personal best. But no, quite the contrary.

The fast marathons are the easy ones – easy because all those controllables and uncontrollables have deigned to converge in your favour. We're talking about those countless factors that come together to shape the overall result, from route to crowds, from general well-being to ability to take on water, from shoes to temperature, from clarity of thinking to the moon rising in Venus – factors which unite in your favour simply because you got out of the right side of the bed.

The tough ones are the hard ones, the ones where you lose the plot, lose your time and lose all sense of perspective in a slog which becomes mind-numbing and knee-knackering in its intensity of effort and endurance.

All of which explains why, once you are hooked, it's so difficult to give up marathon running. If you achieve a personal best, then you will have done so because everything has conspired to make it all go well for you on the day. And that's why it won't be long before you start thinking, 'Well, that was pretty straightforward – so straightforward I really ought to have done a better time than that.' Dissatisfaction creeps in precisely because you've had a good day. You start telling yourself it was all so stacked in your favour that in reality you underachieved. A good marathon always leaves you feeling that somehow you didn't try hard enough, that you didn't capitalise on a great opportunity.

And so you push on – just as you do after a shocker or a moderate marathon. You'd think that an experience such as Amsterdam would be the end of it. Far from it. You don't want disappointment to be your last experience and so you book up for another marathon in the hope of erasing the memory. You tell yourself: 'I'm better than that.' A bad time leaves a bad taste, and the only way to rid yourself of it is to sign up for another. You need to show yourself – and a world that isn't remotely interested – that the bad one wasn't representative. You had put in the training and yet, for whatever reason, you didn't realise the potential it gave you.

Fiona has long since learned the pattern. On marathons abroad when she's not been there, I've phoned home and been either satisfied or disappointed. The only certainty is that by the time I get back satisfaction will have turned to disappointment and disappointment will have turned to dejection. Fiona knows not to say, 'That was a good time!' She's realised it's far better to ask, 'Are you pleased with it?' And even then, she knows that the answer will be different a couple of days later. And it's that, as much as anything, which keeps you going.

It reaches the point where, whatever you do, you aren't pleased – something Fiona and my mother-in-law Stella have grudgingly learned to accept. Whatever they achieve, marathon runners are far more likely to grunt in disappointment than whoop with delight – a fact which doesn't necessarily make them easy to live with. In the end, you become so hooked that, whether you do a good time or a bad time, your only response is to want to do another. And so it goes on.

Fiona asked me whether I'd been wishing I was at home with the children during my Amsterdam lows, and sadly the answer was no, not especially. My only wishes were that I'd been running faster and hadn't felt so awful, which probably illustrates the strange position that marathon running had come to occupy in my life. It was a huge part of my life, but at the same time, it seemed to stand wholly outside it. The training was a big commitment which had to be accommodated within all the usual home, work and family constraints, but the marathon itself was an absolute, standing apart from everything else.

In a way, my marathons didn't relate to my day-to-day life, and maybe that was the whole point. They weren't rooted in what the French like to call *métro, boulot, dodo* – that daily routine which supposedly taps out the rhythm of our workaday existence. By now my marathons stood wholly apart from my own daily slog, existing entirely in their own right and subject to their own set of distinctly peculiar laws.

Training, especially in the darkness that I was still enjoying at this point, had a crucial function in helping me sleep, keeping me energetic and happy, and also obliterating all the nonsense and hassle that go hand in hand with work. But the marathons themselves were more than that, existing on an entirely separate and elevated plane. What drove me on was the desire to feel worthy of that plane a couple of times a year. Amsterdam had been a nightmare in so many respects, and as the grim reality sank in, I told myself endlessly that I was a much better runner than that.

Logically perhaps, this was the point at which I should have joined a running club. There are thousands of runners who will insist that you cannot possibly consider yourself a serious runner unless you are a club runner – and maybe they are right. It's manifestly a great way to learn to push yourself and to raise your game, but club membership seemed to me too much of a negation of the many reasons I ran. I was unaffiliated, as club runners like to call non-club runners. Unaffiliated and proud. For me running was a freedom, not a tie to a particular group of people once a week in a particular location.

One of the great attractions of running alone was that I didn't have to drive anywhere to do it; I just seized the moment and dashed out the door. The run began the moment the door clicked behind me.

Inevitably, my running fell into a pattern, but I could still persuade myself that there was something vaguely spontaneous about it.

Of course, I wanted to get faster, but just as important in my day-to-day existence were plenty of other considerations. For work, I was at the theatre reviewing once or maybe twice a week; the last thing I wanted was another definite commitment on top of that. If something cropped up at home to stop me running, then home would come first. If I joined a club, then I would be taking on a new set of obligations, bringing other people and other places into the equation. I needed to keep running simple to make it fit alongside job and family. Joining a club would have taken my running to the next level, but I just felt I couldn't do it – and nor did I particularly want to. Specious nonsense, club runners would say, I am sure. But that's how I saw it.

It's great in life to set yourself goals and targets, but you do need to keep half an eye on the extent to which you become selfish in your pursuit of them. I'd learned by now that a marathon is a selfish taskmaster. It can be run properly only if you accept that it demands a selfish attitude requiring regular and time-consuming attention, but what you need to guard against – especially if you have a young family – is allowing that selfishness to start with you, as opposed to it emanating from the marathon itself. It's an important distinction, and it seemed to me that if I joined a club, then I would risk losing my perspective on this. Far better to run when I could fit it in around family life than run when a club dictated, especially when my reviewing commitments were already a heavy demand.

Maybe this is why I haven't turned good times into genuinely impressive times. I have needed to retain a freedom which wouldn't have sat terribly easily within a club-running format. But even just saying that makes the decision sound far more conscious than it ever really was. The fact is that club running didn't appeal. It was never a serious consideration.

But, as ever with running, it's very much a case of 'to each his own'. By now, Michael was very much a fan of club running. After his London Marathon in 2002, he decided to enter again in 2003, but this time on the back of some rather more serious training, if only to minimise the aches and pains. He had found a 10-mile race organised by the Great Bentley Running Club and, on finishing, was promptly asked if he had ever considered joining a club.

Michael doesn't consider himself a clubbable person but agreed to think about it. He looked at the websites of other local clubs but they all seemed very competitive and rather frightening for someone who was, as he says, so clearly past his prime. He asked at his local specialist sports shop; they recommended the Bentley club as being the most friendly one in the region; and so he joined – a decision he has never regretted. From the very first, he was never made to feel an outsider, even though he was immediately their oldest and least experienced runner. Michael doesn't train with them, but he runs their races and participates in club functions, enjoying all the encouragement they freely give. The club willingly worked out new handicap tables to accommodate his advancing years. As he says, they have helped him in every way possible to improve and, more importantly, to enjoy his running. All of which makes Michael a model runner – and a great advertisement for joining a club.

But it just wasn't for me, and so, instead, I had to find other ways to make up for the disappointments that marathon running was clearly going to bring. Amsterdam was a setback. That was all. I had to prove that it wasn't typical, and the only way to do that was to make the next move – one made all the easier when a colleague told me that her husband, also a working journalist, ran most of his marathons on 'press places'. It had never occurred to me that they existed, but indeed they did.

The deal was that, in return for your press place, you wrote about what a great event it was. For the 2005 London Marathon, I promptly secured myself just such a press place – much to the annoyance of Michael, who was by now progressing nicely with his world-record bid – still ongoing – for the most number of times anyone has ever been rejected by the London Marathon.

However, my 2005 London Marathon would turn out to be a different kind of marathon. I decided to run it with Jane, a friend of Fiona's with whom I trained for a few months leading up to the race. As a relatively experienced marathon runner by now, I was going to help her round on her marathon debut – a different kind of challenge for me. But because she was slower than I was, the pressing need in the early months of 2005 was to find a marathon or two which I could run semi-competitively. There was another requirement. After the disappointment of Amsterdam, and given that I was returning to London in April, the new marathon had to be a step away from the big-city treadmill I'd launched myself onto.

To an extent, I wanted a no-pressure marathon. Having got too hung up on beating my previous times, I'd gone astray. I wanted a marathon that I could run simply for the sake of running it, one where I wouldn't be obsessing about elapsed minutes and kilometres which started to seem like miles.

That's when the wonderfully named Steyning Stinger entered the frame, a marathon which carries a clue in its title. And therein lay the appeal. How could you not want to do a marathon called the Steyning Stinger? Even better, it was close to home, convenient and cheap – important considerations, given that I had just booked a big-treat marathon for the autumn of 2005. Dublin, centred on a half-term holiday for all of us, was the appealing prospect for the back end of the year.

And so, for all these reasons, the Steyning Stinger in March 2005 was just what the marathon doctor ordered. I wanted a new marathon experience, and the Steyning Stinger promised to deliver: one of those middle-of-nowhere odysseys which are generally labelled 'cross-country'. There's a perverse element of self-flagellation to events such as the Steyning Stinger which, sad to say, appeals to the twisted side of my brain. If you're going to flog yourself, flog hard. And if you want to take masochism to the next level, search out the conditions we had on that mad March day.

Cross-country horror is actually the simplest of recipes. Take a cross-country marathon and just add water. You can add it during the race, or for even better (or should that be worse?) results, you can add it in torrents the day and night before. Either way, the outcome is a marathon in which you will constantly revise downwards your possible finishing time, a race in which the struggle is simply to finish; a race where there's every reason to soldier on. If you don't, you'll risk spending all eternity in a lonely, windswept field with not the foggiest idea where you are.

The Steyning Stinger is organised by the Steyning Athletic Club, and in 2005 the race took place on 6 March, after the soggiest of weeks which mixed snow with deluge and then served it all up with heavy frost on the day. The day itself was moderately bright, but by then the elements had done their bit to make tough terrain as tough as it possibly could be.

The route takes you from Steyning to Chanctonbury Ring Road and Washington, then on to Cissbury Ring and then a circuit around Steep Down. The return is via Chanctonbury and Wiston and then back to Steyning – all places I can barely picture now. If I think of the race, all that comes to mind is snow, ice and mud.

I am sure there was an impressive amount of outstanding natural beauty en route, but the beauty isn't the memory. Yes, of course, this was picturesque West Sussex at its absolute best; unspoilt fields stretching down towards the coastal towns with the sea beyond; patchwork greens of all hues in the foreground suggesting all the luxuriance which follows a damp winter; all promising the rapid growth to come. Snow was still thick on the high ground; lower down were the shoots of new life. Small wonder Sussex has attracted poets, painters, musicians and novelists down the centuries. Few counties have proven themselves more fertile when it comes to sparking the imagination of our artists and writers. Anyone who has ever set foot in the county could wax lyrical for ages about its splendours and its glories; a great tradition of art and literature has striven for years to do them justice.

But on 6 March, all the beauty was wasted on a day which was simply about keeping your footing while all around were losing theirs – if Rudyard Kipling will forgive the paraphrase. Belloc and Co. had wandered across Sussex collecting its folklore and lauding its idiosyncrasies. We were about to skid across it collecting bumps and bruises.

The race began from a field opposite Steyning Leisure Centre, launching you off into the unknown in the most relaxed and friendly of ways. After all the pressure of the big-city marathons, all the formalities, all the jostling, it was lovely to get back to something chilled (in every sense) and informal. The organisation was excellent, with no need to be oppressively so. This was small scale and inviting.

It was an early start to the day, being an hour and a half's drive away, but I got there in good time and was just settling down for the usual lengthy pre-marathon wait when word was passed around that you could go whenever you were ready – an astonishingly laid back approach to marathon running. I kept wondering how they would do the timing, but that wasn't my problem. And nor was it theirs. They managed it efficiently. What it did mean, however, was the chance to get up, off and out well before the designated start, one of a trickle of runners setting out on the most monumental of treks.

I ran it in a T-shirt and running jacket and never once felt warm. There was ice on the ground, and it wasn't long before there were glimpses of snow through the trees, lying in the shade in woodland that the pale sun couldn't reach. Right from the start, I was on my own, and I was immediately rediscovering something rather lovely – just why I wanted to run. Or perhaps it was more negative than that: I was seeing just what I had lost in Amsterdam. There was a newfound freedom. I was off the leash, a feeling which translated into a comfortable start. The thought of all the miles stacked up ahead didn't hang heavy along those opening country tracks. It hovered as a potential delight about to unfurl.

The staggered start meant that we were well spaced out, a fact which somehow added to the camaraderie. There was no way you were going to pass someone – or be passed by them – without a smile, a hello or maybe even the quickest of chats. There was a feeling that this was one for the serious runners. You had to be pretty serious even to contemplate it, and each new greeting with each fellow runner seemed to reflect that. We were the big boys, and we were doing our thing. The field was very, very male, much more so than usual for a marathon, or so it seemed. But, unlike Amsterdam, I felt I had every right to be there. Again, it's all in the mind; but I didn't feel out of place, and that was crucial. Somehow in Amsterdam I had become detached from the marathon; here I was once again in the thick – or perhaps more accurately – the thin of it.

Consequently the whole thing had kicked off with a general, smug sense of well-being – and maybe that's why I have so few impressions of the route from those early miles, beyond track stretching ahead through the trees – and then track slowly starting to rise, which was when the underfoot conditions really did start to become a major factor.

On the flat, there had been some squelching and a degree of hopping to avoid the worst of the puddles, but then as the terrain started to get steeper, so the ground underfoot started to get treacherous. The higher I got, the worse it got – to the point where on narrow paths I had to pull myself up on the branches either side.

There were times when I just stood there and thought, *Well, how the hell am I going to get past that?* It was either ice or deep, thick, cloying mud and pretty much nothing in between. If I attempted to run up the mud, I would be flat on my face in an instant and sliding ignominiously back down, the same fate which awaited anyone foolish enough to take a run at the ice or simply unlucky enough not to have noticed it.

It was no better going down the other side. Gravity working with me was no better than gravity working against me. Once I reached the mini-pinnacles of the frequent ups, I had little choice as to how to tackle the downs. Running wasn't an option. It was more a case of clinging to the branches and trying to slide in as controlled a way as possible. Not so much flying as falling with style, as Buzz and Woody would have said if the *Toy Story* superstars had joined us that day.

Just occasionally at these points, things got as congested as the day was ever going to get: two runners together. I don't remember much conversation by this stage. A certain grim chumminess had taken over. The chat had evaporated. What could you possibly say in the circumstances? 'Lovely day for a 26.2-mile squelch, don't you think?'

We all just had to keep on going. Occasionally it would flatten out and the path would become firmer, but the psychological damage had been done. This was a race in which it was easy to lose your nerve – a race which became less of a race the longer it lasted. It became simply a question of shuffling on. Often where the ground looked safe enough for something a bit more firm-footed, I would quickly discover that it wasn't. The sane runners were running gingerly by now. A few slips, and your confidence would be gone; and even if you didn't slip, just the sight of the path ahead was enough to loosen your assurance.

Inevitably, it wasn't long before tiredness started to become a factor. I was feeling it strongly after perhaps a dozen miles. Running in a cramped, unnatural style is hopelessly enervating. Running is supposed to be all about freedom, about letting rip and letting go, just as it had been for those very early miles. But by now, it was all about caution, not letting slip and keeping upright. That great surge of sovereignty at the start had become as cramping as that damned Amsterdam wristband. For hundreds of yards at a stretch, there was no chance of a sweeping stride. Instead, I had to pull my foot free with each step I took. Hey, Mother Earth, can I have my shoe back? And when she released it, it was caked in mud, heavy, uneven and awkward.

Sod this, I started to think. But then I started to smile.

The strangest thing was starting to happen. The more stupid the whole thing started to seem – and, believe me, it really was stupid – the more the enjoyment started to creep back in. It was a different kind of enjoyment to the off-the-leash burst we'd had at the start. This was now pleasure of a darker kind, much more the perverse thrill of something so utterly pointless that it defied all logic. An early start, a long drive… and all for the purpose of mud-coasting and ice skating. In the end, the only reason to be doing it was because it was so difficult to do – and for me, that was suddenly enough. I can't say I surged onward with renewed vigour. But I certainly stopped feeling sorry for myself. I started to chill out. I started to have fun.

The sun never gained much strength as the day wore on. To an extent I could read from the shadows whether it was mud or ice which awaited me, but it wasn't exactly a knowledge I could do much with. I just had to keep on keeping on. I can't even remember whether there were mile markers and I have no recollection at all of the water stations, though there must have been some. It was all about trying to find – and eventually finding – the fun in a race which would have been tough enough on hard ground, but which was now starting to seem like the oddest of lotteries.

Inevitably, the thickest snow was on the highest ground – a point, I seem to remember, where we ran a big loop around a wide-open patch, three-quarters of the way into the race. I hadn't a clue where I was, but here, I hate to say it, I dropped to a walk for about ten minutes. Someone said we were about 20 miles to the good, but the temperature had dropped. Briefly, I lost it, conscious that my walk was probably about the same speed as my run anyway. I let the walk take over for ten minutes, thinking that nothing much – probably not even face – was being lost. But then bloody-mindedness reasserted itself. I cursed myself, told myself I was an idiot, useless, hopeless and worse and forced myself back into a trot, which inevitably was the point at which things started to seem easier again – not for the fact of having had a breather, but more because this was simply the motion my aching body had congealed into before my walk.

Presumably the last few miles were downhill. They must have been. By now I was seriously plodding, but with the plod was growing a kind of smugness. It was tough, really tough, but I was going to get back. There wasn't any point looking at a watch. This was a run way outside anything I had ever done before. Time didn't enter into it. All that mattered was finishing, especially as I was starting to feel uncomfortably cold – which is a rare and worrying thing on a long-distance run. The minimum is always the best thing to run in. You might take along more, but you'll soon discard it or wish you had once you're off. But that didn't seem to be the case on the day of the Steyning Stinger. The route home seemed to be much more in the shadow, the temperature seemed to be dropping all the time, and that alone was the best possible reason for shuffling onwards, finally reaching the flat which would take me back to the start for the lowest of low-key finishes. No crowds, no banners, no cheers. Just someone with a clipboard. But that was more than enough. It was all I wanted.

They were serving teas and coffees in the leisure-centre canteen when I finally reached it. A couple of dozen runners were there already, readmitting themselves to the human race, defrosting their frozen bodies and mulling it all over. I've no idea how many runners completed the course, but it can't have been many. I grabbed a drink, sat down and started chatting with the others.

I couldn't take my eyes off the hands of the chap sitting opposite me. They looked like dead flesh. They weren't just colourless; they were lifeless. He couldn't help but see me staring, and he started to explain the circulation problem which he suffered from in low-temperature conditions. I went to get him another cup of coffee. It was steaming in a thin plastic cup which he wrapped his hands round without the slightest wince of discomfort. It was obvious that he had almost no feeling in his hands whatsoever. He kept saying that the sensation would come back, but they looked utterly beyond revival and it was difficult to see that burning them was going to help.

'Have you had a good morning?' I asked him. 'Yes,' he grinned. 'Great. Really great.' And the worrying thing was that he meant it – worrying until I realised that I too, despite the mud, the ice, the snow and the hills – or perhaps because of them – had had a great time too.

I haven't kept a record of my time on the Steyning Stinger, but I am reasonably sure it was around the 4:20 mark – nine minutes or so slower than I had achieved seven years earlier on my marathon debut in the wonderfully supportive atmosphere of London.

But 4 hours 20 minutes in such terrain felt good. By now I was generally marathoning at around 3 hours 30 minutes on the flat in the big cities, something I was clearly never going to do in Steyning. But my Steyning time suggested a significant improvement in stamina, which was gratification enough. And I was home for a late lunch, knackered but deliciously invigorated. You're supposed to believe eight impossible things before breakfast. OK, so it was only one. But I hadn't just believed it. I had actually done it.

A month later, I was back for the big one, the London Marathon of 2005. It was a strange affair, run in a time not my own with a knee not my own.

As anticipated, I ran it with Jane, who was making her London Marathon debut. We completed it together in 4:20, a time which didn't stretch me, I am pleased to say – a measure of my progress since my own London Marathon debut. But I am not sure that I could have run it much faster anyway, because I had a bursar. At least, that was what I heard when the doctor first told me. Fleetingly I had wondered what a public school money-man had to do with the price of eggs, but then the doctor explained: not a bursar, but a bursa – the ignominy of housemaid's knee. Chafed nipples had been bad enough, but this really did seem the ultimate indignity. My knee was a squidgy mass of wobbly fluid, a condition more usually caused by too much time down on your knees vigorously polishing and scrubbing. I pleaded most definitely 'not guilty' to that kind of activity, but my knee argued otherwise.

I was lean and fit in every other department, but it dragged me down that I seemed to have borrowed one of my knees from the Michelin Man. It was raw, red, puffy and horribly big. Two or three times in the week before, I had had it drained at our doctors' surgery, trying not to look as vast syringes gorged themselves on the yucky yellow-red fluid my knee was apparently floating in. But still the fluid came back. I started to write the run off, but to my astonishment and delight, the doctor didn't advise against running. I simply ran with my knee tightly strapped, and surprisingly it did the trick – albeit in a marathon in which I didn't have to extend myself fully. If I was ever going to get housemaid's knee – oh the shame! – before a marathon, at least it was this one, one which wasn't about finishing times as far as I was concerned. All that mattered was getting Jane round safe and sound at a pace she was happy with.

I felt in control at every point, which perhaps underlines the extent to which marathons are run in the mind. I was so focused on helping Jane round, sorting out her drinks and her gels, that I didn't think about any tiredness I ought to be feeling myself. Consequently I didn't feel any. Retrospectively, I probably ran it as a 4 hours 20 minutes pacer might have done. Finally I saw how pacers managed it. They ran at a pace well within their natural time. That's why pacers float by, chatting, at ease with the world, untroubled, unflustered, unbothered. That's why they had left me so woefully far behind in Amsterdam. They were coasting; I was clinging on.

And at the end of it, I felt as a pacer probably does. They've run unselfishly in a race which was never about them. Consequently my personal craving wasn't sated. I needed more of that marathon drug. Steyning had been a blast (an icy one); London had come and gone almost unnoticed; and Dublin was still six months away. There was nothing for it but to head overseas. Well, across the Solent. The Isle of Wight is just a short ferry ride away, and the Isle of Wight Marathon beckoned.

The Isle of Wight Marathon is broadly in the Chichester up-and-down cross-country category. Right from the start, I suspected it was going to be a good one. From the outset, you couldn't fail to be impressed by the organisation; nothing fussy, nothing more than necessary, but efficient and on the ball – the perfect cushion for the feat of endurance ahead of us that Sunday morning in May 2005.

The course starts and ends in Ryde; in between times, you run a big circle, starting to the south-west before heading back home from the south-east. The route takes you from Ryde to Newport, through Blackwater, Rookley and Sandford, across to Shanklin, north to Sandown and Brading and then back to Ryde, a description which betrays nothing of the fact that this is a marathon which is relentlessly up and down, a real and persistent drag on your determination.

The hills, many long and steady, begin fairly soon after the start. After a while, you cease to enjoy the downhills that follow, for the simple reason that you know that before long you will be going uphill again.

You also cease to enjoy them for the fact that they actually start to hurt. You tire yourself as you go up, but force of gravity means that inevitably you pound your legs even harder on the way down. Eventually it takes its toll. It's an established fact (unless I've just made it up) that in running you are much more prone to injury on a downhill. The Isle of Wight Marathon is for many the proof of the pudding. Downhill, your stride is that little bit longer; gravity means you crunch your knees and your ankles with greater impact; and the chances are that your joints will protest somewhere along the line. Mine certainly did – and quite vehemently.

But it was a good course, one for the serious-minded marathon runner – good in the sense that it was bound to test your body and also your resolve to the limit. We hadn't even left Ryde and already we were climbing, a foretaste of hills to come. Thereafter we were constantly heading up and down. The roads were good for 6 or 7 miles, all the way to Newport, but after that we were much more on country – rather than main – roads, and the hills seemed to get bigger all the time – a reflection, most likely, of their frequency rather than their actual size.

With a limited field, this was another marathon where the runners were rapidly stretched out, and for long periods there was no one much in front of me and seemingly no one behind, though every now and again someone would storm past, leaving me wondering where they'd been all along. Or if they had suddenly had an excess of renewed energy? If so, how? I wanted some!

Rather worse, from the motivational point of view, was the fact that this wasn't a marathon that impacted much on the island. We were very carefully marshalled and protected from car traffic at every point, much to the organisers' credit, but it was not a day which brought the islanders out in support. For the most part we were running on an island going about its daily business, rather than making us its daily business – a sobering little thought for any marathon runners who get their kicks from the big cities and their crowds.

Run the London Marathon and you'll feel like you are the centre of the universe. Run the Isle of Wight Marathon and you'll feel like you are on a back road between Rookley and Sandford, which is precisely where you will be at one point. There's nothing to lift you out of the here and now – though, in fairness, the marathon never actually claimed that there would be. All I mean is that this was a different kind of marathon, one where the route was actually working against you. In New York and Paris it helps you glide, just as it does at significant points in London. Similarly Steyning, in all its ludicrousness, had a certain quality which urged you on. But here, there was no boost from the seemingly endless up-and-down dreary greyness of the Isle of Wight on a dreary grey day.

The morning had dawned dull and had proceeded to get duller still. The route from Ryde to Newport isn't exactly the island at its most attractive, and Newport itself isn't exactly the most beautiful of places. We weren't going to be seeing the lovely coastline, but I would have hoped for a few more of the picturesque villages. Sadly, they were in short supply. I had to fall back on my old habits of creating significance for the numbers from one to 26, getting ever more obscure in my reasons for enjoying them. When I got bored with that, I made the mistake of trying to reel off Aussie opening batsmen – a task I soon abandoned. There is something about that kind of exercise that I simply cannot cope with in a marathon. I always hope that it will ease the passing of the miles, but it doesn't. Instead, it replaces grind with frustration as I struggle to retain names I know I can list easily in other circumstances. It simply makes a bad thing worse.

So instead I tried to let my mind wander, eventually meandering to the conclusion that there are actually two types of marathon runner. There are the big-city specialists who love the roar of the crowd, and then there are those who actually relish the loneliness of the long-distance runner. You're either London or you are Isle of Wight. On that May morning on the island, it seemed to me that it was hopelessly overambitious ever to aspire to be both.

Certainly I remember the Isle of Wight as a heads-down, no-nonsense type marathon, with the runners clearly committed types, presumably knowing precisely what they had let themselves in for in a way that I didn't. This wasn't a marathon with a great deal of chat, not even at the start as we waited for the off. Instead, it was a marathon where we dutifully got on with it, and for a long time it went well – not so well, however, that I could be bothered to write it up afterwards in the top-secret Dear Darling Diary section on my computer. I have to therefore rely on memory for my account of it here, but it does come back to me as a marathon that flowed past reasonably satisfactorily for the first three-quarters. Oddly, it was once we were back in civilisation that it started to seem tougher.

Once we reached Shanklin and Sandown and the more built-up area on the east of the island, the hills seemed to go beyond relentless, towards impossible. None of them was huge, but the cumulative effect was taking its toll. I felt increasingly on the wrong end of an interminable, body-sapping succession. I doubt I was alone in approaching the downhills fairly gingerly by now. The uphills were hurting, but the frustration was that there never seemed to be any reward at the top. I remember several times experiencing a kind of leg spasm as I tried to open my stride on a summit – a reaction against the cramped, closed style of running that the uphills had forced me into.

The mythology is that you are supposed to welcome hills; you are supposed to look forward to them and attack them. Opinion is divided as to whether you stare at your feet as you ascend, carefully avoiding any sight of the ordeal ahead, or whether you boldly pitch your eyeline on the horizon and drag yourself up to it. Some people will tell you that you are supposed to imagine you've got ski sticks in your hands and that you are pulling yourself up with them. Certainly your upper body comes into it more as the incline forces you to dig deeper and, in stamina terms, hills are said to be excellent training.

When the numbers of hills are within acceptable limits, then there can indeed be something masochistically pleasing in imagining that you are a rubber band being stretched with every step as you head upwards, ready to ping forwards when you reach the top. In those first few steps at the crest, it often feels as if you've built up some kind of credit in your legs as you surge forward. But on the Isle of Wight, the sheer frequency of the hills means that the credit dwindles, diminishes and disappears. Hill after hill after hill in the end wears you down.

I walked for maybe five minutes in all across two or three little troughs of 'What the hell am I doing here?', but just as I had felt in Steyning, walking was the harder option for legs that had got into a groove and couldn't get out of it.

Eventually, as it always does, the finish started to close in and then, quite suddenly, Ryde boating lake was in view for a final little loop round to the finish, a choice of location presumably supposed to create a little more sense of occasion. On the far side of the lake, I could see people gathered and when I reached where they were at their densest, I stopped, thinking I had finished. I'm sure I must have seen some kind of line on the ground. I can't be that daft. Something must have made me think I was there. But instead, all I heard were shouts of 'Keep going!' There were a few more yards to go, but the false finish had been a strange, slightly deflating experience, as were the couple of minutes which had taken me past the four-hour mark.

I completed the course in 4:02:09, finishing 66th out of 119 male finishers – not great, but reasonable enough on a hard course. The next day, my boss, an Isle of Wighter through and through, told me that the Isle of Wight Marathon was generally believed to add half an hour to your normal marathon time. It seemed to me that his words were spot on.

Looking back, I was guilty of not adjusting my expectations to the reality of the course. On a new marathon, it's vital that you recompute and rethink as you go along. I hadn't done so. Hence the initial disappointment with my time, but once I started to think back on the course, I realised that my time hadn't been bad at all. I was well down in the field, but my time was respectable given the serious nature of the runners who turned out that day. I suspected I had run with a lot of seasoned club runners. The Isle of Wight Marathon is not for wimps, and I had shown that I wasn't one.

I can't imagine any possible reason for ever wanting to do it again, but I'm glad I did it – a hilly, testing marathon in the Chichester mode, but one where I felt I could trust myself to the experience of the organisers. After all, the Isle of Wight marathon has been run continuously since 1957, making it the longest-running UK marathon – and that's something worth shouting about. If it keeps going, perhaps one day it will flatten out a few of those hills.

For me, though, it had been just the job – my third marathon in four months. After the horrors of Amsterdam, I was back in business. Steyning, London and the Isle of Wight, in their different ways, had given me back a sense of perspective. More importantly, they reminded me of the great joy of running. I was never going to give up after Amsterdam, but I had certainly needed to go back to basics. I'd done exactly that, and I was back on track now. And, deliciously, I had Dublin on the horizon.

Chapter Nine: 'Gimme Shelter'
Running Stupid – Dublin 2005

By now, things were subtly changing at home. My marathons – for everyone else, if not for me – had been absorbed into the natural workings of the household, and, somehow, for the rest of the family, the gloss had slipped off them. The cakes and celebratory banners which used to greet me on my return from each new marathon had started to disappear for wholly understandable reasons. If you win the FA Cup twice a year, year after year, the celebrations will inevitably become more muted in the end, I told myself. And I wasn't even winning marathons. I was merely taking part.

For me, however, marathons will always belong, one foot at least, in the realms of the extraordinary – a reflection of the fact that I was experiencing them from the inside, rather than the roadside. It was the extremeness of marathon running which appealed, which was possibly in itself a reflection of my more than modest record in PE at school. In games, I was invariably among the last to be picked for any team sport. I played plenty of cricket and football informally with my mates and did reasonably well, but when it came to organised sport, I was right at the back of the queue.

The low point came at the end of my second summer at secondary school when school report time came round.

Having got over the shock of having to hold a pen, our PE teacher came into the showers at the end of a lesson and asked, 'So which one is Philip Hewitt?' Naked and mortified, I put my hand up and confessed. How dare he write a report about me when he doesn't even know who I am, I complained to friends. I was annoyed – an annoyance which shot off the end of the Richter scale when I eventually read the report. C+ for attainment, C+ for effort. The swine. Even worse was the comment: 'It is felt that Philip is somewhat lacking in co-ordination.' What kind of phrasing was that? 'It is felt'. I ask you! Who by? Certainly not by someone who had only just noticed my presence. 'Huh!' just didn't cover it. But at least I could manage joined-up writing, I told myself in consolation as I looked at the report.

I wouldn't pretend that the slight altered the course of my life. Little swot that I was, I was always far more interested in pursuing the academic side of school life. But maybe, just maybe, the put-down was there, lurking somewhere unacknowledged at the back of my mind, in the marathons I was now doing. It would be wrong to suggest that I was trying to prove something to a games teacher who had long since forgotten me, but possibly the memory heightened my satisfaction when I discovered that I could indeed compete at the upper end of the sporting scale. I had gone off and got a degree. I had even completed a doctorate. And now I was turning on the sporting prowess. I was one of the boys – at last. Maybe that's one of the reasons marathons have never lost their aura for me, no matter how many I have stacked up.

For the rest of the family, however, they were becoming run of my particular mill. For Fiona, Adam and Laura, they were by now simply something that Daddy did. Of course, there was plenty of genuine interest and plenty of encouragement alongside some perfectly reasonable expressions of sympathy/dismay in all the appropriate places, but for the rest of the family the extra special something had tumbled away and the extraordinary had become ordinary.

My brother Jonathan, a doctor, had even stopped telling me that marathons were unhealthy, that our bodies simply weren't equipped for that kind of pounding and that I was daft to be doing them. I'd never taken any notice anyway. Besides, there are plenty of doctors more than happy to run marathons. Plus, I was convinced that general well-being in the moment comfortably outweighed any joint damage I was saving up for later. But by now, not even Jonathan was trying to dissuade me.

I guess people had started to recognise my supreme ability to ignore advice. Some would call it pig-headedness. I prefer to think of it as single-mindedness. But certainly it had started to filter through and affect the way I was regarded.

Fiona had even stopped trying to get me to eat properly in the weeks before a marathon. In the early days, she would mug up on good foods for runners and serve it up religiously in the final few weeks before the marathon. Meanwhile, I'd keep on eating the biscuits and the chocolate, confident that the running would run them off. I am naturally fairly skinny. For me, eating properly simply means not missing my mouth, but in truth, in my view, I was eating well enough. We've never eaten junk food; Fiona has the highest standards in that respect.

But by now, after a dozen or so marathons and the likelihood of marathons stretching long into the future, Fiona had started to worry less about preparing special meals. Again, my marathon running had simply become part of the pattern of our life. If I wasn't in the house, the children would automatically assume I was out running. Even if I was sitting quietly in another room, they would assume that I was out hammering the country lanes – for the simple reason that that's what their dad did.

However, for the Dublin Marathon of 2005, for once running and family life happily converged. Amsterdam had been a lonely miserable slog; Steyning and the Isle of Wight had been renewal runs. It was now time to reconnect running and family. I was going to put the two halves of my life back together in one glorious week in the Republic of Ireland.

It was half-term and we'd booked a cottage in Waterford, where we spent an exceptionally enjoyable eight days, our first time in Ireland, just the four of us in a beautiful converted barn well and truly off the beaten track. None of us really knew quite what to expect. We'd driven off the ferry from Wales late on the Saturday night in urgent need of petrol. It sounds stupid, but I had no idea whether I was going to be understood at the garage. Everything was written in Gaelic, strange combinations of consonants which looked utterly alien. But there was no need to worry. Everyone was friendly and welcoming, and I spent a very happy week practising, and indeed perfecting – much to my children's annoyance – my Irish accent. I was feeling quite the natural by the time our week in Waterford was up and it was time to head north for the Dublin Marathon.

We'd seen a strange mix of run-down towns and wonderful sights. Among the best of the sights was the Rock of Cashel, which we reached by driving over mountains offering beautiful views across the Tipperary plains. At the Rock, a collection of half-ruined ecclesiastical buildings, the wind across the plain was ferocious. The children loved leaning fully into it, trusting their whole weight to the gust hitting them full in the face. The pleasures were rustic, rural and simple, and we had a great time – though increasingly in the back of my mind was the niggling, unsettling thought that we were doing things the wrong way round.

The holiday needed to be the reward for the marathon, not the build-up. Maybe I relaxed too much. Maybe I didn't relax enough, but the marathon the following Monday sat lump-like and immovable on the horizon. I did a couple of runs during the week, nothing too strenuous, but probably not enough. It was far too hilly, and besides I was too much in holiday mood. The thought of exploring Dublin was an appealing one, but I couldn't honestly say I was relishing the thought of running round it, even less so as the clouds darkened ominously as we approached the city that Saturday morning. I registered for the marathon as the rain lashed down outside. I hoped it wasn't a little taste of things to come.

Every single marathon I've ever run has been a Sunday marathon, except for Dublin, which was run on the Bank Holiday Monday, which gave us the whole of the Sunday to get to know the city. And we had a great day – a day of brilliant sunshine during which we fell in love. Dublin city centre isn't just beautiful; it's fascinating. Dublin has got it all – gorgeous parks, elegant classical architecture, a modern buzz, a rich, complex history and plenty of present-day chic. And for the children, to cap it all, it offered the prospect of a hotel breakfast. They could barely contain their excitement

– which probably says it all about the deprived upbringing we'd inflicted on them. There they were at the ages of nine and seven eating a hotel breakfast for the very first time. As parents, we had clearly failed. But at least we let them add a new Pizza Hut to the list they were lovingly building up: Pizza Hut Dublin. Now, how cool was that, at least in their eyes? We were nothing if not sophisticated on holiday. But even as we sat there, I started to think *Uh-oh!*

Intoxicated with the city, we had walked for miles, striding out across parks, strolling down attractive shopping streets, exploring little arcades, haring off after historic monuments, lapping it all up on the tourist equivalent of a trolley dash. Absolutely the right thing to do in family terms; absolutely the wrong thing to do before a marathon. A far cry from the three or four hours of *dolce far niente* which Michael and I had come to regard as de rigueur the afternoon before a marathon. In Dublin, for all sorts of reasons, such considerations went out of the window. I am not saying it was crucial. Or course it wasn't. But it was one of those little controllables that I had opted not to control – a sacrifice which may or may not have made a difference, but one which I was foolish to make as far as the run was concerned.

The real setback came on the Monday morning, however. There was no need to look out of the window to see that Sunday's fine weather had been a false promise. It was tipping it down, the rain hammering onto the streets on which we would soon be running. I wandered down to the starting area in plenty of time, half a mile or so from the hotel. There was no point taking a rucksack with me to leave at the left-luggage. The hotel was close enough. Besides, anything I carried would have been soaked right through by the time

I reached the start. Instead, all I took was a T-shirt, which I discarded, and a bin bag, which I didn't – and therein lay the decision which defined the day. It was my first bin bag – and quite definitely my last.

Bin bags are very much a part of marathon tradition. You need something to keep you warm at the start of a marathon, something you can hurl into the gutter just before the off. Inevitably, you reach the point after a while where you've got no more sweatshirts you want to part with. And so out come the bin bags. I'd never tried one until that day, but I'd often, rather bizarrely, thought that my fellow runners had looked pretty cool as they strolled around at the start sporting theirs. I wanted to be one of them.

But things started badly when I all but suffocated. Being a bin-bag virgin, I imagined that you just pulled it over your head and used your manly strength to push out the arm holes and head hole. Unfortunately, I'd brought along a heavy-duty refuse sack. Those around me must have thought I was chickening out, preferring to commit suicide on the streets of Dublin than to actually run on them in the cascading rain. Eventually, possibly slightly blue in the face, I gave up, pulled it off and did things the conventional way, ripping the holes before putting it on. I can't help thinking that it was my difficulty in getting it on which led to my bizarre decision to keep it on – quite the daftest thing I have ever done in a marathon.

In my defence, I would have to say that it served a purpose for the hour or so we hung around at the start. I was soaked beneath it, but it did actually feel as if it was keeping me warmer than I would have been without it.

The marathon wasn't particularly big, less than a third of the size of the big ones such as London. There were about 10,000 runners, I believe. Consequently, we weren't particularly tightly packed at the start for the wait, which went on forever. I muttered 'Bloody rain' to the guy standing next to me, who replied with the legendary Irish twinkle, 'Well, what do you expect? We're in Dublin!' Oscar Wilde couldn't have put it better. The weather was clearly par for the course in a notoriously soggy city.

And so as we stood there, I could find no reason to divest myself of my plastic coating. We moved off eventually, and still it seemed reasonable to keep it on.

The start would have been impressive had we been able to see more than a few yards in front of our faces. I knew that I would be seeing – or trying to see – Fiona and the children just before the end of the first mile, standing on the corner of the road a few hundred yards from our hotel. It was a great incentive to get cracking – if only to allow them to rush for shelter all the sooner. In the event, they gave me a quick wave and returned to our room drenched and shivering. It was that kind of day – not a day for running. Not even a day, really, for being a duck.

With the rain came an autumnal gloom, which in turn became a slightly more inviting mistiness as the course took us, fairly early on, into Phoenix Park, a couple of miles west of the city centre, north of the River Liffey. Here there were some long straight stretches, and on a clear, bright day, it might just have been a little oasis for marathoners. Instead, under oppressive skies and with the rain belting us straight in the face, it simply seemed exposed.

One good thing was that fairly rapidly in Dublin you could run at your own pace. There was very little bunching. The streets were wide and would have been great in the dry. But on this particular late-October day, we were running through sheets of water, splashed by those ahead as we splashed ourselves and splashed those behind us. But thank goodness for my bin bag, I suppose I must have occasionally thought to myself. I'll show them. I hadn't a clue that I was actually the biggest Irish joke of them all.

After a few miles, there began perhaps to be an element of keeping it on deliberately; once past the half-marathon, the element of deliberateness grew stronger. It started to seem to me that a Clark Kent moment was there somewhere ahead. I was going to rip off my bin bag and suddenly become Superman, whizzing through the last few miles for an extraordinarily fast finish.

All of which goes to show one thing and one thing only – how easily muddled thinking can creep in when you're tired. By keeping it on, I started to think – if think isn't too strong a word for it – that I was somehow keeping something back, a trump card, an ace up my soggy sleeve that would stand me in good stead for the final flourish.

2005 hadn't been a year of competitive running, so I felt I had something to prove. The Steyning Stinger and the Isle of Wight marathons had never been going to be about times. London had been a joint venture. All of which meant that I was pinning my hopes on Dublin, my only genuine race of the year. I blanch, though, at the twisted logic – or lack of logic – that persuaded me that running in a bin bag was the best way to prove myself. Twenty miles became the fixed point in my head. At 20 miles I would rip it off, the crowds would gasp and I would fly. Absurd. And absurd for one blindingly obvious reason.

The fact is that for 20 miles of torrential rain, 20 miles of feeling frozen, I was sweating like a pig beneath my plastic.

I was like a cheese sarnie in cling film. And I didn't realise it. I just didn't have a clue how much I was perspiring, no idea how much fluid I was losing, nor how dehydrated I was becoming. Madness. When I ripped off my packaging, it was too late. I wasn't a tasty little M&S sarnie, fresh and flavoursome, tumbling out of its box. I was weeks past my sell-by date. I ran dressed as rubbish, and I ran a rubbish race.

We were in nondescript backstreets by now, no one around apart from the runners. Pulling off the bag, I shoved it rather decorously into a roadside bin. And then I waited to soar. Nothing happened. The damage had been done, and there wasn't the remotest prospect of recovery. I'd been drinking steadily, but nowhere near enough, and instead of surging, I slumped. Exactly as in Amsterdam. And just as in Amsterdam, there was no chance of any help coming from the course itself.

After the comparative pleasures of Phoenix Park, the route had nosedived into mile after mile of suburban could-be-anywhere anonymity. The day before, under bright blue skies, the city centre had oozed charm with its classical buildings, attractive shops and beautiful parks. In the rain, in the outskirts, we really could have been anywhere, with almost no points of interest for miles on end. Or if there were, we couldn't see them. It was grim, featureless and boring. I don't even remember the mile markers on a course which was unremarkable in the extreme.

The roads merged one into another, undistinguished and indistinguishable. The route felt like the least interesting sections of the London Marathon cut out, elongated and stitched together for the ultimate in monotony on two legs. I am tempted to say it was the middle 24 miles that were the problem, but that's probably being a little bit unfair. The boring bit was probably much less than that, but there was just absolutely nothing for the soul to rejoice in, nothing to send the spirit soaring – just grey buildings on grey streets under grey skies in heavy, heavy rain.

Fortunately, the skies can hold only so much. Around mile 15 or 16, the rain had started to ease, lessening considerably towards the 20-mile marker, where I had discarded my plastic cloak and discovered I wasn't Superman after all. By miles 21 or 22, the rain had more or less stopped, but with the sheets of water we were running through there was never any prospect of drying off. And that's when the cold started to set in. Perhaps the bin bag had actually kept me warmer than I would have been, but this was no compensation for its unnoticed dehydrating effect, which probably also contributed to the coldness I felt in the early 20s.

I started to shiver and could sense that I was not alone. People were dripping and bedraggled. This was another of those marathons where the prevailing mood was a gritty determination, people slogging it out for no other reason than that there was nothing else to do but keep on going.

As early as 15 or 16 miles in, people had been falling by the wayside, pulling up with cramp, leaning against lampposts, stretching legs or sitting forlornly in the gutter. In the 20s, there was even more roadside suffering. Dozens of people were walking. I managed not to; I was hanging on in there. But my run wasn't much faster than a walk. I was shuffling along, dog-tired and fed up, and it was now that my hideous deformity started to take its toll.

Perhaps because of asthma, or perhaps the cause of it, I have one shoulder a few inches higher than the other. I am naturally lopsided, and as tiredness set in, one shoulder rose as the other one sank. I was unaware of it, but towards the end I was running in a horribly hunched position, which added to my tiredness and made my running all the more ineffective.

Bizarrely, it had never been an issue until Ireland. If my shoulder slump had been particularly marked when I first started running, I am sure Pamela would have picked up on it. Perhaps it had simply worsened with the years. Perhaps it was just that I hadn't ever really had any supporters towards the ends of races when the deformity was at its worst. In fact, in Amsterdam, the Chichesters, Steyning and the Isle of Wight, I had had no personal support at all.

But now, suddenly, somehow, here in Ireland, my lopsidedness was indeed a problem – even if it wasn't a problem I was aware of until after the race. Whilst I was still running, it was indistinguishable from the general discomfort I was suffering.

Maybe my right-leaning lurch was worsened by the weather, perhaps even by my bin bag barminess, but more likely perhaps by the sheer amount of running I had done that year. But by the time Fiona and the children, waiting for me at around the 25-mile mark, saw me, it would have been impossible not to notice it. They tell me they were aware of my shape before they were aware that it was me. Staring at the runners, they saw Quasimodo lumbering towards them. My gait was awful; my posture was terrible, any running efficiency long since wrecked by a shape which was hopelessly skewed.

Since then the firm instruction to anyone kind enough to support me has been to shout 'Shoulder up!' when they see me coming. If it's well into the race, it's certain that the shoulder slump will have started – just another of the ways in which the extremity of long-distance running can play havoc with your body. I was almost certainly running like this towards the end in Amsterdam. I just didn't know it then. There was no one there to tell me. No one there to care.

Yes, self-pity was never far away. But here, thank goodness, I had support – terrific support. Fiona, Adam and Laura were there after mile one and there they were again at 25, and I was overjoyed even if I didn't manage to show it. Ideally, it would have been great to have had someone midway round the course as well, but there was no way Fiona could have dragged the children to some remote Dublin suburb in torrential rain simply to stand for hours in the hope of not having missed me. And I wouldn't have wanted her to. I'd wrecked their day enough. It was enough that I saw them with just over a mile to go.

Fiona tells me I looked shot away at that stage, every effort focused on just keeping going, which I did, and slowly the finish inched nearer. Maybe ten minutes before I got there, the sun came out, and by the time I finished, the sky was suddenly as blue as it had been the day before. Dublin was determined to have the last laugh on the toughest of days.

But, as with all tough marathons, I did feel a certain grim satisfaction. You've stopped banging your head against the wall. You've stopped dropping the hammer on your foot, and at last it feels good. And even now, I can't helping smiling at my 20 miles in a bin bag – smiling while at the same time thinking how unspeakably stupid I had been.

Perhaps the point is that when you are tired, you really do stop thinking logically. 'Marathon brains' is the best way of describing it. You enter into a strange, isolated world where you torment yourself about the things you cannot control, but miss the blindingly obvious things you can actually change.

The finish was in Merrion Square, one of the most attractive sights in Dublin; classical, elegant and classy – and so typical of a city centre which once again seemed all of those things in the bright sunshine. It didn't take long to find Fiona and the children, and I am sure I looked quite a state, unable to stand straight, weather-beaten and exhausted.

I slumped down beside the railings which enclose the square. I ached, but not enough to stop me thinking some deeply pretentious thoughts about the healing power of the sun. Sitting on my pavement, I closed my eyes, lifted my face and thought just what a gorgeous sensation it was to feel the sun on my skin. Adam and Laura sat down either side of me. No one said a word for several minutes. I needed time to come back to me before I could come back to them.

But it strikes me now how odd it was that the children never once thought to ask me that question so beloved of children everywhere. This was the first time they had seen me at the end of a marathon, and yet as they looked at me, it didn't occur to them to ask: 'Why?' Perhaps it was because I'd done it all their lives, bar the first two years of Adam's. They accepted it as normal in an abnormal kind of way. You can imagine the playground conversations. 'What does your dad do?' 'Oh, he likes to go fishing. What about yours?' 'Oh, you know, he just likes to run himself into the ground for four hours in torrential rain dressed in a bin bag, you know the kind of thing.'

But even if they had asked me, I doubt I would have been able to frame a sensible answer. Arguably, I still couldn't. 'Because' is the only possible response. 'Because I do.'

My finishing time was 3:40:38, positioning me 1,475th out of just over 8,000 finishers – and as I look at those stats now, a big part of me wants to shout 'So what on earth have you been whingeing about?' I guess the answer is that this was one of those instances where the position was much more satisfying than the time achieved, which is a problem when time is the thing you instinctively measure a marathon by. The placement was impressive for a non-club runner on a tough day, but that doesn't change the fact that placement can never be more than the consolation prize when the golden ticket of a PB has been denied you.

I did the first half of the race in about 1:40. The second half came up in two hours, such was the extent of my slowing. But for hours afterwards people were streaming in, which was gratifying in its way. The Dublin course record for men at the time was ten minutes off the world record and the best women's time was a strangely slow 2:35-ish, so I guess you have to take into account the fact that it wasn't a quick course.

Even so, I look back on Dublin as my stupidity marathon, just as Amsterdam had been my misjudgement marathon. Having perfected in Amsterdam a route to disaster which involved fixating on a specific finishing time, I went for out-and-out idiocy in Dublin, indulging a piece of foolishness so foolish that it goes off the top of the foolish scale. I shudder at the thought of it. What on earth was I thinking? Except, of course, I *wasn't* thinking.

My Amsterdam and Dublin experiences left me starting to think that my Paris time of 3:27 six months earlier was probably an aberration, the kind of result you get only on that rarest of rare occasions when absolutely everything goes right. My Amsterdam and Dublin times were 3:37 and 3:40 respectively, times so closely clustered that I started to think that this was probably my natural time.

But even after 3 hours 40 minutes of grind in Dublin, the day wasn't done yet. This wasn't so much a marathon as a triathlon. Within a couple of hours of the marathon, we were heading home on the ferry, being tossed around by seas so stormy that even the crooner had to give up and stop singing. A triathlon because part two (the ferry) was followed by part three, a 300-mile drive home, from North Wales back to Hampshire on endless motorway in the middle of the night.

And this is where I am prepared to admit to yet more stupidity. Fiona repeatedly offered to drive, but I insisted that I wanted to, and I just kept going – perhaps in expiation for a disappointing marathon. I suppose I wanted to redeem the race – a stupid reaction given that in the cold light of day there can't possibly be any connection between the run and the return home.

I was awake and invigorated, and we got home safely and without incident, but I suppose it does have to count as daft, given that another driver was available and more than willing. Perhaps it's an insight into the marathon mind. Running marathons is all about setting yourself targets and challenges. Marathons are all about the feeling of 'I've got to do it'. Subconsciously, I was trying to make up for the day's setback by setting a new challenge straight away. Foolish. It didn't make the marathon any better in retrospect.

Chapter Ten: 'Like a Rolling Stone'
Thinking a Good Marathon - Paris 2006

When you have a stinker such as Dublin, there's nothing you can do except try to be philosophical. Not in the sense of reaching for Nietzsche. Rather, you just try to put it down to experience and hope you'll bounce back. With Dublin, just as with Amsterdam, the only way to move on was to do another – which suggests a freedom that most blokes probably simply don't have. I'm married with children and have a job, but marathons were here to stay as far as I was concerned. Fiona recognised it too. She doubted my sanity at times, but never for a moment opposed my running.

Thus it became a question of working the running around all the other commitments we had – and if nothing else, the Dublin experience at least suggested one way how. Dublin had been the first marathon I'd combined with a family holiday, and apart from the run itself, it had worked out extremely well.

We'd been wanting to take the children to Paris for a while, and so Paris once again became my next marathon, in April 2006. In my defence, it wasn't simply a question of 'think of a marathon and then tack on a holiday'. It was much more positive than that. The marathon made us get ourselves organised and do something we'd long been intending to do. All we needed now was to reverse the order of ceremonies. Dublin had confirmed the folly of having the holiday first and then doing the marathon. This time we would do things the right way round from the point of view of my running.

Fiona and I are both modern languages graduates, and Adam and Laura, by now nine and seven, had started to do a little French at school. We were keen for them to progress, and it was time for them to get to know one of the world's most beautiful cities, an experience which came with the added excitement of travelling there and back under the sea. For us (older) Brits, it's a truly novel experience to sit on a train and end up in a country which speaks a different language. In our student days, we'd InterRailed to our hearts' content, always more than a little gobsmacked at that great experience of standing in a European mainland train station and totting up all the different countries that you could reach without once getting on a boat.

From a London station, Edinburgh and Glasgow were about as exotic as it got. In Paris or Stuttgart or Vienna, the world (well, Europe at least) was your oyster. But now, since the advent of the Channel Tunnel, we too can be part of that great sense of countries joining together. Those awful coach journeys to Paris were a thing of the past, with all that tedious getting on and off at a ferry port in the middle of the night. Now we Brits had joined the gang. Catch Eurostar and, at the price of having half an hour's worth of sea over your head, you could be in a different land all without leaving the comfort of your seat.

Another big bonus, of course, was that it was so wonderfully easy to sign up for the Paris Marathon with that instant confirmation email. I secured my place soon after we got back from Ireland, and life seemed good. I was twitchy whenever I didn't have a marathon on the horizon, and now I had a good one, along with the perfect pretext for planning a treat for all of us.

We travelled out on the Friday; I ran the marathon on the Sunday; and we then had three days to stroll the boulevards. The weather was perfect throughout, another of those important elements which fortunately slipped into place this time. And just to add to the family feel, we were joined by Fiona's brother, Alistair, on the race day itself. It was another sociable time in Paris, and again the togetherness of it all – just as it had with Marc, his family and Michael a couple of years before – added hugely to the experience. Factor in that base support and you factor in a precious stepping stone on the path towards eventual success – priceless when it comes to knocking off a minute or two.

In the intervening two years, Amsterdam and Dublin had surfaced to suggest, whatever excuses I could offer, that I was definitely getting slower. For that reason, I can't say I was overly confident about my Paris performance. A few days before the race, I had also twisted my ankle, doing nothing more heroic than walking to Marks & Spencer's for a sandwich. Mostly it was fine to walk on, but there was a lateral movement, which I couldn't quite pinpoint, which sent razor-sharp pain shooting up my leg. It gave me grief the day before the race at the Paris Marathon registration, and I started seriously to doubt that I could run at all. In the event, so strange is the world of running, it gave me no problems at all – a great relief and perhaps the final element of good fortune I needed. Another factor was that I went into it with a couple of months' worth of intervals under my belt.

Also helping on the day was the fact that 2006 was the race's 30th anniversary, a landmark which added greatly to the fun and the colour of the event. We were given special 30th-anniversary yellow sunhats, which everyone wore for a picture at the start. It must have looked lovely from above. Down below, there was the traditional swill of piss and ponchos – something which was starting to seem typical of the Paris Marathon. But from above, we must have been quite a sight, resplendent in our matching hats – a fine start to a race which became more and more enjoyable as the morning wore on.

Once again I was back in the world of five-minute kilometres. Rather than focusing on 4:45 minute-kilometres for an eventual 3:20 finish, I decided to look at it the other way. Five-minute kilometres would get me there in 3:30. The task was simply to build up minutes in hand and then not let them go. It seemed a more practical, more encouraging approach, and soon it started to pay dividends

I reached 10 km in 47 minutes, which gave me three minutes in hand just under a quarter of the way round. I wondered whether it was enough, but at this stage the main thing was that I was feeling comfortable and looking forward to the next section of the race, the country trek through the Bois de Vincennes. Even-numbered miles were again marked in Paris, and the 10-mile marker came up in good time. I trotted out all my reasons for liking the number ten. I'd reached double figures and there were just 16 miles left, which always sounds manageable. For once, I was managing to think in both miles and kilometres – a definite rarity in marathon conditions.

Alistair, always superb at judging times and distances and always knowing exactly when to pop up, had been at the roadside at 3 km; he was there again at the halfway mark, at which point I had more than six minutes in hand. Again I wondered whether it was enough, given that I was bound to slow. But, again, more importantly, I knew that for the moment I had the power to add.

The run, however, wasn't entirely incident-free. We were all going at a decent pace in a fairly tight bunch when a silly old biddy in the crowd decided that she was going to cross the road in front of us, an insane move. I remember seeing a vision in pink waving a hand in an 'I am coming across' gesture. *Oh my god!* I thought as I turned to see her flat on her face in the road. I didn't see the impact, and I didn't see whether people were jumping around her or over her, but they must have been. Making matters worse was the fact that it would have been horribly difficult for anyone to wade in and retrieve her. I wonder what the consequences were. It's possible that she was seriously injured. I hope she was OK, but it was such a stupid thing to do; mad, irresponsible and wholly lacking in any sort of understanding of what was happening all around her. With the best will in the world, she was always going to be knocked flying – and she duly was.

It was upsetting, but all we could do was keep going. I had no intention of losing focus. By the time I was down by the Seine, just before 24 km, I had ten minutes in hand. Along the Seine, the support was good once again, with plenty of people by the roadside and on the bridges. I was getting some nice shouts every now and again of *'Allez, Phil'* alongside the Tuileries Gardens, which is where Fiona and Adam and Laura were waiting. I had said to them that I would probably pass by there at about 11.15 a.m. In fact, I passed by at 10.56 – and I am not going to apologise for knowing this. Run well, and these things will lodge in your mind. You need clarity of thinking, and when you get it, you cling to it.

But my earliness caught them unawares. They were waiting by a sponge station and I had to shout out a couple of times to get noticed. They saw me fleetingly, but the important thing was that they did see me – though not as important as the fact that I saw them. I was delighted to have been so far ahead of the game at that point, but my time highlighted the basic difficulty your supporter will always face. When you are trying to work out when you are going to be where for your friends and family, you have to be completely realistic. If someone is asking you what time you hope to finish a race, you might downplay it in the hope of impressing all the more with your actual time. But when it comes to your supporters, you have to be as bang on as you possibly can. But, inevitably, once the race begins, you see that time as a time to beat, a mini-race within the race. When I said '11.15', I suspect I was hoping 11.05, whereas 10.56 was wildest dreams territory.

And there goes another of the great marathon imponderables. If it hadn't been my day, I would be writing now that my time at that point suggests how much I had overcooked it, just how disastrously I had let my ambition run away with me. In Amsterdam I had been brought low by going off too fast; but here, with every other factor working in my favour, speed was a sign of strength rather than a warning that I was riding for a fall. It's the finest of fine lines. Thank goodness I was on the right side of it on that beautifully sunny morning in Paris.

The Eiffel Tower was looming large on the horizon by now and then suddenly it was behind us. At the 30-km marker, I had exactly an hour for the final 12 kilometres if I was going to come in around 3:20. With nearly 11 minutes up my sleeve at this point, it still seemed very manageable. I had stopped adding to the time in hand by now, but it wasn't yet going down.

At 34 km, you reach the Bois de Boulogne, and then the countdown really starts. During my first attempt at Paris, this part had seemed so long, but knowing this was now a key way of coping. I was expecting to feel awful, but the awfulness didn't come. I kept telling myself that all I had to do was just keep going and that's what I did. At 35 km I topped up my water and sipped on a lemon gel; 36 km came and went; 37, 38 and then 39 slipped by. I was feeling strong.

For quite some way, looping around the large lake in the Bois, there was no support, but once we started to emerge, the crowds built up again. Suddenly there was just a kilometre left, and it was just a question of pushing onwards. That's all I had to do. I guessed I was slowing over those last 2 kilometres, but still not significantly, and this time round, it helped massively to know that I was going to be in the Bois pretty much until the end, just before the final turn which gives the first glimpse of the finish.

And that's just what happened. Suddenly the Arc de Triomphe was up ahead and I was plugging away towards it, passing the 42-km marker, knowing that in less than a minute I would be there. I remembered to pull my sunhat off for the final photographs as I headed towards that final beep as you pass over the timing mat: 3:21:44. I'd done it. At last a PB – four and a half minutes faster than my previous best on the same course two years before and a massive 50 minutes quicker than my London debut eight years before.

Of course, it is an utterly unremarkable time which thousands of runners will routinely beat, but for me, never hooked on intervals, running only when the rest of life allowed me, it was a considerable achievement. I was running to my potential and I had hit a time which was to my credit. Not in the 'good for your age group' category perhaps, but good for me and for the effort and time that I was prepared to put into it.

I'd lost just under a couple of minutes from my time in hand over the last 2 kilometres, but I'd never felt in serious trouble. It was a straightforward, no-nonsense run – as easy as can be imagined and one to savour. After the slump of Amsterdam and Dublin, I felt that I was at last back on track, running much more confidently and in fact much more expectantly, hoping for the best rather than simply hoping to delay the worst. With Paris, I felt in the zone again – or maybe even for the first time. Given a fair wind and all those imponderables coming up trumps again, I knew I could build on it.

Looking back, though, the biggest reason for satisfaction was the fact that I could honestly say I had used all my experience as a marathon runner. This time, I had actually *thought* – as well as run – a good race. I had botched Dublin with spectacular stupidity; I had botched Amsterdam by going off too quickly and running out of steam. This time, I had run much more steadily and much more sensibly, helped by not going for a target which was too ambitious.

Of course, I would have loved to touch 3:20 but two years after my best-ever marathon, and after a succession of disappointments, I decided that I wanted above all to get a PB, rather than fixate on a time target and risk going astray. It worked, and the marathon was as easy as you like.

Or perhaps, rather than easy, I should say it was *controlled*. All the uncontrollables had converged in my favour, and I had managed to control the controllables. Even when tiredness set in, I didn't slow significantly, and I reckon I had Pamela to thank for that, encouraging me to do intervals all those years earlier. I am sure they made a big difference in Paris in 2006.

In the past, when I have faded, I have faded because I just haven't had the strength over the final few miles, but that really wasn't the case this time. I never had any inclination to walk. I knew that I had to keep going – and I am sure it was the intervals that gave me the strength to do so in the very last stages.

Another way I turned experience to my advantage was that I kept sipping from the very beginning, not really drinking but remembering to sip when I didn't really feel I needed it – correcting a mistake I made in Amsterdam and Dublin where conditions were poor and I felt I could get away with drinking less. In Paris, the conditions were bright. There was a slight breeze, but it was warm. In fact, the conditions were ideal for running, and in the hope of converting them into a decent time, I made a point of concentrating on hydration – even more so than I usually did, topping up the fluids with a few strategically positioned sports gels, including a couple of super-high-powered ones which Michael had given me for the last couple of kilometres. In so many respects – and so unlike me – I had been the model marathoner.

In Amsterdam and Dublin I got so many things wrong. In Paris I got so much right, which gave me a lovely sensation for the most part of surging forward relative to my fellow runners – a sensation borne out by the stats. For once, I spent most of the race moving forward in the field. At 10 km, I was in 6,302nd position; at 21.1 km, I was in 6,090th position; at 30 km, I was in 5,723rd position; and at the finish, I was 5,076th. I overtook around 1,200 people between 10 km and the finish, and I overtook more than half of those over the final 12 km.

Non-runners will glaze at such statistical overload, but runners will appreciate the story it tells – the tale of a strong run which, for once, got stronger as I ran. In Amsterdam and Dublin I fell further and further behind. But in Paris I more than held my own in the field, improving my position as the kilometres slipped by.

In Amsterdam, I faded badly after 30 km. I also lost Dublin over the final 12 km. In Paris, helped by intervals, by proper hydration, by sensible running, by a stimulating course and by ideal weather, I converted a decent start into an excellent race. In all, 30,772 people completed the course that day. Mine was therefore a top-16-per-cent finish. And I know it sounds nerdy to know this, but run a marathon, and you will see that these things matter.

And better still, the real holiday was yet to come. Three days stretched ahead of gorgeous, glorious Paris. I was on a high – the next day quite literally. We walked all the way up to the second stage of the Eiffel Tower for a fabulous view, and then we walked down again – exactly what my marathon legs needed, but even more importantly, exactly what the whole family wanted as we revelled in a beautiful city that suddenly was looking more beautiful than ever.

Chapter Eleven: 'Around and Around'
To the Brink and Back – La Rochelle 2006

For the past few autumns, my father-in-law, Michael, had been running the La Rochelle Marathon, a race he warmly recommended. He achieved his best-ever result there in 2005, coming in at just inside five hours, good enough in his age bracket to win him automatic entry into the London Marathon. It was a terrific achievement. He was officially 'good for age', something I couldn't possibly hope to get close to, though it remained a dream. In fact, it still remains a dream – a woefully unachieved dream. But Michael had run his socks off in La Rochelle, and that was inspiration enough for me. There was clearly something about the course that clicked – and so I joined him for the La Rochelle Marathon of 2006, a race I look back on as one of the most significant I have ever run.

The race was on a Sunday in November; it didn't coincide with half-term, and so it wasn't possible to turn it into an extended family break, but still we managed to make it very much a family affair. Adam and Laura stayed with my parents, while Fiona and I flew out to La Rochelle to join Michael and my mother-in-law, Stella, who had driven down to the coast from their second home just south of Angers. For them, the La Rochelle Marathon was by now very much routine. They had their preferred hotel nicely close to the finish; they knew their way around. For us, it was like being greeted by locals when they fetched us from the airport.

Registration was efficient and undemanding, conveniently located near the docks, a short walk from our hotel. We settled in and then enjoyed an early pasta meal *en famille* before an early and mostly sleepless night. I knew the score on that one. I just kept telling myself that sleeplessness really didn't matter too much, provided I was reasonably fresh when I went to bed – knowledge which really ought to have made it easier to get to sleep. But it didn't. All you can do is lie there and keep telling yourself, 'This does not matter, this does not matter…'

The start was at 9.30 a.m. and I was over the line within a couple of minutes, heading out under clear blue skies into the heart of this most eye-catching of cities. It's a place rich in history, and most of that history is still standing. A seaport on the Bay of Biscay, and the capital of the Charente-Maritime *département*, La Rochelle enjoys a strategic position, which accounts for its significance down the centuries. Now it's more noted for its bustle, its ancient streets and its lovely eateries – all of which combine to offer the most seductive of vibes, plus plenty of attractive roads to run along, in the city centre at least.

For the first couple of kilometres, it was all very crowded, the roads clearly not having been designed with marathons in mind. In fact, it remained a fairly tight race for most of the first half, the relative speeds of the runners eventually thinning us out rather than any particular breadth on the course. These weren't the wide boulevards of Paris, and the difference was noticeable.

For much of it, rather rudely, I was in my own little world. By now, I was regularly marathoning to an MP3 player, convinced that thudding rhythms would help my feet thud at the right pace. But the fact that the course was so crowded for so long made me nervous about putting the music on. I held off until about 19 km, partly also because I knew it would give me a boost. In a marathon, you need to try to give yourself things to look forward to.

A kilometre or so into the race, I saw the 3:30 pacer ahead of me, which was worrying. I was doing OK time wise, and it seemed to me he really oughtn't to have been ahead of me at that point. It felt like he was setting off too quickly – though it would have been somewhat presumptuous to tell him that. Besides, I was sure he knew exactly what he was doing, so I did the next best thing: I eased past him. It seemed the right decision. Four or five kilometres into the race, I spotted the purple flag of the 3:15 pacer ahead of me. That was my man. I overhauled him and aimed to get a couple of minutes ahead of him, just to have something in hand for when the going got tough, as surely it would.

At a couple of points over the next few kilometres the route curved and I could see him a few hundred metres behind me, which was exactly where I wanted him – incentive enough to keep going on a course which offers every incentive for giving up: a double figure of eight. Lovely for the spectators wishing to see you several times; not so good for runners whose will has wobbled. The day saw an absurd number of dropouts, a direct reflection of a course which brings you back three times to the start before you enter the final quarter – far too much of a temptation to jump ship if you can feel your time drifting away from you.

The first quarter of the run soon saw us leave the attractive centre behind as we headed north through some fairly dull suburbs. The second quarter, the lower loop of the figure of eight to the south of the start, was much more interesting, taking in a fairly long stretch by the harbour. At about 12 km, I saw Fiona, just as I was finishing the top loop first time round, and though she saw me five times in all, this was the only time I saw her. But it was stimulus enough, and I was going well. I started on a lemon gel which seemed to do me some good, and I felt emboldened to push the music back a little further, before finally giving myself the treat just a kilometre or so before the halfway marker.

I spent the next half an hour or so congratulating myself on my great choice of running music including The Stones' 'All the Way Down' two or three times in succession and then 'Start Me Up', another Stones favourite, five times straight off. But then Tom Robinson undid me. 'Up Against the Wall' was pretty amusing when it came on, but maybe, just maybe, it unlocked a little doubt lurking in my mind somewhere. Without any warning I started to struggle at about 25 km – a feeling for which I felt quite unprepared. This wasn't part of the plan.

Earlier, there had been a little boost – something I had never seen before and have never seen since on a marathon. At two or three of the distance markers, a chap was manually turning over numbers on a display to give you your projected finishing time at that point. The first one I saw gave a projected finish of 3:11, which was encouraging. At the half-marathon point a chap was shouting over the microphone '3:10 to 3:15' and later I saw the time 3:18, still reasonably encouraging. I hit the halfway point in 1:36, at that time my fastest half-marathon in any marathon. It was all going so well.

Soon after that, we had headed into the top loop of the figure of eight for the second time, and the route – after the pleasure of the harbour in the lower loop – was soon pretty dull again. I was starting to tire; the route was uninspiring; and then Tom Robinson started singing about walls. The sucker punch came at 26 km when the 3:15 pacer overtook me – a significant psychological blow, even though I still calculated that I had a little bit of time in hand. It seemed to me that he was ahead of his pace, so there was potentially still hope. I just had to keep him in sight somehow. That was all I needed to do, and consequently I mentally abandoned my 3:15 wristband. He was my human wristband.

But very soon I had a horrible feeling of drowning, that feeling of clinging on to something which is pulling away from you and loosening your grip till you are just holding on by your fingertips. Like clinging to a life raft, I am tempted to say, though thankfully I wouldn't really know. The pacer was Kate Winslet, serene on her life-saving bit of debris; I was poor old Leonardo DiCaprio, knowing that the ship had gone down and that I was about to follow. It was my *Titanic* moment. A curious seduction started to creep in. I was clinging on, desperately clinging on, but something, a stronger voice, was telling me that everything would be so much easier if only I let go.

And I did. I let the pacer push ahead, and I drifted backwards as he surged forward towards his brazenly displayed target time.

That's where the pacers have the advantage of you, I remembered once again and far too late. They are running within themselves while you are at the limit of your endurance. Or at least, I was at the limit of mine. 'Just let him go, stop the agony,' the voice said. In truth, I didn't have much choice. And off he went. I hoped I wouldn't lose him completely. He took my chances of 3:15 with him, and I forced myself to try to readjust, hoping that I might salvage 3:20 as a consolation prize.

When Fiona saw me again at about 33 km, she tells me he was probably two minutes ahead of me. Soon afterwards, we were back into the figure of eight's lower loop for the second time. We were entering the final quarter marathon, and I was struggling. I can't really remember what I was thinking – except that in time-honoured fashion I was now losing the ability to think terribly much at all. In Paris I'd been telling myself that the only way to stop is to keep going. I don't know that I had those thoughts this time round. I just kept pounding it out, not looking at the clock, just keeping going and hoping.

I'd had a second lemon gel at around the half-marathon mark and at about 33 km or so I broke into the first of the super-strength OVERSTIM.S gels I had, again a gift from Michael. Maybe I hadn't taken on quite enough water, but the gel seemed heavy on my stomach and made me feel sick. Meanwhile, though, the music was certainly helping, and I guess this is where I started to break through again. From nowhere, I started to believe that I might just be able to hang on in there. I'd wobbled, but I started to feel that maybe I was going to be able to contain it and possibly even overcome it. I forced myself to keep going to the music going through my head, letting it take over my body and willing it to take over my thoughts as well.

It's not necessarily a question of running to the beat, though of course it's great when, somehow, by some happy chance, beat and feet coincide. It's much more a question of identifying the music that will give you a lift. It's perfectly possible to listen to the radio (OK, let's admit it, Radio 2) for hours and barely notice the music. And then, suddenly, along comes a track which forces you to take notice. For me, those sit-up-and-listen songs, more often than not, come from The Stones, The Beatles, Paul Weller, The Who, Bad Company; my rock gods, my idols, the stars who always make me think, 'Yep, that's what it's all about.'

And it's that kind of moment I try to engineer with my MP3 player during a marathon. It's impossible to hear 'Start Me Up' without being started up; impossible to hear 'In My Life' without thinking 'life's worth it'. And that's what happened at around 34km in La Rochelle; something clicked and the music kicked in. Jagger crooned; Lennon went all elegiac on me; and new blood coursed through my tired legs.

Going around the port again was a boost in itself, at last something to look at, and before too long we were curving round and heading north once more towards the distinctive towers which mark the harbour entrance. Just beyond them is the finish. Fortunately, Michael had warned me that you can easily be deceived at this point. Rather like Big Ben in London, you see the towers – but you aren't there yet by a long way, because the route then takes you away again before you finally head towards them for the final time. It was helpful to know, both times round.

With confidence returning, the kilometres were going up tolerably quickly. It was clear that I wasn't going to get the time I wanted, but the pain had gone, replaced by relentlessness. And then great joy. I saw the sign, which I'd noticed first time round, that there was now just a kilometre to go. The final stretch was back by the waterside where the crowds were at their biggest. Suddenly it was all seeming a bit narrow, a bit hemmed in, and as you went into the very final stretch it was even more so as I passed through a constricted entrance to the finishing straight. Suddenly, it was all happening in a rush, but what a wonderful sight it was.

I made my finishing time 3:23:15. It was actually 3:23:14. The fact that I have even bothered to note this sums up – so my wife tells me – the vast gulf between runners and the rest of humanity. But hell, I wanted every second I could get.

I wobbled as soon as I slowed, but an arm came out from nowhere to support me. I felt sick as I went through the finishing area, but then had an experience I never thought I would have – a cup of Coke which I enjoyed. I felt sick of sweet things at that point so I've no idea why I needed that Coke or how I managed to stomach it, but it helped. There was plenty of food laid out, fruit, cake and chocolate, but I didn't feel I could eat just yet so instead I carried on through to find Fiona at the meeting point, which was when I started to realise just how hot the day had been. Once again, it seemed that warm weather was key to any running success I might ever have.

Again it struck me that you can take absolutely nothing for granted in a marathon. I suspect a good proportion of those who didn't finish stopped because their target time had run away from them. After all, it looked an incredibly fit field – which made me all the happier with my time. I had shown genuine grit in the face of looming adversity.

It hadn't been a great run, but it had been a good one. It was 90 seconds off my best, but more importantly, it felt as if I had conquered something. The Amsterdam and Dublin demons had threatened, but somehow I had fought them off. And in that sense, La Rochelle now seems a turning point – a marathon in which I did what I have done so rarely: a marathon that I managed to turn around.

Having seen Dublin and Amsterdam fall away, La Rochelle was the marathon I saved from disaster, pulling it back from the brink, getting back on track and finishing in a time which remains my third-fastest marathon ever. For that reason, it's right up there among the most satisfying I've ever run – one of those rare marathons that you're glad you've done for wholly positive reasons. It's not one of those where the pleasure was simply in stopping. La Rochelle was a good, strong run.

But with running, of course, as our wives know only too well, there is no such thing as unadulterated pleasure. No result stays good for long. At the time, La Rochelle was my second-fastest marathon. I knew, though, that it should have been my fastest. But the satisfaction was that I hadn't come a cropper. I'd had a wobble which threatened to derail me, but I had forced myself to recover.

My times in Amsterdam and La Rochelle were remarkably similar until the 30-km point. The difference was that in Amsterdam the wobble became a big one. In La Rochelle, I held my nerve, regrouped, refocused and came in at 3:23 – 16 minutes faster across the final 12 km. Amsterdam and Dublin were very similar races, similar conditions, similar wobbles, and similar times in the end. La Rochelle could very easily have gone the same way. But I retrieved it, and therein lay the satisfaction.

The dropout rate was massive, and it had much to do with the heat, I am sure. Strangely, I wasn't conscious of it being particularly hot while I was out there, but once I stopped it was clear that it was a very warm day. Fiona and Stella had been uncomfortably hot as they darted around from place to place to see us. Sadly Michael didn't finish, packing it in at about 30 km. He insisted he could have finished but it would have been a bad time, a long way outside what he wanted. It seemed the less demoralising thing simply to abandon it – a very difficult decision which I am sure he called correctly. In all, 1,450 people failed to finish.

As for the finishers, there were 6,600 of us. I was 1,259th, which equates to 19 per cent down the field. If you include the non-finishers (and why not? After all, they started), I finished in the top 16 per cent – perfectly respectable given that this was a very serious race, as seems the norm in a French marathon. There was no fun run element that I saw, just thousands of very lean French blokes running hard. I'd dipped a little in my finishing time, but unlike Amsterdam, it didn't seem a reversal. Quite the contrary, in fact. My confidence was high.

Chapter Twelve: 'Satisfaction'
As Good as It Gets – London 2007

My next marathon after La Rochelle 2006 was London in April 2007, my first return to a competitive attack on the capital since 2003. La Rochelle had been my 'Recovery Marathon'; London 2007 was my 'Got The Training Right Marathon'.

For all my marathons, I had worked on the basis of four months of serious training, but in reality I was running all the year round. It was just that, four months before a marathon, I generally stepped up a gear. My two mid-length runs would be replaced by three very different runs a week: a faster, shorter one; a mid-length one of maybe 8 to 10 miles; and a long one, mostly hitting 15 or 16 miles and quite often 18. Occasionally I also threw in the odd session of intervals. But for London 2007, I gained a crucial new piece in that strange jigsaw puzzle which just occasionally gives you a glimpse of what a marathon should look like.

This time I did my long runs in training with a couple of running mates, Rob and Nick. Fiona had become friendly with Nick's wife, and Rob was a friend of Nick's. Nick's love of running emerged in conversation, and it was agreed that we should motivate each other and hammer out the long run together once a week.

Nick had done a 3:11 marathon on his first London outing a year or two before and was a terrific runner. We'd be running along and then off he'd go towards the end, effortlessly stepping on the gas. Suddenly hundreds of yards would open up between us. He was a real gentleman and would do this only once we were heading home, which double-underlined the gulf between us. He was a very natural runner, and a very pacy natural runner, running within himself when he ran with us, but definitely lifting our pace just by being there.

Rob, on the other hand, was a runner very much in my mould; same build, same hopes. We ran at the same pace and ran well together, lapsing into a conversation which ate up the miles, unaware of the extent to which we were pushing each other and ourselves as we trained that winter. All in all, the preparation was as close to ideal as I have ever managed.

Nick probably gained little from running with the two of us, but we gained a huge amount from running with him, just as we gained a great deal from running with each other. It was another example of getting it right. This was exactly how training should be, not that endless self-centred slog, but a communion of feet and minds as you build up your fitness and, with it, your determination for the big day ahead. Training and friendship went hand in hand; something crucial had slipped into the mix. I knew it, I loved it and I hoped I could translate it into results.

Rob's running days ended later that year with an injury which led to keyhole surgery, after which running was strongly discouraged. But in the first few months of 2007 he was everything I needed – far better in every respect than the Garmin tracking device I use now. My GPS wristwatch is conversationally challenged, to say the least. Rob, who I continued to train with after London, was great company and a spur to my every running ambition.

Fresh from my experiences in La Rochelle the November before, I went into London 2007 feeling as confident as I have ever done at the start of a marathon. Nick and Rob were both running it. We had our very own little race within a race – all part of the games you play to get yourself round the course.

Fiona and I stayed with her brother, Alistair, in Clapham the night before, and it was the usual bad night. I got up at about a quarter to six and left his flat at about 6.30 a.m. to catch a train, which turned out to have been cancelled. A complicated taxi ride, shared with other runners, followed. If it hadn't been my day, that would have been my first step towards a poor time. But it wasn't a factor. I had a good feeling. This was the day it was going to all come together. On another day, the cancelled train would have been a disaster; today, it barely warranted a shrug.

I was at Blackheath for the start in good time. It was still relatively quiet, with the loos readily available in the first half an hour. Later, once the queues built up, that's where – needlessly, but it was something to do – I stayed until about three minutes before the off.

As soon as the gun went, the runners surged forward, and it took me only about 45 seconds to get over the line for a nice smooth start which moved off easily, with no sudden stops. It was crowded and difficult to get going, but at least it was steady. The first mile came up at about eight minutes, a fraction too slow for my liking. I was pleased when mile 2 came up at 15 minutes and mile 3 at 22 minutes. I was picking up the pace.

By now, things were getting distinctly warm, and I was annoyed to miss the first Lucozade station at about 5 miles. Later, when I got my first Lucozade pouch, I was perhaps too eager. I glugged it too quickly and coughed for a while, which was uncomfortable. When you are running, you just can't glug, as I knew only too well, but so often when you're out there, you forget the things you know you know. Fortunately the discomfort didn't last long. Maybe even it helped in the long run – a little reminder to be careful.

I started out with six gels, one in my hand, three wrapped around my arm with a headband and two down my shorts, none of which wanted to stay in place. I dropped two of them at various points and ended up carrying the rest, which wasn't particularly comfortable and meant plenty of fumbling, but at least I kept hold of them. I had the first at about 6 miles. I expect it helped. I had another gel at about the halfway mark and then another at about 20 miles and then most of the fourth at about 24 or 25 miles. Along with the gels, I was sipping water regularly, conscious that it was getting increasingly warm, but only in the sense that the warmth on my skin – after so many big-city soakings – was pleasurable and encouraging. It got hotter and hotter, but my reaction was simply relief that it wasn't cold.

I was pleased to be inside the hour at the 8-mile mark, which is when I first started looking for Alistair, always a great supporter and always so adept at being in the right place at the right time. Eventually I saw him at about 10 miles, and then just after 11 miles I saw Fiona and Stella, which was great. The Cutty Sark earlier on had been a non-event, nothing visible of the ship behind the hoardings, not even the masts. It was undergoing some heavy restoration. Not long afterwards, it was almost destroyed by fire. So, given that the Cutty Sark had been no lift at all that day, it was great to have some support in the crowd.

I continued to go well, still not tiring particularly. Mile 12 came in at about 1:27, soon after which we were on Tower Bridge. You turn a corner and there it is – a genuine highlight followed by a slight trough. I had forgotten that mile 13 is still a long way once you leave Tower Bridge. But it was around about here that Rob touched me on the shoulder and said 'Hi!' I replied, but I felt the need to push on. I didn't want to be third out of our little running trio if I could help it, so I gave in to the urge to keep going.

Looking back, it's clear that just having Rob and Nick there sharpened my competitive edge, but running is like that. If you sense any kind of incentive, you can't resist trying to turn it to your advantage – and Rob's friendly 'Hi!' was effectively a spur at a time of need. I passed the halfway mark at 1:36.

I had been steeling myself, from past experience, for the fact that the first section after the halfway mark is really boring, but it wasn't too bad at all this time. The uninspiring little alley that they used to take you through is no longer on the course. Instead it is much more major roads all the way through, and soon we were in Docklands. I had put my MP3 player on just after the half, and around mile 14 or 15 I discovered the delights of running to Dire Straits' 'Walk of Life', a terrific song to run to which I played twice, tried to play again and then lost. Instead, I had three-quarters of an hour of Oasis, again terrific running music.

Docklands is a place where you seem to be weaving in and out and just making up distance, but the support here was strong, almost oppressively so. We were doing it a different way round this time, apparently, all part of the changes brought about by no longer going over the cobbles at the Tower of London, or so a chap had explained to me on the train on the way to the start.

But still, I was feeling good. I choked a little and coughed painfully on the Lucozade at 15 miles in a little lapse of concentration, but at least the miles were still going up steadily. I was rapidly chipping into the second half, and I was pleased when I crossed 16 miles with something like two or three minutes to go to the two-hour mark – seriously good progress. I was running at more than 8 miles an hour at this point. Ten miles to go and I had about 1 hour 18 minutes to do it in if I was going to do 3:15, 1 hour 23 if I was going to do 3:20. Again, I make no apologies about citing the times. It was the way I motivated myself – however anorak-ish it might seem in the cold light of day.

For me, all that mattered was that the times were stacking up nicely, and I was becoming increasingly hopeful of achieving a PB. All was going according to plan – so much so that I wasn't actually bothering to look at the 3:20 pace band I was wearing. The novelty of pace bands had worn off by now. In fact, I was starting to dislike using them. If you are going well, you can get by without them. If you're not, the gutter is the only place for them. I don't think they can lift you, but I know they can bring you down.

I don't remember much about miles 16 to 20. They were uneventfully steady, but I was certainly glad to see mile 20. From about 16, I was imagining running to Wickham and back, a 10-mile route from home. At 20 miles, my mind was on the hill just past McCarthy's, a roadside fruit and veg shop I could picture so well from countless training runs. I was feeling fine, especially when I reached 22, effectively the start of the long home straight. Here the support was amazing. By now it has always built to the deafening crescendo which it stays at until the end of the race. My own personal soundscape at that moment was George Harrison singing 'My Sweet Lord', an inspirational song which it was easy to tap into.

I was in control, and I was going strong with 3 miles to go. I was looking forward to seeing the Thames, and soon we were running alongside it. It seemed to me that we joined it a little later than in previous years, which probably wasn't the case. I suspect I'd just got it into my head that I mustn't be deceived by my first sight of Big Ben and so started to misjudge distance. In the event, the confusion worked to my advantage. I was further along than I thought – and that in itself helped me to run strongly.

With the crowds roaring, with the music helping (The Stones, Paul Weller, plus an extended stretch of Bad Company), I kept on keeping on and was staggered at about 24 miles when Nick tapped me on the shoulder and said 'hello'. He looked like he was struggling. It was a big surprise, and just as with Rob at the halfway mark, it was the trigger to a competitiveness I probably hadn't completely unleashed in previous marathons. I had just assumed that Nick would be well ahead by now. And, even after seeing him, I assumed he'd soon pick up pace and pass me by, gliding Nick-like to the finish. He didn't.

In the event, Nick came in a couple of minutes behind me. But just seeing him was crucial to my finish, opening up the prospect of something I had never dreamt of. Never for a moment had I imagined I could beat Nick. Once he was behind me, it was one hell of a spur to keep going at a point when you need every spur you can get. Nick's struggle helped me surge.

Twenty-four miles came up in about 3:02, so sadly the big target had slipped. It was clear that 3:15 wasn't on. But – and here's a sign that the marathon was going well – I was sufficiently *compos mentis* to do some rapid recalculations. I needed to be within nine minutes a mile to come in sub-3:20 – an easy enough calculation to make, of course, but not the kind of number-juggling which is generally within my reach at this stage of a marathon. But this time, the number crunching urged me on. Going along Birdcage Walk, I was still thinking that sub-3:20 was on.

Sadly, any time in hand I had just wasn't enough in the end. It evaporated. You turn and then you turn again before you reach the home straight, and I guess that's where the time went. I expect I was still just about sub-3:20 when I saw Buckingham Palace, but those precious seconds trickled away from me. I came in at 3:20:25.

As so often, I wobbled and was supported by a marshal for a while before leaning against some railings. My recovery was rapid. It was the emotion of the moment that caused the wobble, and when it passed, it was clear that I wasn't in bad shape at all. I was wandering around imagining I was worse than I was before I realised that I was actually fine – the point at which I could start beating myself up about the time I had just done.

My best marathon. But probably the one I was quickest to criticise. Annoyingly, I was just over something rather than just under something, just over 3:20 rather than 3:19 something. Was it good enough? I look back on it now and I am impressed. Seriously impressed. But at the time, the doubts soon set in. Which was probably a good thing. I guess if they hadn't, I wouldn't still be doing marathons now.

My aim had been to complete the course in under 3:20; the outside hope had been to do under 3:15 and so be 'good for my age'. In the event, I did neither, but there were plenty of pluses. 3:20:25 was – and remains – my fastest-ever marathon, beating Paris 2006 by nearly a minute and a half. My placing of 2,528th out of more than 36,000 runners was very respectable indeed. By 6.45 p.m., 35,674 runners had crossed the finish in the Mall, a London Marathon record at the time by more than 400 people. And that's a figure that puts me in the top seven per cent on the day – a position reflected in the fact that I really didn't suffer at all, despite having run in very high temperatures at the end of a very hot week.

On the back of turning it around in La Rochelle, this was the London where it all went right, where none of those last-half agonies dragged me down, where marathon running on one glorious day was the easiest it will ever be. I was only 79 seconds quicker than my previous fastest marathon, and it was hugely annoying not to break 3:20. But even I had to admit that, on the whole, the positives outweighed the negatives. It was boiling hot, the hottest London Marathon ever, and yet I didn't run into any serious discomfort. Instead, I did my best time ever, beat both Nick and Rob and finished 33 minutes quicker than I had ever run London before.

So what was I complaining about? Nothing really. A healthy dose of discontent is simply the natural state for a runner who hasn't run his final race.

Chapter Thirteen: 'Paint It Black'
When You Just Shouldn't Run –
Berlin 2007

Hindsight, great thing that it is, makes me look back moderately fondly on the Amsterdam and Dublin Marathons. However much I love to hate them, I still love them grudgingly, just a little bit. Berlin – in October 2007 – was an altogether different kind of experience, one that makes me shiver even now whenever I think about it.

My marathon-running career has been remarkably free from injury provided I change my running shoes fairly promptly once my knees start aching. I also have to transfer across to the new shoes the little inserts which correct, to a degree, my bandy legs. Decent shoes and a little bit of in-shoe support have kept me running through the years, for which I am eternally grateful.

However, it's not just about the aches and the pains, the twists and the stresses. It's also about the sniffs and the snuffles, and when they hit you, there's really not much you can do about it. Marathons are set up to make sure you run only if you are fit; London Marathon places are much prized things, but the organisers really, really, really don't want you to attempt it if you aren't fit, and they will do everything they can to put you off. They don't want you keeling over any more than you want to – and they do all they can to encourage you to be pragmatic in the face of illness. If you're not well, you simply post off your postponement form before the race starts and you get your place back the following year. You shouldn't risk yourself, and the London Marathon organisers don't want you to either. Pulling out couldn't be simpler – and, in the vast majority of cases, effectively it's a decision made for you by the nature of your injury.

But colds are something else altogether, putting you in the shall-I-shan't-I middle ground where doing the sensible thing isn't always the easiest thing. Well, not if you are me. Berlin was a case in point. After the usual three or four months training, after all those long, tedious, Sunday stamina runs, I succumbed to a heavy cold a week or so before we were due to fly out to Germany. Common-sense runners take their vitamin C all the year round; I never get round to it until two or three weeks before the race, if at all, and then I simply hope for the best.

However, for my autumn marathon of 2007, hoping wasn't enough. I was a snuffling, hacking wreck; dosed up, spluttering and shivering. Had the marathon been in the UK, I like to think I would have thrown in the towel and never even started. But Berlin had been on the horizon for months. I was to fly out with Michael and with Rob. We were all going to run it. It was our great adventure, three lads together for a weekend away.

From 2006 to 2007, I was in the running form of my life, consistently pulling off marathons which reflected well on my ability, especially given the fact that I was juggling training with my job and home life. Berlin offered itself as an alluring next chapter. More than ever, by now, running had become a quest for the new, and Berlin, traditionally flat and fast, appealed to all three of us as we contemplated our invasion of Germany.

Sadly, a few weeks before our departure, the three had been reduced to two when Rob couldn't ignore any longer the serious knee pains which eventually meant surgery. Gamely, though, tickets booked and paid for, he decided to come along anyway. Michael too was suffering. He was recovering from an injured ankle but intended to run just within the time limit, the point at which the organisers reopened the roads. Our trip seemed ill-fated before we even started.

And then it was my turn. With ten days to go, I started to feel ropey in a different way; heavy, lethargic, dull-headed and snotty. However, bloody-mindedness kicked in. To an extent, I was influenced by Rob's enforced abandonment. As the week of the marathon dawned, I was damned if I was going to allow cascading snot and aching limbs to reduce our gang of three just to one injured septuagenarian. I thought of all the hours spent training and I resolved to run through the pain barrier.

Oddly, on the Thursday and Friday, my cold lifted, but on arrival in Berlin on the Saturday, I was feeling worse again – worse than I let on. I was coughing; I felt feverish; and I felt the time had come to add another act of gross stupidity to my roll call of marathon debacles. Starting too quickly in Amsterdam had been an error of judgement easily made. Running 20 miles in a bin bag in Dublin had been idiocy on a grand scale. Now it was time to run while palpably unfit – the daftest crime of all.

Berlin had been a pleasant discovery on the Saturday afternoon, but, as seemed par for the course on my big-city marathons, the weather deteriorated as the day wore on. We explored a super-chic shopping arcade and emerged to discover that the rain which had been threatening all afternoon was now coming down in torrents. Continuing along the road we ran into the crowds gathering along the marathon route, waiting for the late-afternoon roller-skating marathon. It was exhilarating stuff to watch as the skaters sped by, the puddles growing ever greater and the splashes ever higher as the skaters zoomed through them. It was not a particularly good omen, though. Not least, it was unwelcome exposure to the elements in my fragile state, and by now I was feeling decidedly sorry for myself.

As it happened, the marathon morning dawned bright, but by then the damage had been done – a phrase I know I keep using, but the fact is there are so many points in a marathon from which there's just no coming back, and I had definitely passed one before I even reached the starting line in Berlin. Stubbornness is a vital weapon in the marathon runner's armoury, but there are times when it will count against you. If anyone had said, 'You mustn't run,' I know I would have ignored them.

As you'd expect – if you like following the stereotypes – the start of the Berlin Marathon was excellently marshalled, and organised with the maximum efficiency to minimise the hassle for everyone concerned. The bag deposit was easy and obvious, and there was plenty of room to hang around in comfort as we waited for the off, just to the west of the Brandenburg Gate, a few hundred metres from the Reichstag – buildings rich in history and, on any other day, doubtless magnificently inspiring.

We were gathering in the shadow of places which had shaped the destiny of Europe, and the Reichstag was certainly imposing, just to our left – an immense, brooding presence from which so much had so fatefully emanated. We were in the heart of what had once been Third Reich Germany. Now it was the heart of a confident, reunified Germany – a Germany which was in itself an astonishing achievement. In 1986, for my finals in French and German at university, I had been given ten minutes to prepare a speech to a couple of be-gowned dons on whether *Wiedervereinigung* was possible, let alone desirable; five years later, reunification actually happened. To those of us brought up in an era of cold war, the speed – and indeed the success – was mind-boggling.

But that counts for little when you are mentally wading through snot.

Michael and I bade each other 'farewell' and 'good luck' and set off for our respective starting pens, but already I had a bad feeling. After all the rain of the day before, the weather was just perfect for running, fresh and invigorating, but I was starting to sweat and shiver before we had even started – which was all the more galling for the fact that the race offered a splendid opening kilometre or two, straight onto wide roads which allowed us to spread and find our own pace quickly. Within minutes, we were racing through the Tiergarten towards the Siegessäule, one of the city's great landmarks, an impressive column, 69 metres tall, featuring a statue of Berlin's 'golden girl' on top.

We were on the move, and it was straight, fast running on a course known for its speed. Turning right at Ernst-Reuter-Platz, we headed towards Alt-Moabit for a stretch, which took us deep into the old East Berlin before we headed south again for a huge loop south-west of the city centre, which eventually took us back to the start.

To begin with, things went well, and I enjoyed that usual off-the-leash sensation of running strongly while the early kilometres slipped past nicely, but all the time I was conscious that I was sweating far too much. I tried to compensate by taking on extra fluid. I knew I absolutely had to, but by about 5 to 6 kilometres, my stomach was sloshing unpleasantly and uncomfortably. I had reached a kind of saturation point, and yet still I sweated. I tried to drink, but it simply made me feel worse, and I started to remember all the tales of the dangers of hyponatremia or 'water intoxication', the potentially fatal condition which can result from the consumption of excess water. Apparently, it's a condition which has become increasingly prevalent as more and more people have taken up endurance sports.

In the early days, all the emphasis had been on drinking and drinking, never allowing yourself to dehydrate. But it was clear that some people had overdone it. It never occurred to me that it was just as dangerous to go the other way until I stood at the start of the New York Marathon. There, all the announcements – despite the hot day – were geared towards the dangers of overdrinking rather than not drinking enough. It seemed reckless, given how hot New York was on that November morning. But clearly it was an issue, and in the intervening years it had become increasingly recognised as a marathon peril. And it was very much in the back of my mind as I tried – and failed – to force myself to drink as I shivered on Berlin's streets.

Everything felt wrong. The sweat was making me shake; I was feeling colder and colder. And yet I wasn't feeling any less full. Normal bodily processes were suspended, and a glimmering awareness of my foolishness started to descend. I was mad to be out there.

All of which meant – given that I wasn't going to give up – that I needed some help from the route. I wanted to be inspired, lifted and launched forward. Seven or eight kilometres in, it was clear that this was not going to happen.

Berlin has got some fascinating areas and many beautiful areas, but the marathon route was essentially through huge, wide streets – the nondescript cityscape of could-be-anywhere Middle Europe. There were flutters of excitement at recognised street names and squares, but one kilometre was undistinguishable from the next in an unending, slowly passing succession of grand buildings, imposing but grey, with nothing about them capable of raising flagging spirits.

Support along the route was sketchy, to say the least, and from just a few kilometres in, I can remember almost nothing of the course. I wasn't motivated later to pour my thoughts into a post-marathon diary, and few lasting impressions took root at the time, save for the overriding impression of the relentless big-city anonymity of it all, undifferentiated *Alleen* and *Straßen* merging one into the next in a panorama so unchanging as to be almost disorientating. But perhaps that was the fever taking over, exactly as it was always going to.

Disaster struck somewhere between 25 and 30 km. I can't remember the preliminary. I can't remember the event itself. All I know is that all of a sudden I was half-sitting at the side of the road. I couldn't remember being sick, but evidently I had been. I must have blacked out very briefly. There wasn't any question of anyone having to bring me round. I came round naturally and swiftly, but somewhere a few moments had been lost, not least the one in which I decorated my very own little section of Berlin gutter.

The spectators were sympathetic, remarkably so in the circumstances. After all, it can't have been terribly pleasant to have a sweaty Englishman lurch towards them and vomit. However, they were solicitousness itself as they eased me to my feet again and gave me the once-over.

I remember feeling quietly pleased with myself as I remembered that the German for 'to be sick' was irregular in the past tense. I conjugated it perfectly as I apologised for my antisocial behaviour. Perhaps they took my spot-on grammar as proof that I had recovered. They asked me if I could continue. Maybe they just didn't want me to linger. I assured them I was fine, and I felt it. Throwing up was the best possible thing I could have done.

Cough, cold and too much fluid had reached the point of return, and return they did – in spectacular fashion. Purged, I pushed on and started to feel much better. I felt a general weakness and a slight wobbliness, but this was infinitely preferable to sickness and confusion. Far better to feel fragile than to feel nauseated, and as I ploughed on, I became increasingly conscious that the nausea, now lifting, had been with me for several kilometres. I now noticed its absence much more than I had ever noticed its presence. It had been part of a general discomfort which was now evaporating.

The ability to think started to return, and I remember thinking how strangely easy it was not to notice things when you're tired. I have finished several marathons with a sock full of blood. Once I stopped, my toes did indeed hurt, and so they must have hurt while I was running, but the pain hadn't differentiated itself from the general fatigue at the time. You really do enter a strange realm when you hit the marathon route.

But now, on the streets of Berlin, a different problem set in – that depressing Amsterdam feeling that my time had gone. My pit-stop puke had been the culmination of progressive slowing over several kilometres. By the time I was back in the land of the living and pushing on, my target time was well adrift. As ridiculous as it may sound in the circumstances, I'd been hoping to equal or beat my 3:20 in London earlier that year. But by the time I'd recovered a degree of control, I was clearly looking at 3:40 plus. And, as ever, as soon as you know your goal has slipped away, it slips away all the quicker.

But I soldiered on and started to recognise the area we'd walked through on the way to our hotel the day before. The end wasn't so very far away now, just a couple of kilometres at the end of a stretch I'd been particularly looking forward to – Unter den Linden.

I'd found it surprising just how many of the well-known Berlin landmarks were in the former East Berlin. It was as if the former West Berlin hadn't really had too much to offer. We were in the east for most of the final part of the race, and it seemed that here was the historic heart of the city. Best of all was Unter den Linden, Berlin's most impressive boulevard with its lines of lime trees standing proud in front of the city's most elegant, most classical architecture. The day before, it had felt like the city's cultural centre. Much more importantly on marathon day, it was the home straight.

On the Saturday we'd seen the barriers being erected in readiness for the race's showpiece finale, and this was what I was trying to picture, hoping it would give me the lift I sorely needed. Sadly – no fault of Unter den Linden – it simply seemed long, stretching on forever towards the

Brandenburg Gate, just beyond which lay the finish. It was a huge struggle. Light-headedness was taking over, and I just didn't have the strength to force my pace. This wasn't so much fatigue as weakness. I was more debilitated than knackered.

As it so often is, it was simply a case of keeping on keeping on and trusting to the fact that if I did, then eventually, however slowly, I would get there. Almost imperceptibly, the historic Gate was growing larger; we'd very nearly come full circle. Pass through it and you get your first glimpse of the finish, just 400 metres away. It would have been a gorgeous sight on any other day, but today it left me feeling deflated. I was spent. There was nothing left. I had started to sweat again far too much over the final 4 or 5 kilometres; stupidly, I couldn't even find the energy to drink. It was too late anyway. I tried to push forward, but no acceleration came, just an increasingly ragged and lopsided hobble as I inched towards the line and all but tumbled over it.

I had been one of 40,215 runners taking part. I came in 11,018th in a time of 3:51:42. I did the first half in just a fraction under 1:40 and the second half in an awful 2:11. My time was 12 minutes worse than Amsterdam, more than half an hour slower than the London I'd completed so happily six months before. The great god Marathon had slapped me down in all my presumptuousness. Part of me must have thought, *Yeah, I'll knock this one off.* Marathon smiled wryly and watched me suffer. My presumption was in starting at all.

I was back in the realms of the 3:50s – a time zone I'd hoped never to see again in a flat, big-city marathon. But at least I'd done it. I'd finished, and I'd done so with a monumental stubbornness which started to make me feel just a little bit better. I was just outside the top 25 per cent, but there were still very nearly 30,000 runners behind me, so the run couldn't, I told myself, be regarded as a total failure. But I knew I was guilty of sophistry. As soon as you start talking about your position overall, you're conceding that your time wasn't good; you know you are searching for consolation.

The very best marathons you sum up with a time, absolute and unqualified. London 2007 was 3:20. With the very best, the time speaks for itself.

However I computed it, I wasn't happy. Maybe I could take out five minutes for the puking, perhaps another ten for the pre-puke nausea and post-puke wobbliness. But none of it added up to the half an hour I'd added to my marathon time since April. I finished the damned thing with a monumental 'Huh!', voiced with disdain and dejection.

Fortunately two other runners were about to come to the rescue; two runners – sharply contrasting in their finishing times – who would save the day for me: Haile Gebrselassie and my father-in-law. And it's not very often that the two of them get mentioned in the same sentence.

One of the greatest pleasures of marathon running is that you really do get to race with the big boys. However far behind they leave you, they're still running the same race as you, and I felt immeasurably proud to have been there that day as I did my bit towards a men's world record marathon time. There was an hour and three-quarters and 11,016 other runners between us, but I can still look back and say I ran the race in which the astonishing Gebrselassie fulfilled his dream.

The Ethiopian runner ran a phenomenal time of 2:04:26, beating the world record 2:04:55 set by Paul Tergat on the same course four years earlier – times we mere mortals can only marvel at. Gebrselassie was running at very nearly 13 miles an hour for two hours plus – a mind-boggling feat of pace, stamina and skill, a wonderful achievement by one of sport's greatest ambassadors. How superb it was to have been there – even if the record has since been beaten, not least by Gebrselassie himself on the same Berlin course the following year. On that same course again, on 25 September 2011, the Kenyan Patrick Makau ran a staggering 2:03:38, the current world record.

According to the news reports, Gebrselassie cried out to all the other runners on his world-record day: 'You were my tailwind and are all record-breaking runners, too!' I can't say I heard him. But thanks, Haile, I appreciate the sentiment.

The reception he received must have been incredible. So too, at the other end of the day, was the welcome accorded my father-in-law, who came in more than four hours later. After my travails on the course, I did my usual routine of suddenly feeling a genuine, sentimental bond with everyone else out there. Rob found me near the finish. We went back to the hotel where I freshened up and rested a little before heading back out in search of Michael. I found him close to the turn into Unter den Linden and accompanied him to the finish, keeping a respectful distance behind him, which gave me a chance to take some good finishing photographs of him. And what a finish he had.

The crowds, mostly patchy throughout, had been great the length of that final 400 metres, once you have passed through the Brandenburg Gate, and there were still plenty of people there when Michael made it through. Throughout the whole weekend we were repeatedly impressed with the friendliness of the native Berliners, and for Michael's final stretch, the crowds were at their magnificent, generous best. It helped that a presenter-type chap, microphone in hand, dashed onto the course for a quick word with Michael, who initially couldn't hear the German that was being shouted into his ear. I stepped up, translated, told the guy to speak in English and then peeled away to become a delighted spectator at the scene which unfolded.

The chap relayed to the crowd that Michael was English and 75 years old. The crowd roared – a fantastic moment that even now gives me a lovely tingling sensation as I think about it. Great times, great courses, they've got their place, but it's that human element which completes the picture. It was a moment to cherish. The response from the spectators was tremendous, and as Michael acknowledged it, so it grew. He waved to his fans, and the fans cheered as one – a surreal scene. He milked it, and good for him. He deserved every second of it.

It made me feel a total also-ran, but in the best possible and happiest way. I was two hours too slow to get the Gebrselassie treatment, two hours too quick to get the welcome Michael was getting. More than four hours after the record had been set, Michael was being treated as if he'd won the whole damned thing. Which of course, by Gebrselassie's reckoning, he had.

It was a fantastic, uplifting couple of minutes – minutes which transformed my own perception of the day, underlining one of the great truisms of marathon running. You hammer yourself as you go round, but the basic fact remains: we're all in it together. Some marathons turn out to be stinkers, and this one did for me, but it's that togetherness, at times genuinely spiritual, which lifts you up and keeps you coming back.

Afterwards we lingered, lapping up the atmosphere which was still strong. We phoned home and sat on a wall for a few minutes before heading to a cafe where we revelled in one of the most enjoyable times we have ever spent together. Neither of us could stop smiling at the reception which had greeted Michael. After all the selfishness and self-obsession of my run, it was lovely to rediscover a few of the pleasures of selflessness. I couldn't possibly have been more pleased for Michael, and he was chuffed too.

There was something surreal about it at the time, something bizarre – but not when you step back to consider the true nature of Michael's achievement. As I have always told him, speed shouldn't be the only thing we judge a marathon by when the runner is advanced in years. Far more relevant – it's worth saying again and again – is endurance. And the same applies to anyone running with a disability of any kind. It's not about your speed; it's about what you are up against, be it age or infirmity. It's about your ability to overcome.

Running less than four hours that day had been an effort so very nearly beyond my capability, but Michael had run four hours and then two hours more. For sheer stamina, strength and grim determination, it was gold-medal running of the very highest order. He wouldn't see it that way. Not remotely. But I felt humbled, weak-willed and lily-livered in his shadow as the crowds roared him home. Humbled but also inspired. I guess it takes a marathon runner to say it, but there are times when I can't help feeling that bloody-mindedness is the highest of human qualities. Friedrich Nietzsche got pretty hung up on the notion of human will; really all he needed were some running shoes, Lycra and a place in the Berlin Marathon.

Chapter Fourteen: 'Little by Little'
Country Roads - Clarendon Way 2008, New Forest 2009

Six months on from the horrors of Berlin 2007, I kicked off 2008 with a return to London, again using a press place, notching up a time of 3:32:05, finishing 4,570th out of 23,680 finishers on a day remarkable for just one thing as far as I was concerned, one of my worst-ever moments on a marathon course.

I'd been listening to Status Quo from the start. They're a great band – not remotely in The Stones or Beatles category, but as a running aid, they are second to none, their chugging rhythm just perfect for running. Up to a point. Perhaps the volume was too loud. Perhaps I'd had too much of a good thing. But at about 23 miles I had the closest thing to a panic attack I have ever had in my life. Status Quo had got inside my head, inside my brain, inside my whole existence; I was tired and probably dehydrated; across several miles, the Docklands had channelled and echoed the noise of the crowd; and then, abruptly, at the start of the long straight road parallel with the Thames, the noise of the crowd rose several notches more.

Suddenly it was all too much for me. Panic took hold. I ripped off my headphones and felt dizzy – dizzy at the roar of the crowd, dizzy at Status Quo who continued to chug inside my head even though the earpieces were out. It was a frightening moment. I stood there and swayed, thinking that any moment I was going to keel over. Noise, emotion and knackered-ness had reached unbearable proportions. It was a monumental sensory overload, and for maybe 30 seconds it threatened to derail me, until I found the strength of mind to stagger to the side and lean against a railing. The poor spectators I nearly tumbled against were lovely, sweet and concerned, and it was almost certainly that human contact which got me back on track again.

It had been the strangest feeling, one of being utterly overwhelmed. I craved darkness. I wanted to cry. I wanted to hide. I wanted to get away from the noise. I felt awful. But fortunately the tide of human kindness turned me round and I carried on, not significantly the worse for wear.

The end result was a good enough time on a good day. Part of the problem, though, was that this was London number six, and it was all starting to seem just a touch déjà vu. Fiona came up to support me and we were joined by Alistair and his girlfriend – now wife – Jo afterwards, going for a lovely pizza to round off the day. But the point was that London was becoming rather routine. Even I wouldn't have baked myself a celebratory cake after this one – even if there was plenty of satisfaction to be had from the fact that, just as in La Rochelle, I had seriously wobbled but then pulled it back.

Far more interesting in 2008 was my return to the kind of cross-country marathon I'd slogged through in Chichester and Steyning a few years earlier – a marathon which answered the need for something different. This time my self-flagellation of choice was the Clarendon Way Marathon, a marathon which will always rank among my most memorable.

A huge part of the appeal was the fact that this is a marathon that goes from Salisbury to Winchester. So many marathons – Paris, Amsterdam, Berlin – take you on a huge loop from A round to A again. You run for 26.2 miles to get back to where you started, part of the seductive perversity of marathon running in general. But every now and again, it's nice to actually go somewhere. The Clarendon Way Marathon seemed to offer something different – running for a purpose, running because you need to get back to where you left your car.

Equally appealing was the fact that it goes between two cities I have known all my life. You have to take your hat off to the runner who dreamt up the race, realising that with a few kinks and loops, you can make Salisbury and Winchester exactly 26 miles 385 yards apart, an approach to map-reading which I find thoroughly laudable. Those less in awe of marathons will argue that you could do this for any two points 26.2 miles apart, but you'll struggle to find too many marathons that go from one city to another; even fewer that link two cities by an almost entirely cross-country course.

For me, it added to the point of it all. The Clarendon Way Marathon was a marathon I simply had to tackle. I wanted to know whether actually going somewhere would be a good way of getting there. And indeed it was. But what a day it proved.

The event is impressively organised. You start from the King's School in Winchester, where one of several coaches takes you to Salisbury if you are running the full marathon or to a village halfway between the two if you are a spineless faint-hearted good-for-nothing chicken contenting yourself with a half-marathon – which is what I did the following year.

It should have been lovely, but in the days before the race, the heavens opened, and boy, did it rain. It rained and rained and rained on the Saturday and then rained some more overnight. When I woke up, there was no need to open the curtains to see what the weather was doing that October Sunday. Dublin here we come. As my great-great-aunt in Yorkshire would say, it was bouncing. It wasn't just hitting the ground, it was hammering into it with such force that it jumped up to meet the next drop on the way down.

Fiona kept telling me not to bother with the marathon, just to stay at home, but I don't suppose for a moment she ever thought I would listen. She said I was stupid even to try it, but my view was that there was no backing out. I didn't want all those miles of training to count for nothing; they had to count for something whatever the weather on the day. And I suppose that's why it's so hard to pull out of a marathon. You invest so much in it, you focus on it so hard, that it's going to take something rather more than a bit of rain – or in this instance an almost biblical downpour – to keep you away. Even staring at the rain out of the window that morning, I knew I would be unbearable within the hour if I didn't at least try. There was never any question that I wouldn't. Not running was unthinkable.

Even so, it was the most apprehensive of drives to Winchester. Then came relief as I made it from the car to the coach, for this was when it really started raining. It had been mucking around until then. Now it was raining like some huge celestial plug had been pulled, and so it continued all the way to Salisbury. We really ought to have been travelling in a World War Two DUKW, that boat-like amphibious thing that I used to love making Airfix models of. We were crawling along the road, the windscreen wipers at full pelt barely clearing anything in the rainstorm we were heading through.

Inevitably, everyone on the bus was chatty. There was a great feeling of togetherness. I remember speaking to a guy contemplating his first-ever marathon and thinking, without saying it, *Blimey, I wouldn't want to start with this one!* The camaraderie was the best I have ever known it before a race. The windows were steamed up. We were sealed in, getting ready for a soaking. We were back in the realms of those self-loving adverts I hate, the smug 'We must be mad!' ones. Except that we really were mad, sitting there on a coach in torrential rain for three-quarters of an hour simply so that we could run all the way back.

Our Salisbury destination was The Godolphin School, a starting point with excellent facilities and the air of an Oxford college. The organisation was excellent in every respect, leaving us nothing to do but hang around for the big adventure, an off-road extravaganza which is probably around 85 per cent trails. Kicking off from the school, the route headed off under the Salisbury bypass and then very quickly out into whatever countryside hadn't been washed away in the meantime. In all, we were probably several hundred runners.

An online reviewer of the race two years later in 2010 summed it up perfectly as 'Mud, mud, mud, mud, mud, hills, hills, hills, mud, mud, hills, hills and bananas'. I don't remember the bananas. Otherwise that was precisely the experience we had in 2008. I can't imagine anyone set off with a finishing time uppermost in their mind. This one was going to be all about just finishing – which suited me perfectly.

By now I was doing two marathons a year, one of which was generally a marathon in which time was never going to be the major consideration. Partly a defence, I am sure, against the fact that by 2008 it was getting ever harder to knock any time off a fully competitive marathon, but partly also for the stimulation of trying something different. Marathons don't have to be about big cities and running on the flat. There are kicks enough from 'up hill and down dale' in mud you could drown in – not that that was how the organisers sold the event.

However, within half an hour of the start, something entirely unexpected started to happen. Imperceptibly at first, the rain started to ease. Imperceptibly because by then we were so used to it that we imagined it going on forever. I could easily envisage people in their back gardens building arks. But then, suddenly, a few miles in, I became aware that the battering was diminishing. By mile 5 or 6, as we skirted yet another sodden field, the rain had more or less stopped, and from then on the sun started to break through. This was October. It was never going to be hot, but the skies cleared as an impressively bright day started to take ever-stronger hold.

The temperature was just on the comfortable side of cool, but by the halfway point the skies were blue and the sun was high. Suddenly everything was looking much rosier in our countryside garden. In fact, it was all rather attractive as we followed the dotted arrows which took us across fields, down valleys and through woodland, the gently varying kind of rich-green, luxuriant landscape which seems so quintessentially English. It was beautiful in a way which was undemanding, until you tried to run through it.

I don't know the overall gradient, but there were some stiff climbs, and with a decent number of runners out there, there was bunching at a few points where the route thinned to go uphill or down. We were in the middle of nowhere, but for several minutes I couldn't go at the speed I wanted as we ascended a narrow path which skirted a hillside. There were brief windows of opportunity where you could nip past the slower runner ahead, but it generally meant clambering onto a slippery bank and hoping not to slide down into their footfall.

Things weren't helped by the fact that the half-marathon runners joined the route pretty much as we were going by. Suddenly we were running with far more people around, runners inevitably far fresher than we were. Would it have been better to let the half-marathon runners loose earlier? Or was it better to have them coincide with us and so increase the overall density of runners at the finish? I don't know. And I still don't know, having joined the race as a half-marathon runner at this point the following year. Maybe it adds to the atmosphere, but the moments of congestion were an irritation, albeit a mild one. In any event, there was no hope of a personal best. It was never going to be like that.

Instead, on this kind of course and in these kinds of conditions, it was like a rerun of the Steyning Stinger. It was heavy, hard work, the drain on tired legs all the greater for the endless ups and downs, made all the more difficult still by the fact that your shoes were heavily caked in thick, cloying mud. And you couldn't just run it off. Time and again, you had to flick it, rub it, do anything to it just to loosen it.

One particular hill is scored into my mind. It was 16 miles in as I lumbered up it, squelching and slipping backwards as I hauled my body against gravity. It was like trying to run up a banana skin. Maybe that's what the online reviewer had been talking about. And a splashy, uneven banana skin at that. If your foot didn't slip backwards, it slipped sideways. Each step was tentative. Each stride was a hostage to fortune – which was precisely why a photographer had positioned himself at the top of the incline, strategically surveying us all as we waded through the mud up towards him.

It was steep. Very steep. So steep that you were putting your hands out in front of you, and that's when I went over, just a few yards from the photographer's feet. Maybe it was because I glanced up at him. Maybe I was always going to go. But I lost my footing and crashed down in the mud chest first. I held my head up as my arms shot out, and I fell – not very far, but far enough. And this really wasn't falling with style. If I'd had any pride left by then, I would certainly have hurt it. But the only sane response was to laugh – as doubtless others did.

'Don't you dare!' I shouted at the photographer, who must have thought Christmas had come early. He dared, and then dared again, producing a lovely sequence of photographs of me on my way down and back up again. The photographs now adorn the wall in our downstairs loo – an appropriate place for images of me in the mire.

A feature of marathons these days is that the official race photographs are up and ready on the website within a day or so. These particular photographs were hilarious. Even funnier was the fact that mine featured in a special subsection of photographs simply called 'Slips', or something like that. Even funnier still was that when a friend and I were registering for the half-marathon the following year, one of the photographs of me was on the home page of the website. I must say I took it as a tribute. How could it be anything else? We all did a daft thing that day in the daftest of conditions. And I am all for celebrating that.

I don't remember getting seriously tired during the Clarendon Way Marathon, though I do remember a degree of disorientation when trying to work out how far we had gone at various points towards the end. It took me a stupidly long time to tumble to the fact that, very unusually, the final half-marathon was counted down rather than counted up. I suppose it makes sense when you remember the half-marathoners who had joined us by now. But it did add to my confusion to be reaching what I knew to be 16 miles and seeing the number 10 by the wayside. Finally the penny dropped. Ten miles to go, after which it all started to seem endless.

We endured an unrelenting stretch of forest and woodland in the final quarter, still moderately hilly, but above all everlasting. One of the most enjoyable things about doing the half-marathon the following year was recalling how I had felt at various points the year before. At the same time, I also felt a bit of a cheapskate. I felt as if I had gatecrashed somebody else's party. Half-marathon running is an immensely respectable discipline, but it has never grabbed me. A half-marathon is too much of a halfway house to my way of thinking, something you can knock off in a time which makes you question whether it was worth all the hassle of getting kitted out and numbered up in the first place.

OK, that's probably being rather unfair. Very unfair, in fact. All I am trying to say is that, to my mind, only the full marathon distance justifies all the effort. And on that rare half-marathon the following year, which I did with a colleague from work, I was looking out for the full-marathon runners, feeling a little bit of awe towards them, deeply impressed that they had gone so far on so challenging a course. And I mean that in a loving, caring way, as Dame Edna would say. I am not talking a self-satisfied 'that was me last year' type feeling. It was a lovely warm feeling of solidarity, a kind of 'I know exactly where you're coming from and I know exactly how tough I found it' type feeling.

It sounds trite, I know, but for me this is once again where marathons lift you out of the here and now, where somehow you move above your own feelings in the moment and partake of the great shared endeavour which brings everyone together on race day, full of hope and full of an energy which will be increasingly depleted as the miles lengthen. And yet, however tired we get, the links between us are never broken, the marathon binding us all in an unspoken brotherhood.

Yes, OK, that really is trite, but the point is that exhaustion, with all its attendant confusion, so often heightens the emotions, and few things make me quite as emotional as a marathon. It can be your pain or someone else's pain, but there are moments when it feels like it is hurting us all. Of that half-marathon, my enduring memory will always be seeing a full-marathon runner, high in the woods, possibly 6 or 7 miles from the finish, stagger to the side, veer towards a marshal and collapse against him. Maybe the runner said it. Maybe the marshal recognised it. Cramp.

The marshal eased him onto his back, cradled his outstretched foot and tried to ease his silent agony. The marshal pulled and it was silent no longer, a scream of pain filling the woods as we ran past. He screamed for all of us, and we felt it with him. I'd love to know whether he finished. I'm sure he did. Long-distance runners are made of tough stuff. He wouldn't have got that far without the stamina to finish. Besides, there was nowhere else to go. Only one trail was taking us back to Winchester.

And so on we ran in 2008. And on. And on. The forest trails on that marathon morning were attractive, a variation on the more open scenery we had been through so far. But this was hardly the moment to enjoy them. My legs were becoming wobbly – though not to the extent that I wanted to walk. I was determined not to, and not just because it wouldn't have helped. But certainly tiredness was now my constant companion. The remaining distance was unyielding. One path led to another path, which dipped, rose and then twisted before leading to another, which then darted down to the next. It seemed like it was never going to end.

Finally, though, we started to approach Winchester. Isolated buildings started to become slightly less isolated; fences appeared, and behind them were rows of houses, not yet urban, but somewhere in that middle ground where city and countryside merge.

And then, not long after that, we started to hear the finish. We began to see a few runners who'd already crossed the line and were now ambling back to find friends. And then we realised that the fence to our right enclosed the school where the finish lay. Even so, it seemed to take forever to reach the gap which would take us onto the field and into the grounds where the running would finally stop.

But I could hear the crowd. That was the main thing. I could hear the cheering. And then came the turn. And beyond the turn was the final stretch diagonally across the playing field where ropes and spectators narrowed the route and funnelled you over the line. Fiona and the children were there just to my right, with just 100 yards to go. They shouted out. They gave me the lift I needed as I pushed myself over the finish.

Annoyingly, I have no record of my actual finishing time – which sounds bizarre for a time-obsessed runner. But this one really wasn't about the stats. I suspect I was somewhere between 4 hours and 4 hours 20 minutes, much closer to the 4:20 no doubt, but respectable, highly respectable, at the end of a stupidly tough course; one where, quite literally at times, you were taking a couple of steps forward and one step back. Gravity always seemed to win, just a little, as we tried to defeat inclines which gave us absolutely no purchase.

There had been no snow, no ice, just mud, mud, glorious mud. Mud that spattered up your legs, engulfed your shoes, caked your hair, shot up your arms and entered your head. Mud which I wore with pride across a chest which had hit it full on. And I was happy. Very happy indeed. I don't remember the shock of stopping, something you invariably feel much more strongly on the pacier marathons. But I do remember just easing out of the whole thing very nicely. Quickly I felt fine. Rapidly I started storing it all away. I was going to dine out for years to come on this one – the tale of the day we braved torrential rain and slimy, slippery mud to run all the way – don't ask why – from Salisbury to Winchester.

The following year my country slog was the New Forest Marathon. I had wanted something for autumn 2009; the New Forest fitted the bill, not least for the fact that it was close and convenient. The big-city overseas marathons were by now firmly established as my favourites, but I had run Paris (for the third time) in the spring of 2009 (a top-20-per-cent finish with a time of 3:33:57), and I was looking to run one abroad in the spring of 2010. I wanted something different in between, and I was happy to fill the slot with another cross-country toil – another marathon where my finishing time wouldn't be the be-all and end-all, a marathon where simply finishing it was challenge enough.

I knew from running the New Forest in 2004 that we weren't talking massive hills, but we weren't talking flat either; so not Chichester, and certainly not London. Somewhere in between, it was a consistently undulating course which would be rugged and fairly wild and probably also fairly lonely, which suited me perfectly.

I had my entertainment all mapped out – something to take my mind off an injury which I expected to hamper me seriously on the physical front. I'd tried running with a bin bag; I'd tried running with the snots. This time I thought I'd try running with a cracked rib. I'd slipped on a rock during our family holiday that summer and fallen quite heavily. I'd had a camcorder in one hand and a camera in the other. As I fell, I saved both, instinctively stretching out my arms, which meant that I took the rock full on the chest. It hurt. It really hurt. And five weeks later, it still hurt. My big fear was that the pounding of the race over such a long distance would open up the break or at the very least produce a pain so intolerable as to make it impossible to continue.

Fiona's view was simply 'What on earth possesses you?' For her, my behaviour was unfathomable, if not exactly unpredictable. For me, opting out was never an option. I knew I would have been in a foul mood if I hadn't at least given it a go. Fiona tried to dissuade me from running on this occasion, but in time-honoured tradition, it was advice I was never going to take.

I had launched into the training several months before our holiday that summer, and four times during our two weeks in North Wales, I had hammered out 15 miles on the hills – tough running which was a good test of stamina. I didn't want those miles – and all those that had preceded them – to count for nothing. In preparing for a marathon, you give in to a rhythm; you push the distance and then you start to ease off, and though I had probably lost a couple of weeks because of the break, the training had gone reasonably smoothly.

Fiona's view is that running a marathon with a cracked rib is screamingly abnormal behaviour; my view is that I had cracked it six weeks earlier, that the pain was by now more of an ache, and that I was just about fit enough to have a go. It wasn't just a perverse habit of never doing what people tell me to do: the rib was throbbing, but I had never pulled out of a marathon, and I wasn't going to start now.

In the event, it was uncomfortable, but not overpoweringly so. I am not even sure just how much of a factor it actually was. The ache did become pain again about halfway round, but the jabbing in some ways helped me to keep going before, in the final miles, it slowly merged with the more generalised pain of running a marathon.

Even so, I approached the whole thing with a degree of caution. Given the rib, and given the relative difficulty of the course (relative to the big-city marathons where I was now hitting 3:20–3:30), my aim was to finish within four hours. My determination was not so much to run it, but simply to enjoy it. The big-city marathons were the ones where I had a chance of beating my best. There was no hope of doing so in the New Forest, and the cracked rib lowered ambitions still further.

No, for me, the whole point was to fulfil a little ambition I'd been harbouring for years, one which meant that on the day I took in very little of the scenery. I'd always been a huge Beatles fan, and ever since George Harrison's death on 29 November 2001, I had wanted to pay my own tribute. A marathon nut, I let that tribute take marathon form.

My idea was to run against a soundtrack of continuous, chronological Beatles tracks and see on which album I would finish. It took me until 2009 to work out how to do this. It then became a question of just how many albums I needed.

The worst scenario would be not to put enough on, run a horribly slow race and finish in silence. Using the wonders of iTunes, I hedged my bets and stuck on everything up to *Magical Mystery Tour*, The Beatles' second 1967 recording after *Sgt Pepper*. The aim was to finish well inside that. I wanted to hit 1966. To finish close to four hours would be to finish somewhere during the *Revolver* album, an appealing prospect because it had always been a favourite of mine.

By now I was routinely running to music. In my early marathons, I had felt it would be impolite to do so. It felt wrong to be shutting out all the people who were roaring us runners on, but after a while the need for a relentless running rhythm took precedence. Besides, for the New Forest Marathon, there really wouldn't be many people to shut out anyway. Plus, I felt sure that my Beatles tribute would be a huge part of the fun. Perhaps the only part.

In the event, it provided plenty of moments of quiet amusement. The Beatles, so they say, are the soundtrack to our lives. They've got a song for every mood and every moment, or so it seemed as I ran along. 'Misery' as the second song was premature, but 'Ask Me Why' was appropriate. I still don't know the answer. Maybe the answer lies in 'There's a Place' if you take it to refer to the finish.

The Beatles' second album, *With The Beatles*, offered similar moments with the encouraging 'It Won't Be Long', the reassuring 'All I've Got To Do' (i.e. keep on running), and the worrying 'Not a Second Time' (not what you need on your return to a race).

The third album, *A Hard Day's Night*, had the bonus of a vaguely appropriate title track. It also offered another imponderable with 'Tell Me Why', and then quick-fire pessimism and optimism with 'I'll Cry Instead' and 'I'll Be Back', plus the ominous 'I Should Have Known Better'. 'You Can't Do That' was a bit of a downer; 'When I Get Home' offered hope.

The next album, *Beatles For Sale*, threatened 'I'm a Loser' before concluding 'I Don't Want To Spoil the Party'. It also pondered 'What You're Doing'.

Album number five said it all in the title track 'Help!', before *Rubber Soul* offered a sane alternative, 'Drive My Car', rapidly followed by the sublime and wonderfully appropriate middle-of-nowhere song 'Nowhere Man'. 'In My Life' will lift any moment in my life, and it was followed by the stop-start contradiction of 'Wait' and 'Run for Your Life' – by which time the finish wasn't so very far away, signalled by the start of the *Revolver* album, offering Paul McCartney at his upbeat best with the cheery 'Good Day Sunshine'.

And so The Beatles dragged me to the finishing line. I crossed it as Paul, as jolly as ever, blasted my lugholes with 'Got to Get You into My Life'. Marathon done; *Revolver* still rolling; mission accomplished.

The start had been in New Milton, and the route had taken in various places, including Wootton, Burley and Sway, along the way. The course was resolutely rural, some main roads every now and again, but a lot of tracks through the woods and endless country paths. Unlike the Isle of Wight Marathon, we were in company for the most part. I remember passing a wizened little man in a home-printed T-shirt proclaiming that this was his 157th marathon – an astonishing achievement, though you couldn't help wondering what he would have looked like without those 157 marathons. But more power to his knees – and he was still going at an impressive rate.

From time to time, mostly on the decent roads, we could see a long way ahead, often a good thing, inspiring almost, especially as the weather was bright, the conditions were good and the temperature was perfect. As I have said, the course certainly undulated and there were a couple of steady uphill drags, but never to the extent that it wore me down in the Isle of Wight way, and with the miles clearly marked, the distance soon started to stack up.

The water stations were good; I stayed ahead of looming dehydration and somehow, urged on by The Beatles, simply kept going, and this, apart from The Beatles, is my main memory of the day. There were several moments in the last quarter where I felt drained, but I never felt as if I was running on empty. I found a rhythm and I stuck to it, turning in a workmanlike performance during which I never set a cracking (or even rib-cracking) pace, but nor did

I slow. It was a steady-as-you-go performance, which didn't significantly diminish. I didn't fade. The Beatles and plenty of water did the rest.

Coming 195th out of 514 finishers, I completed the course in 3:54:54. Job done. Rib not significantly worse. I was satisfied. I'd done something I'd been intending to do for years, and in the process I'd come up with a novel approach to marathon running, definitely a way to renew the interest. And by the end of it, marathon number 21 was in the bag. Thank you, The Beatles.

And thank you, Fiona, ever-forgiving of my stubbornness, who was there with the children to greet me. It was terrific to see them just a few hundred yards before the finishing line. Knowing they would be there had been a help, and it was great to be looked after once the race was over. Instantly, I felt frozen, shivery and decidedly fragile. I had a craving for a hot drink, and Fiona went off into the school, where the race starts and ends, to ask for one. The receptionist suggested she try the next village, which amused us hugely.

Presumably the receptionist thought we wanted cream tea with the full works, which conjured lovely images of me sweating into bone china amid all the gentility of little old ladies on their afternoon out. Fiona explained the need was rather more pressing than that and was directed to a vending machine, from which she returned with the most welcome cup of coffee I have ever had.

Maybe it was a reaction to the rib; maybe there was an element of shock to the body from finally stopping, but I felt chilled to the core. The weather had been fine, but I wasn't. Slowly, though, with that coffee, the warmth flowed back into me; it was wonderfully restorative and exactly what I needed.

Chapter Fifteen: 'Losing My Touch'
When It Just Isn't Your Day - Rome 2010

By now, country collecting was a big part of my marathon running – partly a reaction to the fact that it was getting so tough to knock time off, and bound to get tougher. My thinking was that I might as well measure my marathon pleasures in some other way. In March 2010, Rome added Italy to my list. It also added one or two standout memories – though perhaps not quite for the right reasons.

Rome was also my first Garmin marathon, the first I had run with that high-powered GPS wristwatch which tracks your every route and then throws it all up on your computer screen in glorious Technicolor. I'd been wanting a Garmin for ages, but until I actually got one, I had simply no idea just how much it would transform my running, changing my approach in ways that I could never have imagined, and releasing the anorak inside me and giving him a field day.

There are all sorts of ways you can measure your running on the mind-bogglingly brilliant Garmin 305, a fact which is doubtless true of all sorts of other makes and models. The way I quickly focused on was minutes per mile, in other words pace rather than speed (miles per hour). My mission in life became to run miles in 7 minutes 30 seconds; in other words, at 8 miles an hour. More specifically, the aim was to do so for as long as I possibly could. The closer I could come to doing so over marathon distance, the closer I could come to achieving marathon times of around 3:20. It was as simple as that.

By now I had long since abandoned running in the dark in favour of early-morning midweek runs, plus a long weekend run. The ability to measure every step along the way brought renewed focus and intensity to my running just when I needed it.

But at the same time, it soon became clear that there was something just a touch double-edged about running with a sports watch. Having your very own GPS tracking system with you at all times is a liberation in all sorts of ways, creating and sating a craving for all sorts of instant information. I wished I'd had one years ago. But alongside that freedom, it also introduced a constraint. It meant that every run mattered, which meant that every run was tough. Maybe it was just me. Maybe it's that the novelty of the Garmin hadn't worn off. But the Garmin brought an end to coasting and, with it, an end to some of the pleasure of weekly training.

Its mere presence started to force me down very narrow lines. When it's suddenly all about measuring pace and/or speed, I found myself thinking twice before heading up a long hill, even if it was the way to some of my favourite running country. Slog too long up a hill, and I'd never have decent stats at the end of it. Slowly and subtly, my sports watch started to dictate my path. Given half a chance, I opted for the flat – which proved extremely limiting in the heart of rural Hampshire, where there really isn't too much flat to be had. I started to become terribly bored of the few bits I could find.

There are all sorts of fantastic things you can do with a sports watch. You can run against a set pace or you can run against yourself over a previous performance on a route you've already recorded. But the basic measurement of minutes per mile struck me straightaway as the guiding principle that I needed, and my training became rooted around it. And because of it, my running routes suddenly started to seem a bit pedestrian. There wasn't any longer any great scope for the dash-down-here invention which meant a run could take you anywhere. And if I did factor in a few hills, I then felt obliged to run the same route the following week just to measure myself against it. It wasn't enough just to do a route. With the endless scope for comparison that a sports watch sets up, I had to do it quicker. Otherwise, what was the point? It all became rather too regimented for my liking.

My training for Rome fell into a pattern: two 8-mile runs during the week, where the aim would be to get back home inside the hour. I measured success by just how far inside the hour I was. For the weekend long run, I persisted with my usual pattern of mostly 18-milers, and then for the final six weeks or so before Rome, I introduced a Saturday session of the intervals which I loathed, where the aim would be to average – including a gentle mile to the start and then back again – around 8.4 miles an hour across the 40 minutes it took me to complete the whole exercise.

It meant, so I told myself, that I had jettisoned what the serious runners dismissively refer to as junk miles, something I'd long suspected I was guilty of. They mean those miles that you churn out by the dozen, simply piling them up and reaping no benefit. For years, I imagined that I was running comfortably at about 8 miles per hour, however far I went. I imagined I could tell how far I had gone just from the time

I'd been running, so metronomic did I fancy myself to be. Mr Garmin soon told me just how generous I was being to myself. In the very early days, I had consistently run further than I thought, but somewhere down the line, I'd started to run much shorter than I thought. Mr Garmin delighted in pointing out the error of my ways.

Yes, I could run at 8 miles an hour, but it was an effort – a real, sustained effort, in which I couldn't allow myself to drop back for a minute. But the benefits were evident. Finally, after all those years of junk miles, this was proper, directed training, and it worked, with a noticeable improvement in pace creeping in, even on generally undulating terrain. The downside was that this progress came at the expense of a great deal of the fun and almost all of the variety.

To start with, it was a relief to complete my 8-mile route in an hour; within a couple of weeks, it was an expectation. By late February, I was looking to do it with a minute and a half in hand. The Garmin had been a Christmas present with my March date in Rome in mind; by the time the race arrived, I was generally clocking up my 8 miles in 58 minutes. Every step, every mile had counted.

My best-ever marathon had come after I had trained with Rob and Nick, and it had been no coincidence. The sports watch effectively replicated the act of running with someone just a bit faster than me, someone who ensured I never drifted; it meant that I pushed myself all the time. And I suspect that approach carried through into my long run, where I discovered that in training I could keep up those 7-minute-30-second miles for 12 miles, just slipping back a bit at around miles 13 and 14. The pattern became to hit mile 16 somewhere between 2:02 and 2:05, depending on the route I took.

The Garmin gives you a wonderfully colourful record of exactly what you have done, especially if you bypass Garmin's own boringly utilitarian software and load your runs into the superb (and free) running site Running Free. There you can amuse yourself for hours. You can view your route on a map, or overlaid on satellite images, or a combination of both. You can view the route with each mile coloured differently, or with your pace coloured differently as your speed varied, growing darker as you slowed. Or you can even follow your route on a line colour-coded according to elevation. The permutations are endless. And it is blindingly obvious: if you are going to take your running remotely seriously, a Garmin or something similar is absolutely essential.

A few weeks later, Michael also bought a Garmin, which turned out to be another spur for me. We signed each other in as friends on the Running Free website. I could keep an eye on what Michael was doing 140 miles away in Colchester; he could keep an eye on me. I've almost never ducked out of a run, but plenty of times I haven't fancied going. Just knowing that Michael had been out already was incentive enough. His runs were also a motivator in terms of distance. At 31 years younger, I felt I had to go considerably further than he ever did to match his achievement.

The downside, though, was that I was allowing the device to take control of me, rather than me keeping control of it. Something in my make-up meant I took it far too seriously, allowing it to become a nag. Obviously, one answer would have been to leave it at home every now and again, but that wasn't a real solution. Leave it at home, and obviously the miles wouldn't count towards your weekly and monthly statistics. Slowly, but surely, if you let it – and I did – a sports watch can tie you up in statistical knots.

Even so, those first three months of 2010 seemed to me, in the context of years of erratic and slightly idiosyncratic training, to be three months of the closest thing I was ever going to get to model training – certainly now that the great London triumvirate of 2007 was never going to reunite, with Rob *hors de combat* and Nick now living elsewhere. The sports watch was a reasonable, if very much less enjoyable, substitute.

I'd been egged on to do the Rome Marathon by my running friend Marc, who I'd run in Paris with six years earlier. Paris had been terrific, all going swimmingly well. Annoyingly, as soon I arrived in Rome, things started to go wrong.

A good time will always owe as much to luck as judgement. Your training is all about trying to control the things that you can control, chief among which is your own basic fitness. But you can do little about coughs and colds, as I had discovered in Berlin; you can't do much about injury (London, New Forest); you can do nothing about the weather (Dublin, Amsterdam); and you're defenceless when it comes to the quality of the race organisation (Paris). Worst of all, you are utterly powerless against the feeling – fortunately rare – that, for whatever reason, today just isn't your day.

That feeling started to take hold when I couldn't get through to Marc on my mobile the day before the race. It was my only way of contacting him. He was out there already on an extended birthday break, and I didn't have a clue where he was. His phone number wasn't summoning him, possibly wasn't even getting through, and there wasn't a thing I could do about it. Mobile phones are no substitute for proper arrangements and, as a mobile phone novice, I had been too trusting, never for a moment thinking that I might need a fallback plan. Travelling alone had often been a prelude to a tough marathon, but I hadn't for a moment intended to be alone once I was actually out there. Sadly, that wasn't the way it worked out.

On another day, in another mood, it was something I would have shrugged off. But not that day. It meant that I was completely alone in a city I didn't know, just as I had been in Amsterdam. It didn't worry me unduly on the surface, but it niggled away in the back of my mind where the fact was firmly logged. There is a definite connection between good finishing times and personal support at a race, by the roadside and at the end. For Rome, I wasn't going to be getting any at all.

Perhaps as compensation, perhaps simply because of the buzz of being there, after registering on the Saturday afternoon, I set out for some sightseeing. I had no intention of walking as far as I did, but my sense of direction, usually strong, abandoned me completely – again, just as in Amsterdam. I didn't have a decent map. The one I had was too small. I couldn't read a word on it. Time and again, I would be striding out in completely the wrong direction. It was infuriating. Nothing was where it ought to be; my every intuition was wrong; and the miles stacked up as I slowly went nowhere. I've since bitten the bullet and bought reading glasses. How I needed them then.

In the end, I made it to most of the places I wanted to see and ended up chilling out over a pizza, but I was tired, frustrated and actually just a little lonely. I'd been looking forward to a sociable time in an exciting city; instead, all I had achieved was to get miserably and repeatedly lost all on my tod. But at least the hotel was comfortable, and I slept moderately well, having studied and restudied and then studied again my route to the start, down by the Colosseum, about 20 minutes away. I'd bought some croissants and honey for my feeling-sorry-for-myself marathon breakfast, and then I set off, wondering if a little bit of exhilaration was going to steal in from somewhere. I felt quite flat – a flatness which was soon replaced by fury.

The start was a nightmare, an awful crush which was allowed to deteriorate by an absence of anyone to police the starting zones. I had left it fairly late leaving the loo area to wander to the start area, thinking I would be fine, given that Rome isn't a huge marathon. But even medium-sized marathons require the strictest of surveillance, and there was none of it here. It was a battle to get to my starting group (the one corresponding to an anticipated 3:00–3:30 finish), and then once I'd got over the barrier (the only way in by now), I discovered that I was surrounded by runners (you can tell from their numbers) looking at finishes of upwards of 4 hours 30, which was infuriating.

Everything conspired to take away the magic of the fact that, if I glanced to my left, I could see the Colosseum. It ought to have been an inspiring sight. It wasn't. It simply left me reflecting that Ancient Rome surely wouldn't have offered such a chaotic start to its chariot races as modern-day Rome was now serving up to its showpiece marathon.

The whole thing was abysmally handled – all the more irritating for the fact that the starting area offered plenty of natural advantages. We were on a wide, wide street. If it had been properly policed, we could all have moved off comfortably and on time. But, sadly, there was no effort to spread us back into a long column ready to roll. Instead, everyone just bundled in as tightly as possible as close to the start as they could get, never mind who they crushed along the way. It was possibly being a little harsh, but I couldn't help reflecting that Rome was playing up to the national stereotypes as surely as Berlin had done. The only difference was that the Berlin stereotype was by far the more appealing.

Distinctly gladiatorial, it was the worst possible preparation for the run. The scrum left me hassled, weary and wound up before I'd even started, and certainly the first mile was an effort, trapped behind slow-moving, shall we say larger, runners who should never have been where they were. *Why am I even doing this?* was a constant thought as I slogged away amid the chaos.

Consequently, my first mile was way outside my hoped-for 7:30. I completed it in 7:59 (with the sports watch, I was now in anorak, time-obsessed mode, very much focused on miles rather than kilometres). I then embarked on a determined policy of weaving in and out, desperately trying to leave the slow coaches behind me. It wasn't so much a marathon as an obstacle course, but the tactic worked, with the next 7 miles coming up within 7:30. I was relieved to have done my first 8 miles within the hour, just as I had hoped. It seemed I'd got over the frustrations of the start.

Helping considerably was the fact that the course was by now definitely in the mouth-watering category. Properly organised, the start could have been terrific; but once we were properly underway, there was every chance to appreciate that this was a marathon which offered something rather special, courtesy of a proud city determined to show us something of its importance, its charm and its romance.

After the Colosseum, we had headed south roughly parallel to the Tiber for the opening few miles, after which we turned to head north, hugging the river, towards St Peter's and the Vatican. Just clipping the square, we continued for a long stretch on the western side of the Tiber until, turning at our northernmost point, we headed back down the eastern side of the river to re-enter the city centre. We reached Piazza Navona just before the 35-km marker and then Piazza di Spagna at around the 38-km marker. We passed the Trevi Fountain soon afterwards, before heading back towards a finish which half-circled the Colosseum, which had of course been our starting point.

Two or three miles in, I had turned on the MP3 player. Today was going to be a Status Quo day again. Several hours stretched ahead of their greatest hits, all of them solidly thudding, their rhythms cascading down into my shoes to propel my feet forwards. The Beatles don't thud; nor do The Stones; but Quo have the right beat, and there was something slightly otherworldly when 'Mystery Song' – always a favourite – struck up just as I got my first glimpse of the Vatican. When the song had finished, I jumped back to the start (of the song, that is) and played it straight off seven or eight times more. But, towards the end of my 'Mystery Song' replays, I realised it wasn't masking what I was subconsciously wanting it to mask. I was getting tired – prematurely so.

The 11th mile proved to be the last I did under eight minutes. With mile 20, I slipped over into nine-minute miling and worse. The low point (and thank you, Garmin, for telling me this) was an 11.5-minute mile, a time worsened by a failed attempt at a roadside puke. There's nothing worrying about a failed puke in itself. It's just that a successful one – not to put too fine a point on it – gets things out the way and lets you move on. I can't claim vast experience, but 'better out than in' would seem to be the maxim, after which inevitably you will start to feel better. In Rome, feeling nauseous and knackered, I was left in vomit limbo and my sports watch spared no detail as I faded and started to fail. On the computer, my speed line for that run gets darker and ever darker as my efforts threatened to tail off entirely.

Dehydration became a big factor. I'd taken several sports gels, which my body didn't seem to want to dilute. They just sat on my stomach, immovable and nauseating; anything I drank seemed simply to slosh around on top of them, which made me less inclined to drink for the simple reason that drinking made me feel worse. It was like filling an overfilled sink. Consequently, I felt more and more revolted at the thought of the warmish sweet stuff in my water bottle – a once-fresh sports drink which I had been topping up at the water stations. It tasted horrible, and yet the remedy was so obvious. At one point late on, I took a swig of lovely, cold, fresh-tasting water from a fresh bottle and realised that this was what I should have been doing all along. It was so invigorating. But by then it was too late.

For the last 6 miles, the sights stacked up impressively, with plenty of support and even more to look at. This was a fine course, one of the best. But somehow, none of it was quite enough. It felt that nothing I had done in training helped me remotely once I had passed 20 miles. Those final 6 miles took me well over an hour – a serious deterioration from a position of relative strength.

I had managed to overcome the slow start; I was running at just inside 8 miles an hour at the hour mark, just outside 8 miles after 90 minutes and then passed 16 miles at 2:03. I was still going well after that. At 20 miles, I should have been looking at a 3:25 finish. But when it came to it, I had absolutely nothing left for those final six.

Towards the end I had the awful sensation of going backwards, simply because of the surge of all the runners going past me. The Rome Marathon website offers you the chance to watch video footage of yourself at various points – desperately unedifying in my case. My shoulder had risen dramatically, and I crossed the line with a gait that was an exhausted, camp prance delivered in slow-motion action replay. It looked as if I had deliberately dreamt up the most tiring, inelegant way of running and was determined to stick to it. I'd entered the Ministry of Silly Runs.

Even worse, I was entering uncharacteristically defeatist territory. For much of the last 5 miles, I found myself thinking – if disconnected, ratty snatches of consciousness can be considered thought – that a marathon is an absolutely stupid distance and that anyone who completes it has done well, whatever their time. To an extent, I was thinking all my usual thoughts at this stage of a marathon. But this time there was something different going on, a loosening of my love of marathons perhaps. I had always adored the perversity they bring out and celebrate, but now the perversity seemed to be perversity and nothing more.

And to add insult to injury, when my sports watch finally conceded that, yes, I had now done 26.2 miles, I was still way short of the finishing line. Finally, I finished after 26.64 miles. It never occurred to me just how much you can add to a marathon by not following the thin blue line. All that weaving in and out early on, plus some fairly erratic meandering towards the end, had added nearly half a mile to my ordeal. Not that it made a huge difference. I can't claim that my time would have been wonderful if I'd stuck to the required distance. My time was very much in the C+ should-do-better category, whichever way I looked at it.

When I did finally cross the line, I had no little tear of triumph or relief. All I thought was a big Berlin-style 'Huh!', and the 'Huh!' stayed as the defining word for the entire experience. Sadly this time there was no one there to lift the day. Michael's finish had transformed my day in Berlin. Rome remained a 'Huh!' with a 'Harrumph' on top.

I finished in a time of 3:48:46 – not in the 3:50s but nowhere near the 3:30s which would have justified the day. I finished around 3,400th out of about 11,000 runners, which was just about tolerable in terms of positioning, but you know what I think about positioning by now. Time wise, it was so far off what I had hoped for as to rank as miserable failure.

Never has a marathon seemed so long. Not for nothing do they bill it as a race through the heart of the Eternal City. Eternal summed it up precisely. On another day, the fact that I ran 26.64 miles on a 26.2-mile course would have seemed part of the quirky pleasure of this most quirky of pastimes, all part of my why-I-love-marathons mythology. But today it simply pissed me off. I could hear Pamela, my first and only marathon trainer, telling me years before that the thin blue line painted on the course is the only thing about a marathon that is 26.2 miles long. I half expected my sports watch to flash up 'Well, don't say she didn't tell you' when I glanced down at it. Wristbands have been thrown in the gutter for less.

But more frustrating still was the fact that this had been a good course – an excellent course even. It was striking that my other poor times or bad marathons had been in Amsterdam, Dublin and Berlin, where the courses were dull – 75 per cent dull in Amsterdam, 90 per cent dull in Dublin, and 75 per cent dull in Berlin. Rome was 75 per cent good, a course dreamt up by a city exceptionally keen to show off its superb sights.

Sadly, the experience was all about to get significantly worse. I am sure fondness for the event would have filtered through if I had hung around at the finish, or even returned to the finish once I had freshened up. But the bag retrieval process knocked out of me what little stuffing I had left. By comparison, the organisation at the start had been a model of efficiency. The bag retrieval area was like every worst nightmare come scarily true.

There was zero respect for fellow runners as everyone piled in around the lorry which held their bag, pushing and shoving quite violently. Eventually I made it to the front and handed over my number, but the people behind me were shouting in Italian, stretching over me and jostling. For fully half an hour I was pinioned against the side of the lorry, looking helplessly up at the bag handlers who were working to no discernible system. They were taking the runners' numbers and heading off to find the runners' bags, an approach which might have made sense if they did them one at a time. But every time they found a bag, they collected a few more numbers.

My only connection with my bag was the number they had now gone off with, and I certainly wasn't in a position to remember it, certainly not in Italian. Everyone else took the view that their only hope of retrieving their bag was to shout louder than everyone else. Absolutely not my forte, especially as I was no longer sure I even knew what my number was. Bear in mind, we were looking into a lorry stacked high with official-issue, identical Rome Marathon luggage bags.

I felt as if I was going to be standing there for the rest of my life. It was an awful way to end a marathon. Several times I felt as if I was going to pass out. If I had done so, I would have remained standing, so tightly was I being pushed against the lorry.

Sheer lack of organisation and the appalling behaviour of my fellow runners resulted in a shambles which was an insult to the whole spirit of marathon running – and it was that as much as anything which stopped me going back afterwards to commune with those still out there on the course.

Having at last retrieved my bag, I got back to my hotel and thought about heading back down after a shower, but I felt so battered and angry by then that I just couldn't be bothered – a big mistake, in hindsight, though comprehensible at the time. Consequently, I didn't do the one thing which could have lifted the negative vibe that the whole memory still gives me.

However, my return to the hotel had been enlightening in itself. The receptionist was a friendly, chatty guy who instantly asked me how I had got on. I told him that I had been disappointed, that the last 6 miles had been terrible and that I just couldn't fully explain why they had been so tough. Articulating a thought that had only now crystallised, I told him that I just couldn't fully get my breath towards the end, at which point he looked at me with that recognisable 'It's Dublin! It's raining! What do you expect?' type look. He gave a very Italian shrug and said 'Well, it's the pollution.' He told me that Rome was so polluted that in certain conditions you can actually see it just sitting there like a blanket over the city.

And so the penny dropped. The conditions had been the same for absolutely everyone, but with a long history of asthma, I was bound to feel it more acutely. It was 50-per-cent excuse, 50-per-cent reason, but the immensity of the struggle I'd endured at the wrong end of the marathon suddenly started to seem explicable. I hadn't been on top of my running. It had run away from me. Suddenly that feeling of being sucked back as everyone else was sucked forward made sense. It really hadn't been my day.

In a sense, though, my folly had been to allow negativity to creep in. I was definitely breathing too shallowly towards the end, but contributing too was a lack of desire. The start had been so awful that even before the off, I was wondering what on earth I was doing there. After 8 miles, I was thinking that 8 miles was a decent-length run, and yet there were still 18 to go. And now, after the race, I was thinking that I was 46 years old and to do just over three and three-quarter hours was respectable – which again was a kind of negativity I would never have tolerated before.

As I pondered it afterwards, I was guilty of a kind of indulgence towards my finishing time which I would never have permitted a few years before. I was settling for what I achieved, and I knew that wasn't good. Something had changed, and it made me wonder if I was coming to the end of my marathon running, 12 years and 22 marathons after I started. Was I falling a little out of love with it?

A few years before, I would have considered 3:48:46 for a big-city marathon to be an awful time. Now, so far had

I sunk, I was actually thinking it was OK. I was getting defeatist. Or maybe realistic. Have I passed the point where I have done my best-ever marathon? Quite likely, I suspect. But in Rome that day I was convinced that I had. And that's something that's very difficult to cope with.

Deepening my depression in the race aftermath was one of the most shameful incidents ever recorded on a marathon course anywhere in the whole history of marathons – one which underlined just what a shocker I had had.

The crowds had been good throughout, but in places there were no barriers, which was reckless to say the least. I was 25.5 miles in; I was feeling absolutely shattered; and my mood was thunderously dark when a little old lady – just like the one in Paris – dashed across in front of me just as the route narrowed, in the way that sometimes spectators do, totally misjudging my oncoming speed relative to her speed across me. She saw her mistake, realised that I was very nearly upon her and half-raised an arm in self-defence – an arm which rose into my face. I had to swerve sharply. There was definite grazed contact. If I hadn't reacted so quickly, either or both of us could have been seriously injured. It was a horribly close-run thing – and that was the thought which flashed through my mind. And out it came.

As I swerved, I voiced my infuriation with the entire day. Uncharacteristically, but with the excuse of marathon-induced stress, I shouted: 'Get out of the ******* way, you ******* stupid cow!' As I spoke, I half-turned. And as I turned, I discovered to my horror that she wasn't just any little old lady, but a nun, resplendent in full nun regalia. I could almost see her halo.

I was appalled; all I could plead was that the day had thrown me so deeply into my discomfort zone that I had completely lost touch with the kind of person I like to think I am. Her behaviour was foolish in the extreme, but my rudeness was unconscionable.

Or at least that's the way it seemed at first. I hate to say it, but my horror didn't last long. Within a couple of hours, the incident was becoming the one thing that let me look back on my day with anything approaching a smile – and a deliciously wicked one at that. For a moment, it had been the day's low point. But very quickly, it became the day's high point, perfectly summing up precisely what I thought about the shambolic organisation which marred the entire event.

My shame has long since gone now. Instead I am secretly delighted (don't tell anyone) that I let rip and gave Rome both barrels. Hilarious in retrospect, but at least she was heading for heaven, whereas I'd just booked myself eternal damnation in the Eternal City.

Chapter Sixteen: 'Don't Stop'
The Love Goes On – Mallorca 2010

So, once again, I had to face up to the annoyance of a marathon which ultimately ended in disappointment – one made all the worse for the fact that I had been completely on my own. I'd half expected to bump into Marc at some point, the kind of coincidence that does tend to happen in big crowds, but no such luck. Instead, I was a sad, solitary failure, a fact which did at least spur me on to some vigorous sightseeing the following day. Still wearing my sports watch, I walked a ludicrous 18 miles on the Monday. Or maybe it wasn't so ludicrous. Driving me as much as anything, I suspect, was some kind of desire to compensate for the day before. But the upshot was that any stiffness in my legs was soon dissipated and I had a great time exploring one of the world's most fascinating cities.

Back home, however, I really did start to enter new and uncharted territory. The usual pattern, whether my time had been good or bad, was to feel more and more frustrated with it once I was back in the normal run of things. But after Rome, something rather different happened: I grew increasingly forgiving towards the time I had achieved. Instead of beating myself up about it, I found reasons to believe I had done respectably, not least for the fact that

Rome was so obviously polluted. By the time I'd finished recounting it, the skies had been black with clouds of filth which threatened at any moment to descend and choke the life out of me. I conjured visions of a marathon in which breathing apparatus should have been de rigueur. Instead of making a good time worse, as I usually do, I was attempting to make an average time better. Something had indeed changed.

I was winding down. Without realising it, there was an element of signing off in my behaviour. After Rome, my couple of weeks' lay-off stretched towards a third as I found more and more reasons not to go out running. One marathon is usually the spur to the next. Not so Rome. It started to seem as if I had roamed enough.

In the end, it was Michael who rescued me from my self-indulgence and sloth with the kind of plan only a marathon runner could come up with. Fifty years before, he and Stella had honeymooned in Mallorca. In their golden wedding year, any normal husband would have taken his wife back there. Instead, after an anniversary party for family and friends in London that summer, he suggested that he and I go out there to run the Mallorca Marathon in October. I liked that man's thinking – the kind of warped thinking I could relate to.

At last, I had a purpose again. And so it was that in June 2010 I resumed training. However, that's when I started to get seriously worried. Something grim started to happen. I found myself once again in new and unexpected territory. Suddenly, I found myself really hating the training. It had never happened before. There had been times in the past when I had endured it without enjoying it, but I always did it. And in truth, I didn't duck out of it this time. But I started to grab a few extra minutes in bed. I would always go in the end, but procrastination was creeping in. There was no spring in my step, and no enjoyment either.

Over the past four or five years, I have invariably announced my next marathon as my last – and at first, I imagine people believed me. But then, the marathon over, I would always book another. I couldn't stand the thought of being someone who 'used to run marathons'. Stopping running altogether seemed to me the most monumental defeat. It seemed like saying goodbye to everything. But still, as some kind of self-defence mechanism, I would spread the word that I would be quitting after the next one, and at times I probably even managed to kid myself.

After a while, whenever I said it, I was met with disbelief, groaning and 'I've heard that before'. It was annoying because part of me meant it. But others had seen what I was slow to see – that announcing my imminent retirement had become part of that complex package which counts as training. It was one of the ways I psyched myself up. Believe it is your last and you make that extra effort. Announcing my retirement had become a way of saying 'this next one is special'.

And so the marathons came and went, and always I added a next one. Always the thought of stopping was worse than the thought of continuing.

Then came the run-up to Mallorca 2010. It felt different. Much more of me meant it this time when I said it would be the last. The training simply wasn't fun anymore. For each new marathon I had taken to inventing a new 18-mile route going out in a different direction from Bishop's Waltham. For the Mallorca training I lumbered myself with an absolute rotter, pleasant enough back roads to begin with, taking me to a new town which I always got lost in while trying to find my way through to the other side. It was infuriating every Sunday as I hit this bizarre mass of identical houses plonked in the middle of nowhere. All I wanted to do was to emerge on the far side, but time and again I would run down blind alleys, run into building sites or simply end up where I started, all without seeing a single person up and about. I started to wonder whether the town was inhabited at all.

I was going nowhere – and it seemed somehow symbolic.

Each week I would get a little bit further before getting lost, but there was no pleasure in it. It was just an annoyance. Eventually, I started to make it all the way through, thanks to the ruse of treating the whole thing as a maze and making a succession of left turns on the lifeless, deserted, early-morning streets. It wasn't the most direct route, but it got me through. But even then, there was no pleasure in the run.

Again, it's behaviour that normal people would find baffling. Fiona insists it's pretty weird. Surely the obvious thing would have been to find another route, but not being able to get through the town annoyed me, and so I kept going back. I didn't want to be defeated by it. Just as a cat returns time and again to the spot where it deposited a bird on your carpet long after you've disposed of the corpse, I kept niggling away at my route – behaviour which some might consider appropriate given that the name of the town is synonymous in local folklore with the asylum which once stood there.

Also, I felt locked in. I was recording good times over the first 8 miles of the route, and my sports watch made me want to stick to it. Stubbornness and stupidity played their part as I pursued a course that was so obviously sapping my will to run. Maybe I kept at it for the reason that I was actually falling out of love with running. By heaping up the frustrations, I was subconsciously making it easier to hang up my trainers for good.

Interest was sparked a little by the fact that Michael and I, using sports watches and computers, were able to follow each other's progress as we counted down to the selfsame race. But after a while I took myself in hand. I was being stupid. I had to make it more fun. Having cracked my labyrinth at last, I did finally resort to variations and combinations of my previous long routes, but none of it quite worked. Not even the change could bring back my desire. It was a grim few months in my running schedule.

I looked forward to the chance to revive my running on holiday in France that August, a way to step things up a fraction before the October marathon, but once again I stalled. We stayed just south of Limoges in a gorgeous cottage and had a fabulous time, the whole family together lapping up all the pleasures of *la vie française*. But as a place to run, it was duff in the extreme. The routes were hopelessly hilly. This was going to be my second sports-watch marathon, and my sports watch didn't mince its stats: my French runs were just as poor as my English ones.

And then I hit a new and utterly unexpected low. I was running through a deserted French village, the kind of village that looked as if no one had lived there since the war. The shutters were up; no humans were around; the only sign of life was the barking of dogs, that low-level yapping so typical of rural France. But I was experienced in these things. I knew that all the *chiens méchants* would be slobbering and slavering behind bars. Except that this time one of them wasn't. A ghastly nippy little thing, it shot right out and bit deep into the flesh just above my left ankle, sinking its teeth into me just as I was going through with my stride. In that split second, the dog hung on and the flesh ripped – a V-shaped tear which bled profusely.

I paused to look down at the back of my leg in shock and horror. I could hear the owners shouting. I didn't want to find out whether it was at me or at the dog. Instead, I fixed my eyes in the middle distance and hobbled on. Glancing back, there was blood on the road.

I didn't have a phone with me. That would have been far too sensible – all too counter to that great spirit of running (or at least my conception of it) that I was just starting to stop worshipping. By the time I got back to our holiday let, the bleeding had eased, but the back of my leg was a mess.

Clearly I needed to go to the chemist's. Fiona came with me, and in my best French I explained what had happened. The chemist leapt backwards in terror and told me to go straight to the hospital, where I was seen quickly and treated with a lovely mix of efficiency and friendliness. The doctor explained that you don't stitch up wounds made by animals. You allow them to drain and heal naturally. She also explained, when I asked perhaps slightly tactlessly, that no, they no longer had rabies in France, only in certain illegally imported Eastern European dogs and in wild bats. Clearly I just had to hope that my dog was as French as a string of onions. The doctor put all sorts of plasters on the wound to hold the sides together, and off I limped – with two months to go until Mallorca.

In the event, I was running again within a few days – much to Fiona's disapproval. She thought I was crazy to attempt it so soon after such an unpleasant injury. My view was that I had a marathon to do. As far as Fiona was concerned, my attitude said it all about runners. In the event, the wound healed quickly, and I was running without pain within ten days. However, I couldn't help but see an underlying significance in what had just happened. It seemed to crystallise the way I was heading. Whichever way I looked at it, running really wasn't any fun any more, and that was the thought that stayed with me as the marathon approached.

For Rome earlier that year I had churned out two 8-mile runs a week, plus an 18-miler, plus intervals. For Mallorca, I continued with the long run, but I dropped the intervals and reduced one of the 8-milers to six. I continued to push myself on the shorter runs, aided by my sports watch, but while I put in the effort, I was conscious that I was marking time. More than ever, I was ticking off weeks, forever counting up how many runs remained until I could stop. Rome had been a tough one. Something had snapped, and now it was obvious, even to me: I'd run my course.

Mallorca was a last marathon which really was going to be a last marathon. Mixing up my sports, I even started telling myself that I'd had a good innings. I'd had a good run for my money. All things must pass. And all the other clichés.

In the final few weeks, I knew. Mallorca was to be my farewell to running – and it was a relief to realise it because with the realisation came a resurgence of energy. In the final ten days, just a little bit of the buzz crept back in. I wanted to sign off in style.

Michael and I flew out on the Friday for the Sunday start, which was from the main waterfront promenade in

Palma, just opposite the Parc de La Mar. The Parc offers an attractive lake which stands in front of La Seu Cathedral, a building which reflects gorgeously in its waters. It was instantly obvious: this was going to be one of the most picturesque starts to a marathon you could wish for.

The registration was novel and exotic, open air in tents under palm trees at the north-eastern end of the lake. As we registered, we could see – across the water – the finishing area being constructed on the southern side, on the seafront. Later that day, still the Friday we arrived, we walked right by it, seeing the final few hundred yards all laid out, still protected by polythene. It's always good to get an idea in your mind of what the finish looks like. A clear image of it will help once tiredness sets in, and here it really did look enticing – several hundred yards of raised gangway, the cathedral standing proud above the lake to our left. It was the kind of finish I could happily envisage; I could imagine how much just the thought of it would help weary feet towards the end.

Importantly, we were beginning to get an idea of the beginning and the end. Now we tried gropingly to get a feel for the rest of the marathon route, very grandly bringing the fruits of our combined experience to bear on the course ahead. We came to the conclusion that it wasn't going to be a good one.

The first quarter was a couple of seafront loops, at the end of which the 10-km runners would leave us. The second quarter was in the Old Town centre, after which the half-marathon runners would leave us. At 13 miles, the marathon runners embark on quarter number three, 6 or so miles eastwards and slightly inland on roads parallel to the coast, occasionally glimpsing the sea to the right. At about

18 miles, the route twists back on itself to come out on the seafront promenade for the final stretch westwards to the finish, the sea now open on the left until a final turn sees you double back on yourself for the final couple of hundred yards.

Wandering around Palma on the Friday and the Saturday we came to the conclusion that the city-centre stretch was going to be a nightmare, particularly when we started noticing the stripe of blue line showing the way to go – invariably along tight, narrow medieval lanes and around twisty corners. It was impossible not to imagine that we would be horridly bunched, especially as we would still be with the half-marathon runners at this point. Plus a few doubts started to creep in as to just how interesting that third, backstreet quarter would actually be.

Another factor emerged as we looked across to the starting/finishing area. The size of the respective bag deposits suggested the marathon runners would be outnumbered three to one by the half-marathon runners. We'd imagined there was going to be around 7,000 or 8,000 doing the full marathon. In fact, that was the total number of runners across all three races, with the marathon comfortably the smallest element. As it turned out, there were 1,372 marathon finishers; 2,977 half-marathon finishers; and 1,795 10-km finishers, plus various walkers and Nordic walkers, who presumably had a fine line in knitwear. It was clear it was going to be a very different kind of marathon to the vast city slogs we'd become used to.

The night before, as almost always, was bad. It was difficult to get to sleep and then even more difficult to stay asleep. We left the hotel at 8.15, just three-quarters of an hour before the start but still in plenty of time. Funny when you think how early you have to get up in New York; how soon you have to get cracking in London; and just what an awful crush it is in Paris. This was leisurely indeed. It was barely ten minutes' walk to the start, and it was all terribly relaxed, no wait to hand over the bags, everything calm, unflustered and simple. The queues for the loos were long and slow, but there was a huge city wall you could use instead, and plenty of people did. Mallorca has probably suffered worse indignities in its long and sunny history.

From there it was a gentle amble around the eastern end of the lake and up onto the seafront dual carriageway to assemble at the start. I left it a little bit late. The runners were quite tightly packed at the front by now, which meant a quick clamber over the barriers. But plenty of people were doing the same, and it was all very friendly as we stood shoulder to shoulder. Michael was already in his group further back. I was a hundred yards or so from the starting line, and it wasn't long before we were off – the usual process of standing still, shuffling forward, increasing in pace and then getting into your stride as you cross over the timing mat.

Once again, armed with my sports watch, I was most definitely running in miles whatever the roadside markers said. Annoyingly in the first mile or so, however, quite a number of people were running several abreast or in little groups, which made them difficult to get round. There were also plenty of people who had started too far forward for the pace they were now running at, and so the first mile seemed comparatively slow. I was quite surprised to see it come up in 7:33, far closer to my 7:30 target than I'd expected.

After a while, it was more than possible to run at my own pace, particularly in a temperature which had to count as absolutely perfect for long-distance running. It was bright without being particularly sunny, and it certainly wasn't hot. It was cool and comfortable, and, as usual, there was the lovely release that came simply with the act of getting going.

We started off on the seafront loops which made up the first 6 miles of the course, all on good wide roads. Posh marinas gave us plenty to look at, as did high-rise hotels as we entered the smarter end of town before turning back towards the start. Miles 2 to 6 were all nicely within the 7:30 target.

All in all, it was a good start. The road rose and fell gently, but I had the pleasant feeling that any gradient was mostly downhill, which clearly couldn't have been the case given that we ended up back where we started. But I guess the sensation simply reflected the fact that I was feeling comfortable, particularly as we approached the start/finish area once again. We turned left inland and, almost immediately, the 10-km runners dashed off to our right, down the concourse to the finish.

Of course, every distance has its disciplines and huge challenges, but it was difficult not to feel a slightly superior, totally irrational 'Why did they bother?' as the 10-km runners disappeared. We'd barely been going 40 minutes by then. But it was certainly an important psychological marker. Rather as a rocket sheds bits as it zooms into space, we were saying goodbye to the part-timers; we were clearly well underway; and, more interestingly, we were heading into the Old Town section we'd been worried about.

In the event, it proved absolutely fine. There was limited crowd support; in fact, it's probably fair to say that the whole thing probably didn't impact vastly on the people of the city as a whole; but it was pleasant to be running through the city, particularly early on when we went up one side of the road only to come back down the other side, a chance to see just how many people were behind me – not a terribly sporting thought, but an important way to assess how I was doing at that point. You're always being pulled along to an extent, but even better, if you're doing well, you're being pushed along at the same time, and that was certainly the case here.

I'd hated this kind of doubling-back in Amsterdam; I hadn't much liked it across the lake in Paris. But here, it was fine – another instance of how your feelings on the day colour your approach to everything. On another day, the sight of runners going in the opposite direction would have dragged me down; today it had the opposite effect.

At about 8 miles, I passed our hotel before heading off right on the day's first slightly narrow street, gently uphill for a while before bearing round to the left and then down beside a river which flowed inland at right angles to the coast. And so it continued, some decent straight stretches taking us back into the narrower, older areas before we found ourselves coming out by the cathedral and running along the walkway on its southern side, overlooking the lake with the finish on the far side – an area we'd familiarised ourselves with. From there we headed back into the twisty streets for a bit more criss-crossing.

The fantastic thing was that at no point were the public a problem. We'd imagined it would be difficult to keep pedestrians off the course, but never was this an issue at all. Just as importantly, at no point was bunching an issue either. It was emerging as an excellently thought-out course. The opening 6-mile coastal stretch, along decent dual carriageways, had stretched us out perfectly. Consequently we didn't for a moment get bottled up in the town. And again, even though it was fairly consistently up and down, I still had the impression – again, obviously completely wrong – that it was largely downhill, again presumably a sign that at that point I was still running well.

We took in most of the sites, including Plaça Major and Plaça de Cort, and the miles remained nicely under control – miles 7 to 13 all comfortably under eight minutes. The whole thing was feeling nicely steady as we entered the penultimate city-centre section, a straight road north before a turn to head back south, down to the coast.

Here at the waterfront, the half-marathon runners left us, while the full-marathon runners turned left to head east for that final half-inland, half-coastal 13 miles. With the sea in sight for the first time since mile 6, it was another significant psychological moment in the race. The field had reduced by about a third when the 10-km runners had peeled away just under an hour earlier; now our field was reduced by a third again as the half-marathon runners veered off in large numbers to the right. Turning left, I realised just how well spread the marathon runners were by now.

And the lovely thing was that I had absolutely no sense of wishing to be with the half-marathon runners. All I felt – smug and entirely unjustified – was 'Right, now we're getting down to the serious business!' At 12 miles, I was pretty much bang on the 1:30 time that 7:30 minutes per mile demanded; at the half-marathon point, I was just under 1:40; and now it was marathon runners only as we entered the third quarter of the race – a stretch that proved even more boring than we'd imagined; dull industrial areas with only the occasional glimpse of the sea at the end of side streets to our right.

One point of interest was how low the jets were coming in as we neared the airport, a point at which we seemed to be on an empty main road in the countryside. After that, we simply trundled on eastwards, never more than a few hundred yards from the sea, often much closer, but only ever seeing it in snatches. Occasionally things opened up when we were probably just a block away, and after a while we would catch glimpses of the front-runners coming back the other way – a bit of a double-edged sword. In some ways, it was encouraging, but it made me realise we still had a long way to go.

Towards the end of the inland stretch, we were going through towns, with shops either side which made for a bit more interest, and then finally, finally, we turned to the right before turning again to come out on the promenade, the sea clear to our left now as we headed back westwards on the home straight, all along the coast to the finish. Once again, and quite obviously, this was another major psychological turning point, with about 8 miles to go.

I had been doing well until about mile 16, but then I had started to feel tiredness creeping in around 17 and 18. I was above nine minutes per mile for the first time at mile 18, but the turn along the seafront came just when I needed it. For the next 4 miles, I was well under nine again, helped by a change in the weather. By now, the day had turned cloudy and it was drizzling a bit, which suited me. It was refreshing.

There were various people just wandering along the promenade; very few, if any, were there specifically for the marathon, but there was some good shouted support, and the encouraging thing was that we could see the curve of the coast in the distance, somewhere in the middle of which was the finish.

We were running along in ones and twos at this point in a reasonably steady flow, with no great sense of being in a race. At one point, the route took us down onto duckboards on the sand, and then, for a good mile or so, we were running across slightly hilly sand dunes, followed by sparsely grassed heathland, undulating and starting to become just a touch arduous.

Just as we emerged onto road again, I had my toughest moment of the race, slowing for a minute or two to barely more than a walk as we doubled back briefly and then turned sharp left and uphill. This was mile 23, a stinker and the only one that took me more than ten minutes. But then something suddenly clicked and miles 24 and 25 were fine, among the steadiest I have done at that stage in a marathon, dropping to well under nine for the penultimate mile. In the final mile I started to suffer again as we came back out onto the dual carriageway on which the race had started.

There was just over half a mile to go, and the starting arch came into view in the distance. There were people milling around the roadside with their medals, but it was difficult to know whether these were half- or full-marathon medals. Either way, it was proof enough that the end was approaching. And so I drew level with the lake and passed through the starting arch. Just a few hundred yards more. Turn right at the next corner and then turn right again to reach the final stretch. Finished runners by the roadside were drinking beer, so it seemed. One runner held up his plastic cup to me in a gesture of 'Keep going and this is what you will get', which left me mystified. I couldn't possibly imagine wanting a beer at that point, especially as I could feel myself flagging.

But slowly the corner was approaching, the turn inland very rapidly followed by the sharp turn right onto the finishing concourse, the slightly raised, carpeted metal runway towards the finishing arch, and how lovely it was to step onto it, the rain now falling heavily. We'd looked at it the night before and noticed that it was downhill, and now there it was – so unlike the London finish which you first see from far too far away. In Mallorca, the finish was suddenly there – just a couple of hundred yards away, giving me just enough time to take it all in and try to finish in style.

After more than three and a half hours of Status Quo, still the best thudding running music, the end was in sight. I pulled off my headband, raised my arms and sprinted the final few hundred feet, approaching the finishing clock just as 3:38 came up. My gun time, as they call it, was 3:38:03. My net time – in other words, time since actually crossing the start line – was 3:37:28. I'd done it. Marathon number 23 was completed, and it was great to stop.

I was just under two minutes slower than New York seven years earlier, just over two minutes quicker than Amsterdam six years before; more than ten minutes quicker than Rome earlier that year; and three and a half minutes slower than Paris the year before. It was well behind my grouped 3:20–3:22 times (London, Paris, La Rochelle), but a big improvement on the big-city stinkers; Dublin (2005), Berlin (2007) and Rome.

I remember lurching to the right as I came to a halt, but not worryingly so. I felt fine. I sat for a minute or two, just behind the finish, watching a few more runners come in, before walking on through the finishing section where it turned out that the beer was not only free but also alcohol-free, and lovely it was too. I really enjoyed it, though I remember feeling slightly nervous that in my depleted state it might still have a vaguely intoxicating effect. I nibbled on some banana, grabbed some water and collected my medal before leaving the race enclosure, wandering around the eastern end of the lake and picking up my bag.

The rain had stopped again, and I wondered about hanging around the finish area until it was time to go back along the last couple of miles of the route to find Michael. I got as far as the start of the raised home straight, where I got a chap to take my photograph, but the rain resumed soon after, and I was feeling chilly. I ambled back to the hotel, where I showered and freshened up, before strolling back down to the finish. I retraced my steps along the promenade and was delighted to discover Michael just before 41 km, a lot closer to the finish than I'd dared hope.

The rain had pretty much stopped again by now, but I imagined he would be drenched and frozen. In fact, he'd rather enjoyed the rain. His overriding feeling was relief that we hadn't had to run in blazing sun. I found him after about 5 hours 25 minutes had elapsed, and it was clear he was on track to come in well inside 5:51, the time he needed to achieve if he was to hit 'bronze standard' for his age – which he duly did. He was running steadily and well, just as he had done throughout. He finished in 5:37 – a fantastic result at the age of 78.

This was a marathon in which the organisers had got almost everything right. It was beautifully organised, with the water and the sports drinks frequent and plentiful. I'd gone back with drinks for Michael, but needn't have worried. They hadn't run dry – and neither had we. It's a young marathon but one very much on the up. It was great not to have the awful crush of Rome or Paris; great to be able to move around so easily at the start and at the finish; and great to have done a marathon in a new country. A good result all round.

As I waited for Michael to pick up his medal and collect his bag, I looked around and tried to take it all in, this the most exotic of my marathons. I wanted to register it all in my mind: the palm trees, the lake, the friendliness – all part of the sheer different-ness of the Mallorca Marathon. My last marathon. I wanted to say goodbye.

And as I looked, I started to smile.

The smile broadened. Just who was I trying to kid? The only one who'd fallen for it was me. As I stood there, looking back across the finishing line, I knew I wasn't finished. How could I be? Why on earth would I want to give this up? There was nowhere else I wanted to be at that moment. The only thought of elsewhere was 'Where next?' I knew I couldn't possibly give up the sweet knackered-ness of running.

I was washed and refreshed, but my body was still telling me that it had gone beyond the ordinary, that I had pushed it beyond the point that bodies naturally go. And that was the pleasure. It had been a small marathon, but even small marathons can be great ones.

For this one day, we had converged from around the world; we had attached our microchips and we had pinned on our numbers. We had gone through our pre-race rituals, and then we had stood together at the start, perfect strangers to each other and yet brothers (plus a few sisters) in the maddest feat of endurance known to common man.

With our different-coloured vests, our different hopes, our different worries, we had set off as one. With our different gaits, some super-smooth and slick, others straggly and inelegant, we had surged forward, stretching slowly in the next few hours to cover mile upon mile of Mallorcan road as sweaty humanity pushed itself to the limit. And that was the joy; I realise it now. Not to do well, but simply to be part of it.

As I stood looking at that finishing line, thoughts came back to me that I had had on finishing my very first marathon 12 years before. Thoughts which reminded me why I had become so besotted with marathon running.

All of us have got our lives, our jobs, our families, our routines, our habits, our foibles. All of us work to get from one day to the next. Very few of us hit the headlines. Very few of us aspire to. But train for a marathon, and for one day you can join the ranks of the immortals.

I thought of the distance we had just run and I thought of what we had achieved in covering it. This is the way the common man smashes Shane Warne back over his head to bring up a triple century at Lords; this is the way we mortals smash home that FA Cup-winning penalty. This is the way we become heroes – if only to ourselves. Sporting glory is there for the taking every time you line up at the start of a marathon – and that's the seduction.

I thought of the thousands of people who streamed home in the icy rain hours after me in the Amsterdam marathon; I thought of my Dublin bin bag, my shelter for 20 miles; I thought of my London tears and loud, painful breathing; I thought of the nun I'd cruelly abused in Rome; and I thought of the way I'd pulled myself back from the brink in La Rochelle.

And I then remembered how sweet life had been in New York; how slippery it had been on the Clarendon Way; how hilly it had been on the Isle of Wight. I thought of those Brooklyn firefighters lining the route in the Big Apple. I thought of the man with the boat on his head who sailed past me in the Dutch downpour. And I thought of the little boy who'd really seemed to believe it when he shouted full in my face, nearly two hours after the winner had crossed the line in London, 'Come on, Phil! You can still win this!' This was my world, and I wasn't about to leave it.

And then I realised what had made Mallorca so special. It was my 23rd finish and yet it was the only time I had raised my arms and punched the air as I went over the line. It wasn't a gesture of farewell. How wrong had I been? Instead, in that instinctive gesture, my whole body had been shouting 'Bring it on!'

I was drunk on the whole damned thing, as drunk as I have ever been. It's a world I love right from the nipple plasters through to the blackened toenails, right from the misery of the lonely long-distance training run to the adrenalin surge of the big-city finishing line. As I punched the air, I knew it. I am not done yet. My race isn't run. The best is yet to come – even if, from here on in, the best is likely to get slower and slower.

My Life as a

Hooker

When a Middle-Aged Bloke
Discovered Rugby

'If this is what a midlife crisis does for you, I want one.'
Luke Benedict, rugby writer for the *Daily Mail*

Steven Gauge

MY LIFE AS A HOOKER
When a Middle-Aged Bloke Discovered Rugby

Steven Gauge

ISBN: 978 1 84953 211 2   Paperback   £8.99

In my late thirties, it gradually dawned on me that I had become Jason's regular hooker. It was an arrangement that worked well for a couple of reasons. He didn't need me to dress up in anything particularly risqué or to do anything too vulgar, other than cuddle in the middle of a field with him and thirteen other men on a Saturday afternoon.

Steven Gauge's response to an impending midlife crisis didn't involve piercings, tattoos or a red sports car – instead, he decided to take up rugby. What he found on the pitch was a wonderful game, far removed from the professional televised glamour of international rugby, where ordinary blokes with ordinary jobs (and some extraordinary bellies) get together once in a while and have a great time rolling around in the mud.

By the end of his first few seasons, Steven had cracked his nose and various other parts of his anatomy – but he had cracked the game too, and found a place in the club as Captain of the Fourths.

THE HAIRY HIKERS

A Coast-to-Coast Trek Along the French Pyrenees

GR10

DAVID LE VAY

THE HAIRY HIKERS
A Coast-to-Coast Trek Along the French Pyrenees

David Le Vay

ISBN: 978 1 84953 237 2   Paperback   £8.99

With a glint in his eye, Rob turns and asks me if I want to 'touch his furry puma'. We are only hours into the trip and things have already taken a sinister turn. Thankfully, it turns out he is referring to the little embossed logo on his new shirt.

Fuelled by a degree of midlife crisis and the need to escape from routine, armed with rusty schoolboy French and plenty of schoolboy humour, friends David and Rob set out to walk the fabled GR10 hiking trail. It will take them from Hendaye on the Atlantic coast to Banyuls-sur-Mer on the Mediterranean, through beautiful scenery and one of the most spectacular mountain ranges in Europe. Just about perfect – if you can put aside the inevitable snoring-induced conflict and bad habits that result from two men spending over seven weeks in each other's company.

Have you enjoyed this book?
If so, why not write a review on your favourite website?

If you're interested in finding out more about our books
follow us on Twitter: @Summersdale

Thanks very much for buying this Summersdale book.

www.summersdale.com